Project Management

PROJECT MANAGEMENT

A LIFE CYCLE APPROACH

ARUN KANDA

Professor of Industrial Engineering
Mechanical Engineering Department
Indian Institute of Technology Delhi

PHI Learning Private Limited

Delhi-110092
2025

*In fond memory of **Shri Asoke K. Ghosh** (October 1942 – February 2024), Founder Chairman and Managing Director of PHI Learning, whose vision endlessly inspires.*

The Legacy Continues....

Published by Pushpita Ghosh, PHI Learning Private Limited, Rimjhim House, 111, Patparganj Industrial Estate, Delhi-110092 and Printed by Syndicate Binders, A-20, Hosiery Complex, Noida, Phase-II Extension, Noida-201305 (N.C.R. Delhi).

₹595.00

PROJECT MANAGEMENT—A Life Cycle Approach
Arun Kanda

ISBN-978-81-203-4173-9 (Print Book)
ISBN-978-93-5443-283-5 (e-Book)

The export rights of the book are vested solely with the publisher.

Dedicated to
My Parents, Teachers and Friends
For their guidance and inspiration

Contents

Preface

This book is an outgrowth of my teaching project management courses to undergraduate and postgraduate students for over twenty years at Indian Institute of Technology Delhi. I have also benefitted from numerous short-term courses and seminars for practising managers organized for various organizations like Indian Oil, NTPC, BHEL, BEL, Consultancy Development Centre and a host of other organizations over the years.

Although there are numerous books on project management available in the market, each has its own focus. Some focus on scheduling procedures of PERT/CPM, others talk of the financial implications of preparing a project report, while some others emphasize the human and behavioural aspects of project implementation. I have often felt the need of a unified textbook where all aspects of a project from conception, selection, planning and implementation are dealt with in reasonable detail. The proliferation of software packages in project management has created the impression that managing projects is just the click of a button away. On the contrary, an understanding of basic concepts and assumptions is necessary to use the available software meaningfully.

Moreover, the mathematical rigour and intuitive aspects need to be balanced so that the serious reader can appreciate and delve into the major research issues in project management. This book is an attempt to provide such a need. It is organized to be taught in a full semester course on project management for undergraduate and postgraduate students of engineering or management. It should also be useful to practising project managers to understand the fundamental concepts.

I am grateful to all the students who studied project management with me and provided me an opportunity to learn and grow.

I am especially indebted to my teachers and research supervisors Prof. U.R.K. Rao and Prof. P.S. Satsangi. I must also acknowledge the support of my mentors, colleagues and friends especially Prof. Prem Vrat, Prof. S.G. Deshmukh and Prof. D.K. Banwet for the learning that I have had from their association.

Arun Kanda

CHAPTER

1

Project Management—An Overview

1.1 WHAT IS A PROJECT?

A project is a temporary endeavour to accomplish a need or desire (Fig. 1.1). This need may be economic, social, political, entrepreneurial, philanthropic, environmental or otherwise. Like every thing in life, each project has a life cycle, that is, a beginning and an end. Prior to the beginning is the pre-planning or conceptual stage of any project, followed by the central or active phase of project management. This is followed by the actual implementation including monitoring and control. And finally, the project is wound up, audited and handed over to the client or end-user.

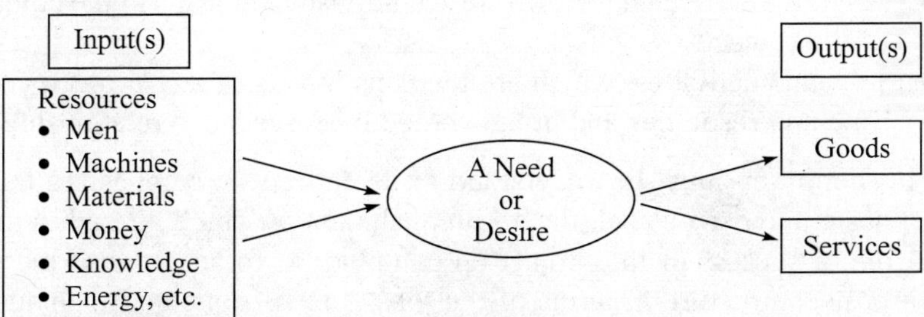

Fig. 1.1 A project activity.

Resources, such as manpower, equipment, materials, finances and relevant knowledge and experience, have to be provided and coordinated as inputs to obtain the required goods or services. Any project may be conceived in terms of a goal to be achieved, a set of interrelated jobs to be done, which constitute the micro-cost centres consuming time and resources (Fig. 1.2).

A project may be conveniently divided into the following four stages:

- Project identification and selection
- Project planning and scheduling

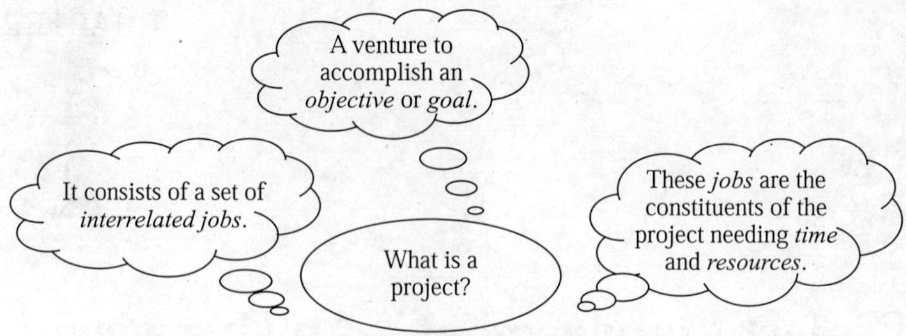

Fig. 1.2 A project defined.

- Project implementation
- Project completion and handover to end-user

In this overview, an attempt has been made to delineate the major activities involved in each of these four major phases of a project. Some examples from the experience of the author have been given and it is hoped that the avid reader would be able to generate new ones from his/her area of expertise.

We are so accustomed to dealing with projects in our daily lives that we rarely regard it necessary to define a "Project". However, to initiate a formal and systematic study of Project Management, it is worthwhile to examine a few definitions that focus on the key elements of a project. A project may be defined in the following way (Fig. 1.2):

- An undertaking or venture to accomplish some objective or goal.
- A set of interrelated jobs whose accomplishment leads to the completion of the project.
- Jobs and activities, which are the constituents of any project, consume time and resources and are governed by precedence relationships.

This definition must be understood in its entirety. It emphasizes that each project has a purpose or goal, the accomplishment of which is used to measure the degree of success of the project on completion. To accomplish the project goal, a project structure in terms of the jobs is to be done and their interrelationships have to be worked out. This is the active phase of project planning where project networking techniques are widely used. At the micro level, the individual jobs and activities of the project are the major constituents which have to be performed to specifications within the restrictions of time and cost. It is important to realize that these activities consume resources and time, and must be performed judiciously to realize the overall project goals.

1.1.1 The Project Purpose or Objective—Change Management

It is important to understand this definition in its entirety. The purpose or the objective actually defines a project. In this sense a project is a temporary undertaking to accomplish a goal. Once the goal is accomplished, the project is over. Construction of a new factory, for instance, is an example of a project. After the activities of planning, construction, installation of machinery and employee training are over, the project is over and the project staff is available to work on the next project. It is for this reason that projects are referred to as *agents of change* for each project transforms the current state into a more desirable state. There may be many paths to move from the current state to the desired state, differing in cost, effectiveness and the skills required (Fig. 1.3). The primary concern of the project planner is to identify the path or project, which is consistent with his/her objectives and requires the minimum cost. A project may, therefore, be viewed as a vehicle to move from one state to another desired state, which is the state in which the objective has been achieved.

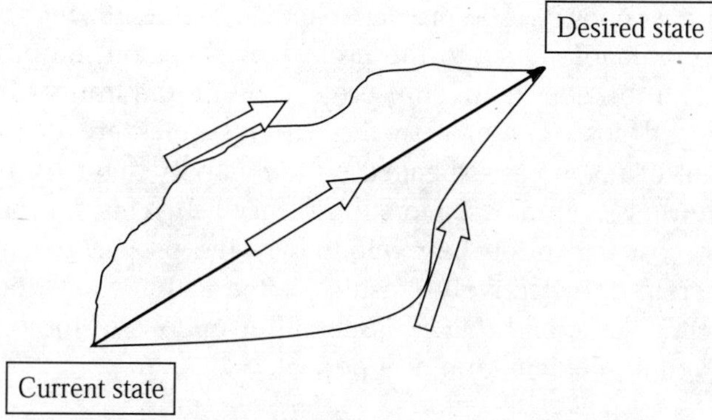

Fig. 1.3 Projects as agents of change.

It is now easy to appreciate that proper choice and implementation of national projects could lead to accelerated growth in the national infrastructure and the economy of the country. Similarly, the proper portfolio of projects undertaken successfully by an organization would lead to the fulfilment of organizational objectives. And at a personal level too, the right choice of projects and their proper implementation would lead to the satisfaction of individual objectives.

1.1.2 The Project Structure

Just as each project has a purpose or objective, it has a structure. The structure of the project is the set of jobs or activities that have to be specifically carried out to complete the project. Quite often the project team would have to debate and discuss to identify the jobs required to be completed in the entire project. Such information is generally available through a Work Breakdown Structure, which defines the major chunks of work to be accomplished in the project. This may take the shape of developing designs, civil work, electrical work, plumbing, installation and finishing for a new factory construction project. The degree of detail to which the jobs may be broken down depends on the purpose—the greater the detail, the better for detailed planning and scheduling, but not so convenient for cost accounting purposes. A convenient compromise is thus needed. These individual jobs so defined have natural precedence requirements, which help in the development of project networks. And project networks become a very convenient means for all project planning activities, such as project scheduling, time–cost trade-offs and resource-constrained project scheduling. The project network is useful not only for project planning but also for project implementation including monitoring and control.

1.1.3 The Project Activities

The project structure identifies the status of various activities or jobs in the project. It is actually through the jobs and activities that the project gets done. The activities consume time and resources and have to be carefully monitored for time and cost control. The project schedule by identifying the critical path provides very valuable clues to the project manager on the priorities that he should maintain to keep the overall project within the limits of the scheduled project time and cost. Quite often the activity times are flexible depending on the amount of resources expended on the activity and may be likened to a spring which can be compressed to a limit (Fig. 1.4). This dependency between duration and cost can often be exploited by the project manager in project crashing wherein by selectively crashing some activities the project duration can be reduced. These and related issues offer options to the project manager in planning and implementation of a project.

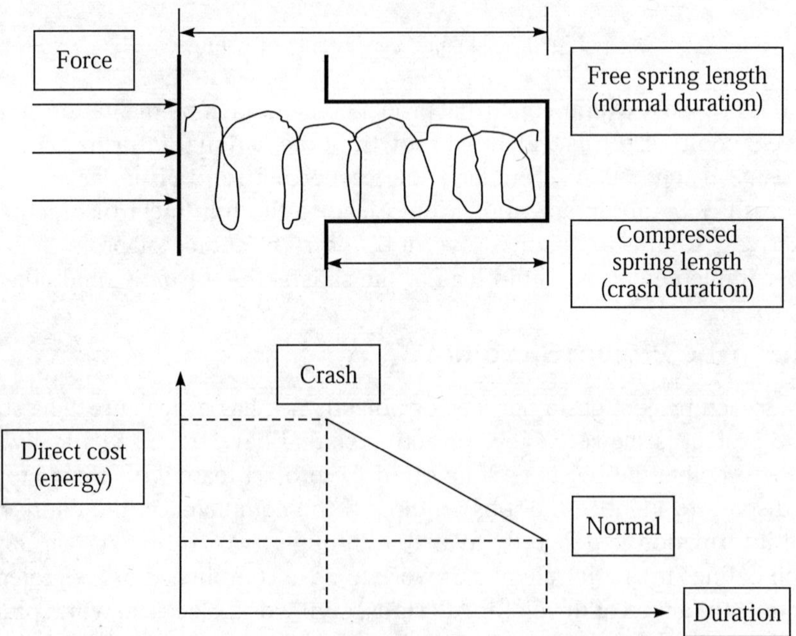

Fig. 1.4 Trade-off between resources and time in project activities.

1.2 VARIETY OF PROJECTS

After having defined a project in terms of its objective, structure and constituents, we will take a look at some examples of projects. It would be instructive while going through these examples to think of what the objective of each project is, what kinds of activities would be involved in the project and what skills or resources would be needed to accomplish the project.

- ***Personal Projects***
  - Preparation for an exam: Such a project would include typical activities as identifying the date and syllabus for the exam, finding out the sources to study from, then scheduling/prioritizing the topics according to expected weightage, studying the topics, doing practice problems, revision and appearing for the examination.
  - A family vacation: Choosing a location within available budget, deciding participants, arranging stay and travel bookings, actual vacationing and return.
  - Writing a book: Decide the topic of the book, divide into chapters, write manuscript and publish the book.
  - Getting dressed: For example, the dressing up of ladies involves a host of activities such as selection of dress on the basis of type, colour, new/old, occasion, etc., then wearing it, make-up, etc.
  - A birthday function: This involves a typical birthday function to be organized for children with all the decorations, arranging menu, cake, organising games for invitees, etc.
  - Wedding in the house: Lot of preparations are involved including setting of budget to be spent and arranging for ceremonies, hosting guests, etc.
- ***Local Projects***
  - A school function
  - Cleanliness drive: A group of people would collect to clean their neighbourhood drainage or waste mounds.
  - Construction of clubs: For example, kitty parties.
- ***Organizational Projects***
  - Construction of a building or a highway
  - Planning and launching a new product
  - A turnaround in a refinery: A turnaround is typical annual shutdown in a refinery. Since the revenue loss per day is phenomenally large in case of such a shutdown, a lot of planning goes into this project to minimize the shutdown time of the refinery.
- ***National Projects***
  - Launching a new satellite

- Literary campaign/poverty removal
- Preparation of annual budget: Involves meeting of finance minister with various industry people and other stakeholders to know their expectations from the budget, then planning various aspects like fiscal deficit, etc. and finally coming up with the budget.

- *Global Projects*
  - Organizing peace missions
  - Space exploration
  - Environment protection

1.3 FEATURES OF PROJECTS

The examples of various projects from different backgrounds considered in the previous section differ widely in scope, complexity, cost and specialty. It is obvious that entirely different sets of skilled personnel would have to be hired to complete some of the projects, whereas others could be accomplished routinely by us in our daily lives. There are, however, some common features in all these projects, which are worthy of note. It is because of these common features that the discipline of project management has come into being. Some of the common features that have been recognized in projects are listed below. It is because of these that the techniques of Project Management have become universally acceptable among project managers.

i. Well-defined collection of jobs: A project can be broken into tasks and sub-tasks whose completion guarantees achievement of objectives. For example, going for a party may be broken into three tasks—getting dressed, buying a present and driving to the party.
ii. Generally non-repetitive, one time effort: The tasks are non-repetitive, i.e. they need to be performed just once as in the above example you dress once, buy a present once and drive to the party once.
iii. Jobs interrelated through precedence: Jobs follow a definite order depending on the phase of the project they are required. For example, in wearing shoes one has to first wear the socks and then put on the shoes.
iv. Jobs otherwise independent: Jobs are independent in the sense that though their order is well defined, they can be done at any point of time if the required order is not changed. For example, it is perfectly alright if you wear the socks in the morning and shoes in the evening.
v. Jobs consume time and resources: As the process advances resources are consumed which is the price to reach a more desired state.
vi. Coordination needed between individuals, groups and organizations: A project may have thousands of interrelated activities and there is a need to maintain an order and communication between them to adhere to the time schedule and optimize the resources consumed.

vii. Constant pressure of conformance to time/cost/performance goals: All is vain if the objective is not achieved which may be anything such as completion before a stipulated time or within a specified budget and with a desired quality.

A production manager does essentially the same kind of job every day while the day-to-day scene for a project manager changes. A production manager faces similar kinds of problems daily like scheduling, delivery of the same products, dealing with the same workers, etc. However, a project manager keeps switching the projects and activities—one day he may have to deal with construction workers, other day with drillers, some other day with transporters and since this brings a lot of uncertainty and running about, his job becomes a nightmare sometimes and is thus more challenging.

Thus, on the basis of classification of projects and their characteristics we can identify a project and the importance of its management in our life. We are now in a better position to appreciate the job of a project manager. Some of the behavioural requirements and the expectations from a good project manager are discussed in Chapters 10 and 11.

1.4 LIFE CYCLE OF A PROJECT

We have already seen that a project is a venture that brings together men, machines and other resources to accomplish an objective. We have also looked at a number of examples of projects at the personal level, in the local neighbourhood, at the organizational level, at the national level and at the global level. Despite their dissimilarities these projects undergo similar phases as the project matures from conception to completion. We may, therefore, talk of the life cycle of a project and identify the major phases in the life of a project as shown below:

- Selection of a project
- Project planning
    - Scope of work and network development
    - Basic scheduling
    - Time–cost trade-offs
    - Resource considerations in projects
- Project implementation
- Project completion and audit

1.4.1 Project Selection

The selection of a new project is a major decision by the top management of an organization. The need for the new project may be created by the desire to place the company in a more favourable financial position by introducing a new product, to ward off competition by creating state-of-the-art service facilities or to introduce e-commerce for online capturing of Internet customers. It is generally true that the success and growth of an organization is dependent on the choice of the right projects at the right time. Project selection can be divided into three major activities: project identification, project appraisal and project selection.

Project Identification

Project identification is the stage where new opportunities and threats emerging in the environment are investigated and suitable proposals that can be adopted by the organization are generated. This is done through the generation of new ideas by the company's think tank. Brainstorming is a very effective technique for doing this exercise in a group. Brainstorming may be structured in which each member of the group is asked for his/her idea in a sequential process, the idea is recorded and the coordinator proceeds to the next member of the group. If an individual has no idea to contribute at any stage, he simply says "pass" to direct the coordinator to the next member. This process continues till the requisite number of ideas is generated (typically 20–30 ideas are common in a brainstorming exercise). In the other kind of brainstorming, referred to as unstructured brainstorming, the procedure is modified to proceed according to the member who gives the first idea, followed by the member who is willing to give the next idea and so on. The process proceeds till the required number of ideas is generated. Structured brainstorming ensures the participation of all members, whereas unstructured brainstorming may be dominated by a few vocal members.

Before initiating the brainstorming exercise, the purpose of the exercise should be explained to the members by the coordinator with an assurance that the ideas generated during brainstorming would be kept confidential and not be used by the company for any personal evaluation.

To encourage creativity and innovation in the ideas during brainstorming, no evaluation or derogatory remarks on an idea are made when the idea is proposed. Even if an idea seems stupid when it is proposed, it is simply recorded. All evaluation is reserved for a subsequent screening of all the ideas.

During project selection the top management has to

- Be receptive to new emerging ideas
- Have a vision of future growth
- Keep long-term objectives in mind
- Conduct a SWOT analysis to map external opportunities and threats with internal strengths and weaknesses
- Perform a preliminary project analysis to assess whether a project proposal is worthwhile or not

Project Appraisal

Before adoption every project needs to be evaluated on various fronts. This evaluation is generally more rigorous than the screening of project ideas after the brainstorming in the project identification phase and considers the following kinds of appraisal:

- Market appraisal
- Financial appraisal
- Technical appraisal
- Economic appraisal
- Ecological appraisal

Market appraisal

Market appraisal considers the following aspects of the market for the project:

- Aggregate future demand
- Market share
- Current and future competition
- Location and accessibility of consumers
- Technological scenario/obsolescence
- Possible pricing options

Technical appraisal

- Engineering aspects
- Locations
- Size
- Production process

Financial appraisal

- Cash flows over time
- Profitability
- Break even point: to decide the volume at which the project should operate
- Net present worth
- Internal rate of return
- Payback period
- Risk

Economic appraisal

Economic appraisal differs from financial appraisal in the sense that it figures out the impact on society of the project.

- Benefits and Costs (in shadow prices)*
- Distribution of income in society
- Level of saving and investment
- Self-sufficiency, employment and social order

---

* Benefits can be seen through shadow prices; after optimizing the model, the dual prices obtained from each equation tell us by how many units the objective function improves if this resource is increased or decreased by one unit. Economic appraisal of large projects like building a dam or something big of that sort involves the use of shadow prices.

Ecological appraisal

- Environment damage
  - Air
  - Water
  - Noise
  - Others
- Restoration measures

Project Selection

Finally, project selection is based on a number of criteria for which a detailed appraisal and evaluation has been carried out for all the candidate project proposals. Some of the important criteria that are relevant in project evaluation are given below:

- Investment
- Rate of return
- Risk
- Likely profit
- Payback
- Similarity to existing business
- Expected life
- Flexibility
- Environment impact
- Competition

Since this is a problem of multi-criteria decision making where a number of incommensurate, often intangible criteria with different degrees of importance are involved for each candidate project, multi-criteria decision-making techniques may be utilized for ranking and selection of the final project proposal.

Multi-criteria evaluation

When we have N different projects that have to be evaluated on M different criteria, we can assign weights to these criteria. Further, each of the project options is evaluated on each criterion. This evaluation results in an Nx M matrix with each entry R_{ij} denoting the score of ith project on jth evaluation criterion. The final score is the product of each entry of the matrix with the corresponding criterion weight W_j. A framework of multi-criteria evaluation is shown in Fig. 1.5.

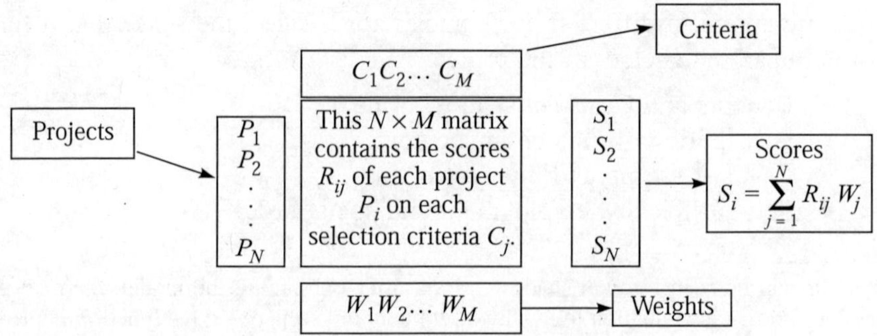

Fig. 1.5 A framework for multi-criteria evaluation of projects.

The project with the highest score is selected. There are a number of multi-attribute decision-making techniques such as Dominance, Cut-offs, SAW, HAW, TOPSIS and ELECTRE which may be employed for this purpose. Some of these techniques are explored in Chapter 4.

The final project selection is based on a feasibility report that considers all these issues prior to project adoption.

1.4.2 Project Planning

Once a project has been approved after all the statutory, financial and other appraisals, it enters the realm of detailed planning where the work breakdown structure is developed, responsibilities for different tasks are decided upon, a timetable for doing various jobs is prepared, the resource requirements of men, machines, materials and money are determined and suitable provisioning for the key resources is done so that implementation could be carried out. Project planning is the active phase of project management in which the project manager and his team have an opportunity to contribute their experience and learning in the development of a realistic project plan. A large number of networking techniques, analysis, simulations and analytical models can provide very valuable clues to some of the typical problems that a project manager may be facing at this stage. Some of the major activities in the planning stage are summarized below.

Forming a Project Team with a Leader

Generally, the most important initial step in ensuring the success of a project is the selection of a project leader who will guide the whole project. The project leader should be knowledgeable, experienced and mature with people-handling skills. Depending on the needs of the project, he would form a team by suitably picking people with the right skills and commitment. The project success depends, to a very large extent, on how this group of people from different backgrounds cooperates as a motivated team under the project manager. Some of the behavioural aspects like attitude, motivation, team working and leadership are explored in Chapters 10 and 11.

Defining Scope and Terms of Reference

The project goal and the terms of reference should be clearly identified and communicated to all the members of the project team. This activity should be properly done to avoid tensions and conflicts during the progression of the project, as a large number of individuals and agencies with conflicting interests could be involved in the project. Quite often the scope and terms of reference in a new project are very vaguely defined. In such situations the project team would do well to evolve a clear scope through mutual discussion. The exercise would help the partners to clearly understand their role in the project and the dependencies on all others involved.

Work Breakdown Structure

The entire project is conveniently broken down into smaller more manageable pieces for effective planning and implementation. Individual responsibility can then be assigned to people or organizations for their share of work. There are many ways of developing the work breakdown structure. For instance, one may go by a functional classification, such as design, planning, procurement, erection and commissioning in a project. Or one may go by a component approach and talk of the propulsion system, ballistic shell, the payload and the launching platform in the case of a missile development project.

The purpose of a work breakdown structure is to identify convenient work packages as units for planning and monitoring project progress. As it happens while cutting a birthday cake, the pieces should be neither too small nor too big, similarly the work packages should be of convenient duration and cost for the handling organization.

Basic Scheduling

The key idea in basic scheduling is to plan the entire set of project activities and set up a timetable for action. This generally involves the following steps:

- Project representation as a network
- Estimation of activity durations
- Forward and backward pass
- Determination of activity floats
- Critical path for selective control and minimum project duration

Time–Cost Trade-offs

Each project activity can be done at a "normal" duration where the direct expenditure is a minimum. However, by investing additional resources in the form of manpower, higher degree of automation or greater number of machines and equipment, the duration may be brought down to the "crash" level. This trade-off between activity duration and cost may take a variety of shapes, such as linear/non-linear/discontinuous/discrete time–cost relationships. The problem in project crashing is to selectively identify project activities for compression/relaxation so that the entire range of possibilities for the project duration between the normal and crash limits are investigated for minimum direct costs. The project cost duration efficient frontier actually summarizes the various possibilities for the project planner. Imposition of the indirect project costs (including fixed costs varying directly as a function of project duration) on the minimum direct costs yields the total project/cost curve. Methods and techniques for dealing with these problems are discussed in Chapter 7.

Resource Considerations

Any project schedule requires resources such as manpower, machines, money and equipment for implementation. How much and when these resources are required is what is determined through *resource aggregation*. The resource usage profile shows the variation in resource requirements over time as the project progresses. A typical profile is depicted in Fig. 1.6. This profile indicates how much manpower is needed at what times to implement the project in duration *T*.

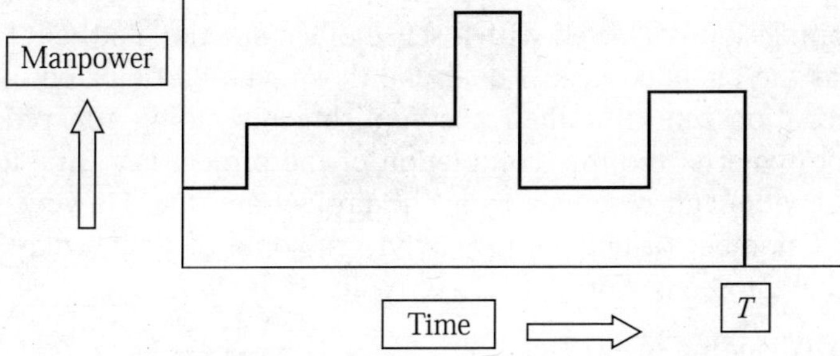

Fig. 1.6 Resource usage profile for a specified project schedule.

If the resource requirements vary in an uneven fashion, *resource levelling* may be resorted to by shifting some activities with float to clip the resource peaks and fill in the valleys. Notice that in this exercise the project duration *T* is not allowed to increase.

Even after leveling, the resource peaks may exceed the resource availability. In such a situation, some of the activities of the project during the resource peaks may have to be delayed, thereby pushing the project duration beyond *T*. This problem of finding a project schedule of minimum duration implementable within the resource constraints is referred to as the *limited resource allocation problem*. Some of the heuristic and optimal procedures for solving these problems are investigated in Chapter 7.

1.4.3 Project Implementation

Project implementation is the stage in the project that turns dreams into reality. The project team proceeds according to the project plan generated in the previous stage. Project monitoring and control using techniques like PERT/Cost help to assess the progress of the work and take timely corrective action. Project implementation is complicated by the coordination between a large number of contractors, suppliers and consultants, the delays in receipt of materials and equipment on site, unforeseen problems in installation and the difficult or stressful work conditions of the project.

Some of the major activities to be looked after during project implementation include

- Organization of project team and proper allocation of work
- Project monitoring with regard to cost, value of work and time
- Effective control action to minimize time and cost overruns

- Updation of project schedules after slippages in time and cost
- Provisioning for financial and other resources needed in the project
- Coordinating with head office, suppliers, contractors and project staff

1.4.4 Project Completion and Review

Project completion is viewed with a sense of satisfaction and relief by the project team as the intended task is over and those who participated in the process of its realization can view their accomplishments taking concrete shape. For the project owner(s) too, the completion of the project is a time to rejoice for now the benefits and revenues from the project are due. However, amidst the euphoria, a number of concluding activities, some of which may not be very pleasant, have to be performed. These typically include

- Disbanding of project team
- Handing over of the project to the user
- Accounting and report writing
- Learning from the experience

1.5 TYPICAL PROBLEMS IN MANAGING PROJECTS

Any project is a collective effort of a number of people coming together for a common goal. Each person is equipped with an ego and a unique temperament. Working together in a team on a temporary objective could lead to conflict and a host of behavioural problems during the initial period of adjustment as well as in the long-term operation of the project. Also there is great diversity in the nature of tasks handled by the project team, where both technical and behavioural problems could surface. Moreover, owing to the uncertainties in the environment a number of unforeseen problems could emerge during project implementation. The following list is only indicative of the kinds of problems that the project manager and his team may face in any project:

- Organizational/behavioural
- Financial
- Legal
- Engineering
- Construction/installation
- Site evacuation/development
- Labour unrest/unavailability
- Non-availability of resources
- Weather conditions
- Ad hoc, on the spot improvisations

1.6 HUMAN PROBLEMS IN PROJECT MANAGEMENT

Since a project manager has to deal with people who do the assigned jobs for him, people management is the key skill needed to get the job done. And quite rightly if a project manager can motivate his team members, obtain their commitment and cooperation, involve them in what they are good at and enjoy doing, the synergy can be tremendous and the project can be accomplished like a well-played game. However, in order to accomplish this, the project manager has to display leadership and maturity to be able to manage his most important resource—his people. Some of the human issues that are important in this regard are listed below and treated in greater detail in Chapters 10 and 11.

- Working together in teams
- Communication
- Conflict management
- Leadership and motivation
- Organizational structure
- Selection of the project manager

1.7 ROLE OF COMPUTERS IN PROJECT MANAGEMENT

The computer is a very valuable aid in project management. Apart from providing computational support in a whole range of network scheduling calculations, it has made possible the generation and distribution of online reports for effective monitoring and control. Since a large number of activities (often thousands) and individuals are involved in a project, keeping everyone up to date and involved is itself a stupendous task. This has been made easier through e-mail, the Intranet and the Internet. Moreover, coordination between the head office and multiple sites is much easier and effective. A number of computer packages used for project management are available. Microsoft Project and Primavera are two of the more popularly used ones. The major advantages of using a software package for project management include

- Easy sorting and listing of activities
- Easy updation and new listings of project progress over the life cycle
- Certain advanced analyses practical only with computer programs
- Many commercially available packages

1.8 SUMMARY AND CONCLUSIONS

In this chapter, an overview of project management has been given. A project is defined in terms of an objective, a structure and its constituents. The life cycle of a project describes the project processes from project selection to project planning to project implementation and project completion. A number of enablers to make the project processes more effective and efficient have also been described. These include leadership and team work, organization and people management, project management techniques of networking and analysis, computers and information systems. Diagrammatically, the project process with the enablers is shown in Fig. 1.7.

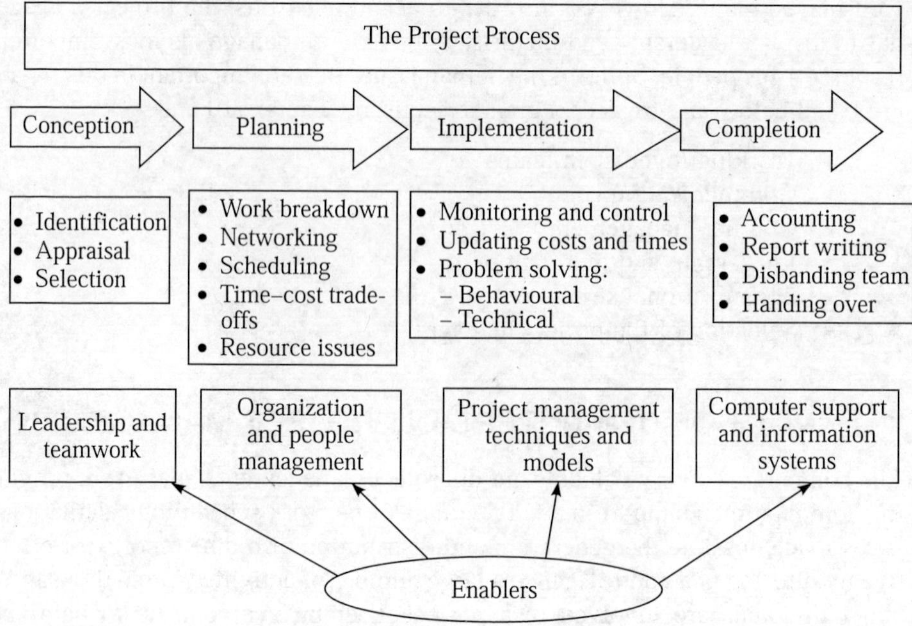

Fig. 1.7 The project process along with enablers.

This book on project management looks at the decisions to be made during the various phases of the project process, examines systematic methodologies and models that help in the decision making, and provides interpretation of results obtained from various models so that they may be intelligently adopted by a practical project manager in the successful implementation of any project. This book offers something for each of the following categories of readers:

For the student: It provides a treatment of the fundamentals of project management, stressing the underlying theory and assumptions for the various decisions to be made in the entire life cycle. There are examples and practice problems to illustrate the concepts.

For the practical project manager: It is a systematic collection of major decisions and solution methodologies available for tackling the problems of project management. The role of human and behavioural factors in managing teams and conflict resolution is emphasized along with technical expertise.

For the researcher: Throughout the text where results are derived, the reference to original sources is included so that the serious reader may pursue those ideas in greater depth. Also hints on the state of the art and directions for research are included wherever appropriate.

PROBLEMS

1. What is a project and how does it differ from routine production in a manufacturing or a service system?
2. What are the different stages in the life cycle of a project? Highlight the major decisions to be taken at each of these stages.
3. Write a brief note on a project as an agent of change giving the role of creativity and motivation in deciding
   - What to change?
   - What to change to?
   - How to bring about the desired change?
4. Comment on the project process and the soft and hard skills needed by the project team to complete the project (the enablers).
5. Taking examples from the manufacturing and service sectors, identify the typical problems that could be faced by a project manager at different stages of a project.
6. Why is the selection of right projects important for a society? How does it contribute to national/international development?
7. Give three examples from personal life about projects
   - You have already undertaken
   - The projects you are currently working on
   - The project you would like to pursue in the future

   What are your observations and learning from the experience that you think make projects challenging?

CHAPTER

2

Project Identification and Screening

2.1 INTRODUCTION

Any project is conceived in response to a need or a desire. This necessitates the undertaking of some task or tasks to be completed, maybe initially very vaguely in the minds of an individual or a team or group responsible for this project. Ideas like what can or should be done, by whom and when invariably crop up and the seeds of a new project are born.

Gradually a picture of the whole task and the partitions appear to clarify after some brainstorming/discussion/negotiation and careful introspection. In Fig. 2.1 is shown a project partitioned into various parts, which could be identified as the major chunks of work to be performed. These individual tasks can later be assigned as responsibilities to different individuals or agencies. This is the pre-planning stage, generally referred to as a work breakdown structure, where a group is typically assigned the responsibility of developing a solution to a perceived need.

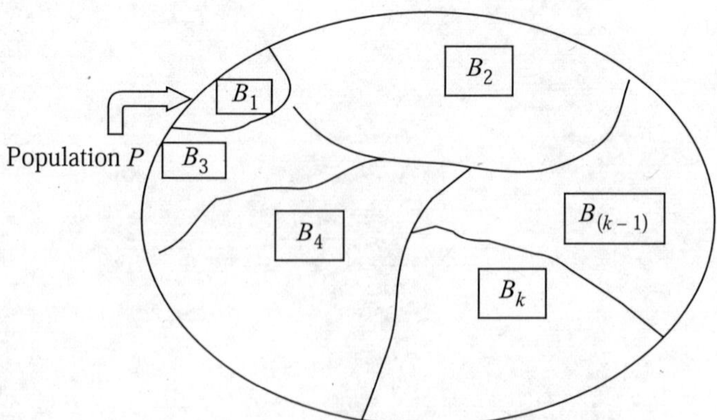

Fig. 2.1 The project components.

The project components are akin to the partition of a population P into sections $B_1, B_2, \ldots, B_k$ such that

$$B_1 \cup B_2 \cup \ldots \cup B_k = P$$

(i.e. the partitions add up to the whole population P)

$$B_1 \cap B_2 \cap \ldots \cap B_k = \Phi$$

(i.e. there are no common points in between various partitions)

To an extent this division is arbitrary, depending on the expertise, resources, human preferences and the natural tendencies of negotiation and aggression. It may be noticed, however, that the second condition of mutual exclusiveness of events is not necessary. If there are some overlaps, the intersecting areas could become the joint responsibilities of different partners.

Once the project has been conceived, comes the phase of planning and scheduling the project. This involves identifying the major tasks or activities to be done, establishing their precedence relations and estimating the durations of the activities. A project network in either the activity on arc (A-O-A) or the activity on node (A-O-N) mode is a convenient mechanism to represent this information. This is generally attained after mutual consensus among the working group. These days, many commercially available computer programs may be utilized to develop a schedule. But primarily the principle is to do a forward and backward pass to determine the critical path, which governs the duration of the project. Subsequently, resource considerations may be added to account for the available resources in terms of money, labour, machines, and materials, etc.

A project is generally represented as a network either in the activity on arc (A-O-A) or in the activity on node (A-O-N) mode after identifying the major tasks or activities to be performed. There are only two kinds of information—the tasks and their predecessors (or successors) required for developing a project network. Because activities are physical occurrences with a positive flow (i.e. they may only logically proceed forward in time, assuming their deliberate delay would be generally wasteful), looping in a project network would be a logical inconsistency. This is one reason why the study of project networks is also termed the study of directed acyclic networks.

Drawing or developing a project network is not a scheduling activity since nowhere yet, have we taken the times or durations of various activities into account. It is only at best the proposed chunks of work with their prescribed predecessor–successor relationships.

The product launch involves selecting the appropriate people to take on the various responsibilities for the tasks conceived ($B_1, B_2, \ldots, B_k$), preparing tasks for any joint responsibilities and appointing a project leader. This project leader should be totally responsible for the project from start to finish.

Generally, the project leader should have experience, wisdom, a long-range vision and an appreciation of the problems and hurdles in the execution of the project. He must be trustworthy, capable of inspiring his team members and providing for their needs with a spirit of understanding and self-sacrifice. Moreover, he must be empowered to take timely decisions without bureaucratic hang-ups.

2.2 EXPECTATIONS FROM A NEW PROJECT

Any individual or organization would think in terms of a new project because the circumstances within necessitate such action. A clear understanding of these circumstances is the starting point to identify the needs and expectations from the new project proposal.

The need could be to *grow* or *diversify.* In that case one could think of newer markets, expanding production facilities, introducing additional warehouses, newer products, e-commerce and so on. And a number of projects could then be conceived for each of these projected directions of growth.

Or the need may be to *counter the stiff competition and survive in the aggressive market place.* The need in such a situation may be to develop attractive and aggressive advertisement campaigns, add to product features, introduce incentive schemes and so forth.

Or the need may be to *close down an obsolete manufacturing plant and replace it with a modern one.* Clearly, the projects identified in such a situation would be to review different technologies, contact different vendors, compare features offered, organize disposal of old plant through auctions, and conduct a cost/benefit analysis before making a final choice.

It is important to realize that projects are a means to accomplish some objectives which may include

- Individual or family objectives
- Organizational objectives
- National or global objectives

Project identification begins in response to the specific need or the objectives. Some of the typical *objectives* in pursuing projects could be

- To increase profits
- To minimize threats of losses
- To become more competitive
- To provide help after a disaster
- To train people in a new area
- To reduce pollution in a metropolis like New Delhi
- To become a successful entrepreneur

The key to the process of growth of an organization lies in undertaking appropriate projects from time to time. Each successful project makes an incremental contribution to the infrastructure, revenues, corporate image and/or position of the organization. On the contrary, a project failure, either in terms of a wrong initial choice or improper implementation or by adverse and volatile market response, could mean a tremendous loss both monetarily and in terms of company prestige. Thus, the task of identifying the right projects for a company to pursue becomes extremely important for the strategic growth of the company. Normally, decisions of what an organization should be pursuing, both in the short term and in the long term, are taken by the top management. Such decisions require a vision of the future directions in which the organization is to be steered, an awareness of the emerging opportunities in terms of new technologies and products being contemplated by competitors, a realistic assessment of the strengths and weaknesses within the organization and a fair assessment of the risks that any new venture entails.

The birth of new projects takes place in the following three distinct phases:

- Project identification
- Project appraisal
- Project selection

Project identification is the stage where new ideas are generated. Normally, the top management with the participation of all the major functional areas such as marketing and sales, research and development, production, logistics and finance involved in the brainstorming exercise identifies the new project proposals. These proposals are screened on criteria relevant to the organization. The set of shortlisted proposals could be mapped using a SWOT analysis based on the intrinsic strengths and weaknesses of the organization and the extrinsic environmental opportunities and threats.

Project appraisal is a more detailed evaluation of a project proposal on its marketing potential, technical features, financial considerations of profitability and return, socioeconomic aspects and ecological dimensions. This phase yields the estimated performance measures of the project on a number of business, technical and financial criteria. Normally, a project feasibility study conducted on a project prior to its launch is nothing but a detailed project appraisal prepared with the intention of giving the top management a clear idea of the inputs and outputs envisaged by the project. The project feasibility report is often needed by financial institutions to take financing decisions for the project.

Project selection is the final stage in which a number of candidate project proposals are evaluated on multiple, often conflicting, criteria to determine a project score or a ranking for picking up the winning project proposal. This decision can be viewed as a decision matrix with project alternatives in each row and the various criteria in the respective columns. The complication in selection arises from the fact that some projects are good on some criteria and not so good on others. If there was a project which was consistently the best on each criterion, it would dominate the selection process and would qualify as the best project. Such situations, however, arise rarely and compromises and trade-offs have to be resorted to. The proper weights reflecting management priorities have to be determined for the criteria and resort could be made to any one of the many MCDM methods available in the literature.

2.3 PROJECT IDENTIFICATION

Project identification is a creative process and like all creative activities it is unpredictable and unstructured. The primary intention in this stage is to generate new ideas that could be considered worthwhile for implementation. The process of idea generation requires a systematic thought process. However, sometimes it may happen that an idea comes to the mind immediately, without much effort, and sometimes on the contrary, despite sustained thinking no idea emerges. This does not mean that the thinking process is futile; it may happen that the thoughts being processed in the subconscious mind may suddenly produce a eureka effect when we are relaxing or doing something entirely different. All new ventures begin with a need. We are not talking here of accidental discoveries. Most projects are initiated to accomplish some objectives. Therefore, the first step is to identify the need or the objective that is prompting the search for the new project. Figure 2.2 highlights the major steps in the identification of new project ideas and their screening to produce a set of proposals for a detailed appraisal.

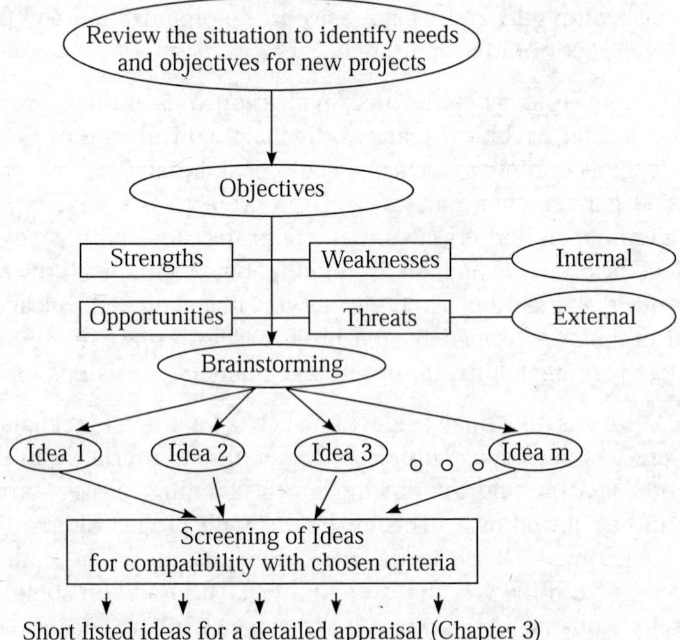

Fig. 2.2 Need identification and project screening.

2.3.1 SWOT Analysis

After having identified the objectives to be achieved by the new project, it is generally worthwhile to conduct a SWOT analysis so that the organization's strengths and weaknesses are highlighted and the opportunities and threats emerging from the environment are viewed in an objective manner. The purpose of this exercise is to be able to generate ideas exploiting the emerging opportunities, guarding against the threats while keeping the organization's strengths and weaknesses in mind. The participants in the brainstorming exercise would do well to participate in the SWOT analysis prior to the actual brainstorming so that they become aware of the requirements and limitations of the system they are dealing with. The extent of conformance of the various proposed solutions with the SWOT profile could also be used to evaluate the various ideas after they are proposed during brainstorming.

EXAMPLE 2.1

Suppose an entrepreneur has been working as a supplier of automobile spare parts to a number of retailers for the last 10 years. He has contacts with major automobile manufacturers from whom he buys the spares at company prices after negotiating suitable price discounts. He has now accumulated enough wealth to contemplate setting up of a manufacturing unit for a suspension unit used in 30% of the cars in the local market. Conduct a SWOT analysis for the entrepreneur indicating how well prepared he is to undertake his decision to switch from his current role as a supplier to a potential manufacturer.

Strengths

- Contacts with automobile manufacturers and vendors
- Good negotiating and marketing skills
- Awareness of market demand for various automobile spares
- Awareness of sources of supply of different products

Weaknesses

- No previous experience of manufacturing
- Much higher investments needed in manufacturing infrastructure

Opportunities

- There is only a single manufacturer of suspension units for the market segment of 30% of cars, and these are often in short supply.
- With marketing contacts, he can promote the manufactured brand with relative ease.
- With a liberalized economy, procurement of loans from banks is much easier.

Threats

- A sizeable share of the market (an estimated 15% of the market segment from amongst the 30% share of cars using the suspension) is manufactured by a Korean company that may wind up its operations from India in the next 6 months.
- There is a possibility of the introduction of a new kind of magnetic suspension by car manufacturers that will make the current suspension system obsolete.

In any realistic situation, considerable thought has to be given to identify the strengths, weaknesses, opportunities and threats that apply for the given situation. The following list is only indicative of some of the factors that ought to be considered while doing a SWOT analysis in practice.

Strengths

- Experience and expertise
- Financial position
- Capital raising capability
- Industrial contacts
- Foreign collaborations

Weaknesses

- Newer unfamiliar technologies
- Inability to raise huge investments
- Lack of experience
- Lack of trained personnel
- Inability to forecast market trends

Opportunities

- Emerging technologies
- New products with new markets
- New processes with better features
- Special financing schemes
- Government and other incentives

Threats

- Competitors
- Poor state of the economy
- Outdated technology
- Unprofessional management skills
- New products and services

2.4 BRAINSTORMING FOR IDEA GENERATION

Since the crucial requirement at the stage of project identification is the generation of new ideas, it is worthwhile to look at factors that improve idea generation capability (Table 2.1) and also at forces fighting new ideas (Table 2.2).

Once the specific situation and the pressing needs of the hour are understood, a concerted effort to discuss solutions and come up with feasible alternatives is the next step. All those concerned with the problem including the general manager, the R&D incharge, the production manager, the marketing and sales personnel,

Table 2.1 Ten ways to great new product ideas

1. Run pizza—video parties, as Kodak does—informal sessions where groups of customers meet with company engineers and designers to discuss problems and needs and brainstorm potential solutions.
2. Allow time off—scouting time—for technical people to putter in their own, pet projects. 3M allows 15% time off, Rohm & Haas allows 10%.
3. Make a customer brainstorming session a standard feature of plant tours.
4. Survey your customers. Find out what they like and dislike in your and your competitor's products.
5. Undertake "fly on the wall" or "camping out" research with customers, as do Fluke and Hewlett Packard.
6. Use iterative rounds: a group of customers in one room focusing on identifying problems, and a group of your technical people in the next room, listening and brainstorming solutions. The proposed solutions are then tested immediately on the group of customers.
7. Set up a keyword search that routinely scans trade publications in multiple countries for new product announcements and so on.
8. Treat trade shows as intelligent missions, where you view all that is new in your industry under one roof.
9. Have your technical and marketing people visit your supplier's labs and spend time with their technical people—find out what's new.
10. Set up an idea vault, and make it open and easily accessed. Allow employees to review the ideas and add constructively to them.

Table 2.2 Forces fighting new ideas

1. I've got a great idea.
2. It won't work here.
3. We've tried it before.
4. This isn't the right time.
5. It can't be done.
6. It's not the way we do things.
7. We've done alright without it.
8. It will cost too much.
9. Let's discuss it in our next meeting.

Source: Adapted from Kotler, Philip, *Marketing Management, The Millennium Edition*, Prentice-Hall of India, New Delhi, 2001.

and representatives of the key customers for the organization could constitute a team which could take part in the brainstorming exercise. Brainstorming is a systematic procedure to utilize the vast knowledge and experience of the experts in their respective fields and come up with ideas that try to address the problem from various fronts.

Brainstorming is normally conducted in a group whose size could vary from three to four individuals on the lower side to 25–30 on the higher side. If the number of participants is 10 or more, it is desirable to form groups of convenient size (say four to eight each) and conduct the brainstorming session for each group separately. Each group has a coordinator, who is one of the members of the brainstorming team who organizes the brainstorming session. After each team is acquainted with the general problem and the need and objectives for the generation of ideas, the coordinator could invite ideas from the members that he simply keeps recording.

The brainstorming could be done in a structured or unstructured manner. In the structured approach the coordinator asks each member in turn to give an idea. If the member has no idea to communicate at that particular time, he simply says "pass" and the coordinator moves to the next participant. During the next round again, the same participant is asked if he has any idea and he may give his idea, since by now something would have struck his mind. It is important to note that no criticism or evaluation of ideas is permitted at this stage as it would kill the creative process of generating new ideas.

In unstructured brainstorming, the ideas are recorded on a first come first served basis. Generally, the more vocal or aggressive members tend to dominate in this scheme and all the members may not get an opportunity to make their point in this system. Generally, the structured form of brainstorming is preferred and the coordinator keeps on making rounds till the requisite number of ideas has been generated.

Normally, 10–20 ideas from a group of about four to six people are considered good enough. If there are more groups participating, the total number of ideas generated would be correspondingly higher. The ideas generated during brainstorming are screened and evaluated later, to encourage creativity and innovative thinking among the participants.

2.5 SCREENING OF IDEAS

The process of brainstorming is a good means to generate new project ideas. It has a focus on uninhibited participation by all members of a group and results in listing of ideas without suppressing creativity at source. This list of ideas is subjected to screening and evaluation subsequently. This screening process is not a detailed evaluation, but is an attempt to select the more worthwhile ideas from the generated list of ideas during brainstorming. For instance, if the cost of the project, the risk, the monetary return and the hazardous nature of work involved are considered to be the four major criteria in the screening process, each project idea could be evaluated on these four criteria. Moreover, if the evaluator considers a weight of 20% for cost, 30% for risk, 40% for return and 10% for the hazard component, this can be easily used in the construction of a common evaluation sheet for all the ideas. Table 2.3 illustrates such a sheet for the example under consideration. It is convenient and adequate to rate an idea as poor, fair, good, very good and excellent on each of the chosen criteria. An evaluation of an idea on a five-point scale is illustrated in Table 2.4.

Table 2.3 A common evaluation format for new ideas

	Screening of Ideas					Weight
	Poor (1)	*Fair* (2)	*Good* (3)	*Very good* (4)	*Excellent* (5)	
Cost						20%
Risk						30%
Return						40%
Hazard						10%

Table 2.4 Evaluation of the score for an idea

	Score Evaluation					Weight
	Poor (1)	*Fair* (2)	*Good* (3)	*Very good* (4)	*Excellent* (5)	
Cost		*				20%
Risk			*			30%
Return				*		40%
Hazard		*				10%
(Score = $2 \times 0.2 + 3 \times 0.3 + 4 \times 0.4 + 2 \times 0.1 = 3.1$)						

This process could be utilized to evaluate all the ideas generated during the brainstorming exercise. The approach could be suitably modified to accommodate different sets of criteria, with requisite weights. The major idea behind the screening is to keep it as simple as possible by ensuring (i) there is one evaluation sheet for each idea, (ii) the evaluation of each idea is done by simply ticking the appropriate category for each criterion and (iii) the idea score is obtained by the weighted sum of factor evaluations.

Some of the criteria commonly used in screening projects are listed below.

- Investment
- Rate of return
- Risk
- Likely profit
- Payback
- Similarity to existing business
- Expected life
- Flexibility
- Environment impact
- Competition

2.6 AN ILLUSTRATIVE CASE STUDY

In order to illustrate the process of project identification and screening, the following group exercise was conducted with a group of students in the class. The problem considered was to identify projects that could be undertaken by citizens, the city and national government authorities to "REDUCE VEHICU-

LAR POLLUTION IN DELHI" and then to screen these project proposals to determine the three best proposals. Brainstorming teams were formed to generate ideas related to the topic. A structured approach to the brainstorming exercise was adopted. The following list of ideas emerged from one such exercise:

Idea Generation through Brainstorming

1. Restrict registration of new vehicles
2. Enforce strict emission regulations for vehicles
3. Ban diesel-run vehicles on road
4. Introduce MRTS for the city
5. Encourage use of car pools
6. Grow more trees/green belts in the city
7. Declare no traffic zones in the city
8. Ban vehicles with an age of 10 or more years from plying on the roads

These and more ideas could be generated through a brainstorming exercise.

Criteria for Screeing of Ideas

For the purpose of screening of ideas generated through brainstorming, the following criteria were considered:

- Effectiveness to achieve objective
- Cost of the proposal
- Ease of implementation
- Time needed

This is an illustrative list. Other criteria could be added, if needed.

Scale of Evaluation

The following five-point scale of evaluation was considered adequate for judging the various project ideas:

Very poor (0)	*Poor* (1)	*Fair* (2)	*Average* (3)	*Good* (4)	*Excellent* (5)
Low			*Effectiveness*		High
High			*Cost*		Low
Difficult			*Implementation*		Easy
Maximum			*Time*		Minimum

Scoring of each alternative was done by the brainstorming teams after considering the effectiveness of the alternative in accomplishing the intended goal, the cost of the alternative, the ease or difficulty of implementation and the time needed for implementation. This evaluation was based on the perceptions of the participants based on the pros and cons of each alternative. The kinds of arguments and analysis preceding the evaluations for each of the eight alternatives considered are summarized below.

1. *Restrict registration of new vehicles:* This alternative was considered to be effective in that it would handle the problem at its source and restrict the indiscriminate entry of new vehicles. However, it was felt that this solution would be costly to implement in that it curbed free customer rights and encouraged corruption in the regulatory bodies. Norms on who would be allowed to bring in a new vehicle could be tricky. Owing to these social factors and cost to implement this solution, the implementation may not be smooth and may even take some time.
2. *Enforce strict emission regulations on vehicles:* This was considered to be an effective means of controlling the pollution levels in the city. Making it mandatory for vehicle manufacturers to conform to the state-of-the-art norms in vehicle emission was seen as a necessary prerequisite to ensure the quality of the environment. Strict monitoring of individual vehicles for conformance to the pollution limits would result in controlling pollution levels within the city. The implementation of this strategy was comparatively easy through the existing infrastructure of traffic police and authorized pollution testing centres spread over the city petrol pumps. The implementation time for this option seemed quite reasonable.
3. *Ban diesel-run vehicles on the road:* Since poorly maintained diesel-operated trucks emitting dense black smoke are a common sight in the city, one suggestion that emerged was to ban their entry into the city. While a total ban may not be feasible as it could lead to inconveniencing the public by depriving them of a viable means of transportation of goods, a restricted entry during lean periods of traffic was considered a practical means to implement this policy. Implementation was visualized to be difficult owing to the strong lobby of transporters and union pressures. Monitoring and implementation of this strategy could be accomplished with the existing infrastructure and personnel.
4. *Introduce MRTS for the city:* For a city like Delhi which is bursting at its seams with growing population, fast increasing private vehicles on the road and a poor bus service, the Mass Rapid Transportation System (MRTS) would be a very welcome alternative. Owing to the huge time and petrol wasted in traffic jams, many people would switch from using personal vehicles or time-consuming buses to the fast and efficient MRTS. Though this would be an effective means to control pollution and provide customer convenience, it is an extremely costly and time-consuming proposition.
5. *Encourage use of car pools:* Considerable savings in fuel and environmental pollution could happen if sharing of cars through car pools could be effected. This is especially true for people residing close to each other and attending the same office or having places of work in

the vicinity. Persons could take turns to pick up and drop the members of the pool, thereby ensuring that only one vehicle is used rather than five or six in individual commuting. This option though inherently simple requires discipline and an accommodating attitude on the part of the partners. Moreover, it ceases to be practical if the residences/places of work of the partners are too far or inconveniently located. However, when implemented properly this strategy can provide an opportunity for encouraging friendships among partners, remove loneliness on long drives and prove economical.

6. *Grow more trees/green belts in the city:* Making the city greener by growing more trees and providing green belts not only would have a positive effect on the environment, but would also beautify the city and improve the quality of life. The launching of a horticultural drive after careful planning of the greening campaign would not be too expensive as it would involve the utilization of the existing manpower and infrastructure. Surely it would take time for the results to show up but the responsibility could be taken up by the municipal authorities and steps initiated in the direction quite easily.
7. *Declare no traffic zones in the city:* Declaration of certain zones as prohibited to traffic or imposing one way restrictions in certain areas could be viable options to control traffic congestion and pollution in the city. These measures do not require additional capital investments and are thus easy to implement. However, these measures may result in inconvenience to the commuters and provide localized relief from pollution to certain areas. But since the total number of vehicles remains unaltered and the total distance that they now have to travel has increased, the overall pollution level in the city may not be significantly affected.
8. *Ban 10-year and older vehicles:* It is generally true that older vehicles tend to contribute to noise and emissions because of natural wear and tear. Thus, banning 10-year and older vehicles from plying on the roads in the city would result in control of environmental pollution. Bringing out a legislation in this regard by the transport authorities and the design and implementation of a proper implementation strategy would be steps needed to implement this strategy. However, the impact on the owners of old vehicles, especially in an economically underdeveloped society, may be rather harsh. Moreover, such steps could encourage the owners of old vehicles to produce fake certificates and indulge in corrupt practices.

Score Card of Alternative Projects

It was assumed in this project screening exercise that the four criteria of effectiveness, cost, implementation and time were equally important. Each project alternative was evaluated on a scale of 0–5, with 0 being the worst performance and 5 the best. The scores of the individual project alternatives on the four criteria and the overall score are indicated below. These scores were derived on the basis of the above discussion taking into account all subjective and objective considerations in mind. (It may be indicated here that any scale such as 0–10 or 0–100 could have been adopted for the screening exercise. Also different weights to the criteria could be assigned and the evaluation done accordingly.)

S. No.	*Project proposal*	*Scores criteria* (1–4)				*Overall*
1.	Restrict registration of new vehicles	3	1	1	2	7
2.	Enforce strict emission regulations on vehicles	4	5	4	5	18
3.	Ban diesel run vehicles on the road	3	1	1	2	7
4.	Introduce MRTS for the city	4	0	1	0	5
5.	Encourage use of car pools	2	5	4	4	15
6.	Grow more trees/green belts in the city	4	3	3	3	13
7.	Declare no traffic zones in the city	2	3	2	2	9
8.	Ban 10–year and older vehicles	3	2	3	3	11

Results of Screening

From the above evaluation, the three best project alternatives can be identified as follows:

Project No. 2: Enforce strict emission regulations on vehicles (18 points)
Project No. 5: Encourage use of car pools (15 points)
Project No. 6: Grow more trees/green belts in the city (13 points)

2.7 SUMMARY AND CONCLUSIONS

- Project identification is generally done by brainstorming.
- Broad objectives guide the brainstorming.
- Introspection is necessary to identify the strengths and weaknesses of the system.
- Looking outside towards the environment provides new opportunities and threats.
- Evaluation of ideas is suspended during brainstorming to encourage creativity.
- A subsequent screening on relevant criteria produces a candidate set of projects for detailed scrutiny.
- An exercise to illustrate the procedure was undertaken.

PROBLEMS

1. Go through a brainstorming exercise (in groups of four to six) to identify a list of 10 projects each to achieve the following broad objectives:

(a) To reduce vehicular pollution in a metropolis like Delhi
(b) To reduce traffic congestion in the city
(c) To improve literacy in the country
(d) To reduce poverty in the country
(e) To improve sanitation conditions in a jhuggi cluster in South Delhi
(f) To become a successful entrepreneur after graduation

2. For each of the projects identified in Question 1, go through a screening exercise based on factors like the following:

   Investment
   Risk
   Return
   Competition
   Difficulty of successful implementation
   Time to implement
   Impact on society
   Impact on environment

   (a) Prepare a list of appropriate factors for each situation
   (b) Assign weights to factors representing your priorities
   (c) Devise appropriate scales of measurement (poor, fair, average, good) for each factor
   (d) Evaluate and rank projects
   (e) Identify the three most important projects under each category of broad objectives to be achieved.

3. Keeping the top project identified in Question 2 in mind, go through a SWOT analysis and list the strengths, weaknesses, opportunities and threats that you foresee in implementation of this project.
   How do you intend to use this information in preparing to undertake this project for implementation?

4. Give five examples each of projects at the following levels with estimates of likely costs and duration.

	Cost		Duration	
	Min	Max	Min	Max
(a) Personal				
(b) Family				
(c) Residential colony				
(d) State				
(e) National				
(f) Asian				
(g) Global				
(h) Solar system				

5. List some possible objectives in project identification and screening.

6. A radar chart could be one means of representing project performance on multiple criteria. Generate three alternative ideas for holiday plans and represent the consequences on a radar chart.

CHAPTER

3

Project Appraisal

3.1 INTRODUCTION

Once a new project proposal is made, it has to be evaluated on a number of criteria to ensure that it is feasible, worthwhile and financially attractive. This detailed and systematic evaluation of the project before an organization commits itself to the project is a necessary exercise that results in the preparation of the project feasibility report. The project feasibility report contains the appraisal of the project on a number of relevant criteria which generally include

- Market appraisal
- Technical appraisal
- Financial appraisal
- Socio-economic appraisal
- Ecological appraisal

3.2 MARKET APPRAISAL

The market appraisal of a project is concerned with establishing the clientele of a project. Some of the important questions that need to be asked at this stage include

- "Who is the customer?"
- "What are his/her needs?"
- "Which are the alternative products or services that satisfy the customer's needs?"
- "What is the competitive position of the product or service vis-à-vis other competitors?"
- "How do we expect the market demand to change over the next few years?"

A market research study based on personal interviews with prospective customers, questionnaire analysis, a historical survey of similar products, information of competitor performance from the Internet or other sources and brainstorming among experts would help to identify the marketing potential of the project by answering the following two basic questions:

- What would be the aggregate demand of the proposed product or service? This would be equivalent to determining the forecast of total demand for the contemplated product or service as indicated in Fig. 3.1 by a solid line.
- What would be the market share of the project under appraisal? This represents the share of overall demand that the product is capable of capturing. (The market share can vary from 0 to 100% and a value towards 100 indicates a market leader, whereas a value close to 0 indicates an unpopular product.) The market share would obviously be affected by a number of factors vis-à-vis the competitors. These would include factors such as the product quality and features, the advertising and marketing efforts, the price and other incentives offered, the after sales service, customer concern shown by the company and the production capacity. The assessment of the market share could be done either from historical data or from estimates provided by experts who are familiar with the market trends and the positions of various players. From these estimates it would be possible to determine the estimated demand for the individual product as shown in Fig. 3.1 by a dotted line.

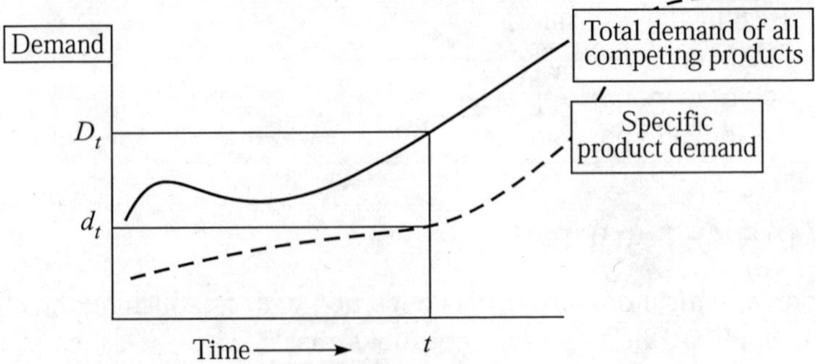

Fig. 3.1 Demand projections.

If d_t represents the specific product demand and D_t the total demand of all competing products at time t, the market share of the product at any time t would be the ratio d_t/D_t. This ratio could be changing over time owing to environmental factors, competitor strategies and the company's own efforts to improve its quality and marketing.

For the estimation of the total demand, resort has to be made to systematic forecasting techniques. Broadly, the following techniques are commonly employed for purposes of forecasting:

(a) Subjective or intuitive methods
  - Opinion polls, interviews
  - DELPHI

(b) Methods based on averaging of past data
  - Moving averages
  - Exponential Smoothing

(c) Regression models on historical data
  - Trend Extrapolation

(d) Causal or econometric models

(e) Time-series analysis
  - Decomposition
  - Stochastic models (e.g. Box Jenkins)

3.2.1 Subjective or Intuitive Methods

The subjective or intuitive methods like interviews, questionnaires and DELPHI are most suited in new product launch situations where no historical data is available about the demand patterns. In such situations, reliance on the experts for their opinions is a common procedure to estimate the demand. The vast knowledge base of the expert, which may include many years of experience in handling similar situations, comes very handy in making an estimate of the demand.

EXAMPLE 3.1 Obtaining an aggregate forecast from opinions of salespersons:

The general manager of a company is interested in estimating the total sales in India of his product (in units) for the next financial year. He has a dialogue with the five salespersons of the company who are responsible for sales in the five regions of the country, namely North, South, East, West and Central and gathers the following data from them (Table 3.1).

Table 3.1 Simple aggregation of forecasts

Salesperson	*Region*	*Sales last year* (units)	*Estimated sales for next year* (units)
Ashok	North	50,000	60,000
Neelam	South	40,000	45,000
Sunil	East	20,000	15,000
Ganesh	West	70,000	90,000
Preeti	Central	30,000	40,000
Total	**All India**	**2,10,000**	**2,50,000**

By a simple aggregation of the opinions of his five experts, the general manager is able to arrive at an estimate of the all India sales of the company for the next year. In producing this forecast, the general manager has utilized the knowledge and experience of his experts, for the salesperson of a particular region knows best both the potential for sales and the limitations in each region.

The general manager may wish to moderate these figures before he decides to project a final figure of next year demand to his boss, the vice president of the company. This could be due to the subjective bias that is likely to be inherent in each individual. Since the general manager has known his salespersons over many years, he has formed some opinions about the reliability and trustworthiness of each of his colleagues. If he mentally incorporates these figures in the analysis, the results could be adjusted as shown in Table 3.2.

Table 3.2 Adjusted aggregate of forecasts

Salesperson (I)	*Region* (II)	*Sales last year* (units) (III)	*Estimated sales for next year* (units) (IV)	*Coefficient of reliability (Subjective estimate)* (V)	*Modified estimate of next year sales* (units) (VI = IV × V)
Ashok	North	50,000	60,000	0.8	48,000
Neelam	South	40,000	45,000	1.0	45,000
Sunil	East	20,000	15,000	0.9	13,500
Ganesh	West	70,000	90,000	1.1	99,000
Preeti	Central	30,000	40,000	0.9	36,000
Total	**All India**	**2,10,000**	**2,50,000**		**2,41,500**

Subjective and intuitive methods of forecasting have the advantage of utilizing the knowledge base of the experts. However, the major drawback in these approaches is the subjective bias that is inherent in dealing with human beings. Each individual is a unique personality entitled to his opinions, prejudices and beliefs. The DELPHI method is one approach that tries to eliminate or minimize the individual bias. This is also a systematic procedure for arriving at a consensus on an estimate and can be used for not only forecasting the demand but also answering a number of questions about market share, global or national trends of new products, services or technologies or the likely outcomes of a political or financial policy of a country.

The DELPHI approach is characterized by

- A coordinator who forms a panel of experts to obtain responses on a particular issue (Fig. 3.2).
- Anonymity is preserved on the panel to remove personal influence and bias.
- The procedure of obtaining responses is iterative in nature. (Generally three are three rounds.)
- A statistical summary of the responses by different experts (without divulging the name of the respondents) is circulated to all respondents at the end of each round.
- At the conclusion, either a consensus emerges (as shown in Fig. 3.3) or divergent viewpoints show up (Fig. 3.4). In either case, useful information concerning the original issue is obtained.

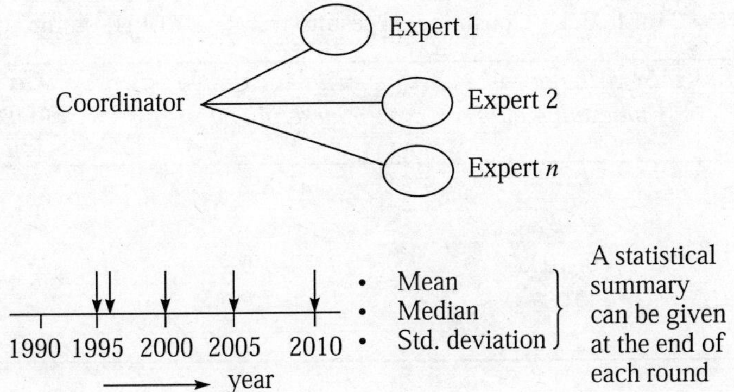

Fig. 3.2 Composition of a DELPHI panel with initial responses.

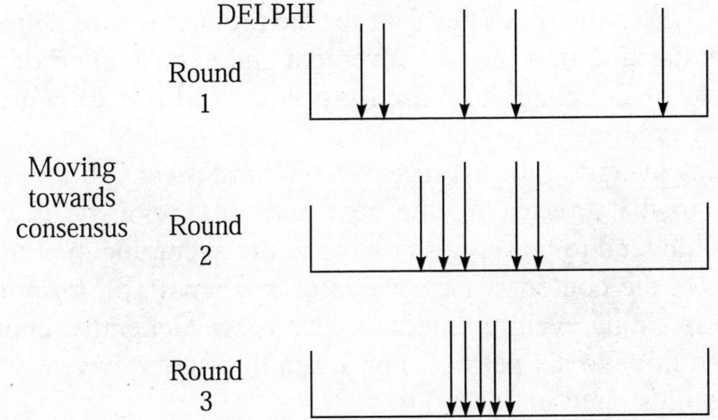

Fig. 3.3 DELPHI panelists moving successively towards consensus.

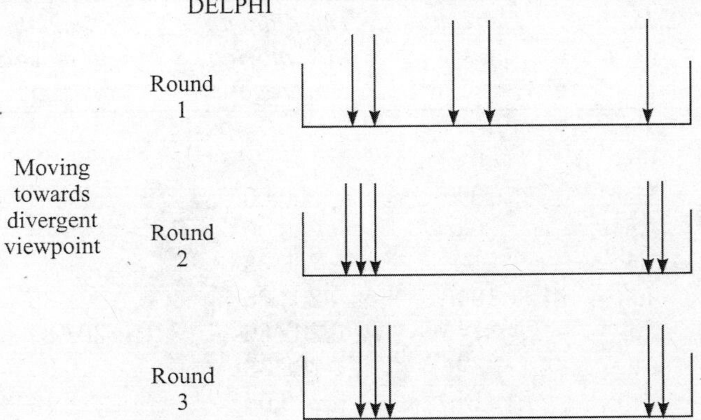

Fig. 3.4 Emergence of diverging viewpoints in DELPHI.

For instance, this procedure may be utilized to obtain the market share of a new product to be launched. Assuming a number of competitors are already there in the field, the respondents may be asked to predict the market share for the product over the next five years. Table 3.3 summarizes the results.

Table 3.3 Consolidated results from a DELPHI study

Year	*With normal marketing effort*	*With aggressive marketing effort*	*Gross total estimated sales* (Rs. in lacs)
1	5–6%	7–8%	20
2	7–8%	9–11%	20
3	9–10%	10–12%	28
4	10%	11–12%	35
5	10%	12%	45

3.2.2 Averaging of Past Data

In situations where the past sales data for the product is available, averaging of the previous demand becomes a convenient and easy method of obtaining the forecast. Two of the commonly used procedures in this category are moving averages and exponential smoothing.

In moving averages, the average of the k most recent observations provides an estimate of the forecast for the next period. Obviously, if k is large, the response would tend to be sluggish owing to the averaging over a large number of periods. On the contrary, if the value of k is small, the response would be sensitive, responding even to random fluctuations. Generally, chosen values of k lie between three to six periods. For a sample history of yearly demand, this procedure is illustrated in Table 3.4.

Table 3.4 Moving averages

Month	*Demand*	*Three-month MA (moving average)*	*Six-month MA (moving average)*
Jan	199		
Feb	202		
Mar	199	200.00	
Apr	208	203.00	
May	212	206.33	
Jun	194	203.66	202.33
Jul	214	205.66	207.83
Aug	220	208.33	210.83
Sep	219	216.66	213.13
Oct	234	223.33	217.46
Nov	219	223.00	218.63
Dec	233	227.66	225.13

In exponential smoothing, each data point in the demand history gets a certain weightage and the forecast is obtained as the weighted average in which all the points contribute depending on where they are placed with respect to the current demand. The weightage is the highest for the most recent demand point and declines exponentially as points recede into the past.

Exponential Smoothing

F_t = one period ahead forecast made at time t
D_t = actual demand for period t
α = smoothing constant (between 0 and 1)
(generally chosen values lie between 0.01 and 0.3)

$$F_t = \boxed{F_{t-1} + \alpha(D_t - F_{t-1})}$$

$$\begin{aligned} F_t &= \alpha D_t + (1-\alpha)F_{t-1} \\ &= \alpha D_t + (1-\alpha)[\alpha D_{t-1} + (1-\alpha)F_{t-2}] \\ &= \alpha[D_t + (1-\alpha)D_{t-1} + (1-\alpha)^2 D_{t-2} + \cdots \\ &\quad + (1-\alpha)^{t-1} D_1 + (1-\alpha)^t F_0] \end{aligned}$$

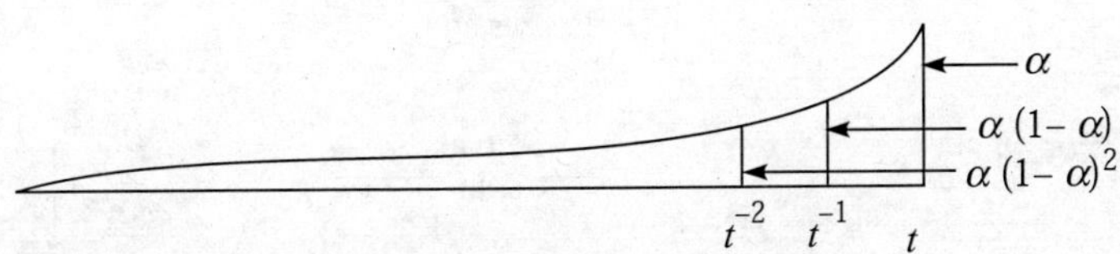

Weightages given to past data decline *exponentially*.

A comparison of the forecast for the demand data of Table 3.4 using

(a) A three-month moving average
(b) A six-month moving average
(c) Exponential smoothing with $\alpha = 0.3$
(d) Exponential smoothing with $\alpha = 0.1$ is made in Fig. 3.5.

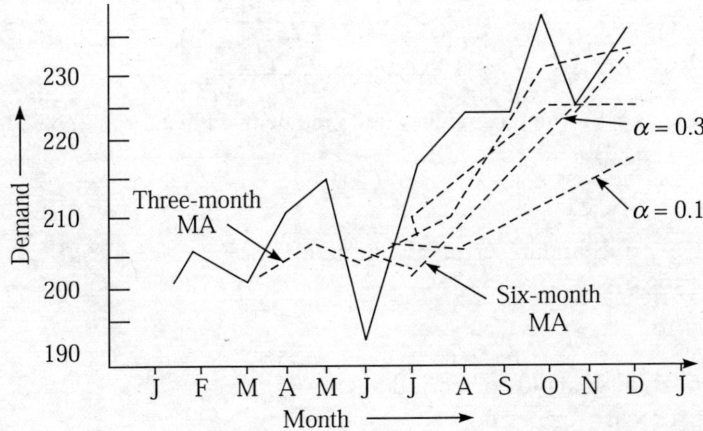

Fig. 3.5 Forecasts using moving averages and exponential smoothing.

3.2.3 Regression Models over Past Data

In situations in which historical data for the past few months or years is available it may be easy to plot the data and see if there are any trends observed in the plot. From these trends it is possible to hypothesize a mathematical function that may be fitted to the historical data. Projections of the fitted function over time give us forecasts of the future value of demand. This procedure essentially assumes that the system of chance causes that operated in the past will continue to operate in the future as well. Also it does not account for any unforeseen circumstances like floods, war or other natural calamities. However, it is a good approach when we envisage continuance of the status quo.

If we consider the same set of data that we considered earlier for illustrating moving averages and exponential smoothing and fit a straight line to it, we obtain the results shown in Fig. 3.6.

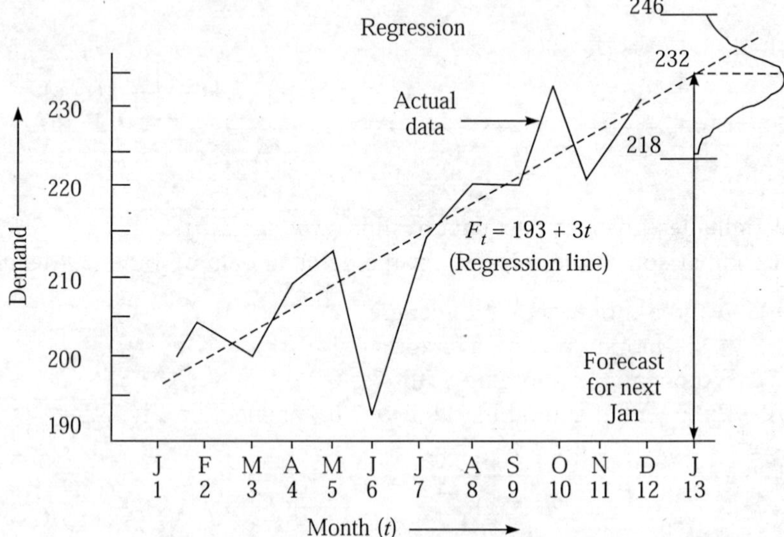

Fig. 3.6 Fitting a straight line to the demand history of Table 3.4.

$$\text{Standard error of estimate} = \sqrt{\frac{\sum_{t=1}^{n}(D_t - F_t)^2}{n - f}}$$

$$= 7.32$$

where

D_t = actual demand for period t

F_t = forecast for period t

n = no. of data points

f = degrees of freedom lost (2 in this case)

95% confidence limits for forecast of next Jan $\simeq 232 \pm 14$ (2 sigma limits)

3.2.4 Causal or Econometric Models

The major assumption in extrapolatory models is that the system of causes operating in the past will continue to operate in the future as well. Thus, the regression model based on past behaviour will apply to future trends as well. Whenever this assumption holds good the forecast based on extrapolation of past trend will continue to hold. However, in certain situations, some or all of the underlying causes may change either by a deliberate attempt on the part of the decision maker or by environmental concerns or a regulatory agency like the government. In such situations, causal or econometric models provide the right framework for making forecasts.

In essence a causal model is one in which the demand or variable of interest is modelled as a function of the causal variables. These causal variables have to be properly identified by studying the dynamics of the process. One useful indicator of whether the chosen variable really affects the demand is the correlation coefficient. Normally it is expected that the influencing causal variables would have a high correlation with the demand. Once the causal variables are identified, regression analysis is used to estimate the parameters of the model from the existing data. The final causal model so constructed is useful for making forecasts under varying conditions that may prevail in the future. For instance, it is common to answer questions such as the following using causal models:

- What would be the demand for car tyres if the government puts a partial freeze (10%, 25% or 50%) on car production in the next three years?
- What would be the annual sales of air-conditioners if the per capita income of the target group goes up by 5%, 8% or 10%?
- What would be the country's exports (in millions of rupees) if the GDP rose by 2%, 4% or 5%?

Causal Models

Here demand is related to causal variables, such as

- GNP
- Per capita income
- Consumer price index, etc.

A causal model for the demand of car tyres would thus look like the following:

Demand for tyres = *f*(Production of new automobiles, Replacements by existing autos, Govt policy on automobilies, ...)

$$D_t = \alpha P_t + \beta P_{t-5} + \gamma$$

is a simplified causal model

In this model, P_t represents the production of new cars in the year t and assuming that cars on the average require tyre replacements after 5 years, P_{t-5} would be an estimate of the replacements.

(Here parameters α, β and γ are estimated by regression from data.)

For a causal model to be useful in practice, the causal variables should be

- Leading
- Highly correlated with the variable of interest

3.3 TECHNICAL APPRAISAL OF A PROJECT

The primary objective in the technical appraisal of a project is to ensure that the right decisions have been made with regard to size, location, process selection and overall layout of the proposed facility. A check is often made to ensure that the project does not violate any well-established scientific laws and the projections of output and consumption of resources are sound and reliable. Decisions pertaining to choice of equipment and processes would involve a consideration of inefficiencies at various stages and an overall optimal choice would have to be made to ensure that the project meets its overall objectives. Since the technical appraisal would be specific to the project—there could be various examples, such as refineries, pipelines, marketing, distribution, construction, highway networks, building of flyovers, building of cement, steel, automobile plants—this appraisal would have to be carried out by the respective experts who are aware of industry practices, international standards and the relevant knowledge base in the field.

Keeping the above general guidelines in mind, the experts would carry out a technical appraisal of a project proposal and comment on its technical feasibility. Only if the proposal is technically sound would it be worthwhile to pursue the project further.

3.4 FINANCIAL APPRAISAL OF PROJECTS

The financial appraisal of a project is generally one of the most important appraisals carried out on a project. The primary purpose of this appraisal is to determine the costs and revenues over the life of the project and see whether there is an adequate return on the investment. Financing the project through institutional loans is also one of the objectives during the financial appraisal. Both these aspects of evaluating return and debt-servicing capability involve the collection of data of the following kind:

- Estimation of cost of the project and its timing
- Estimation of the likely revenues during each period (i.e. estimating the market share and your share in that so that the profit margins, IRR, etc. can be calculated, thereby deciding on the projects)
- The cost of capital (minimum acceptable rate of return as it is generally fluctuating)
- The planning horizon of the project

- The risk in the project as evidenced by the worst and the best values of costs and revenues (i.e. determining the cash flows as a pure optimistic and as a pure pessimistic estimate to get the extreme values of the cash flows and then applying the probabilistic models to calculate the cash flows)

3.4.1 Financial Criteria of Interest

All the following are concerned with the return on the investment:

- Net present value
- Internal rate of return
- Simple before/after tax rates of return
- Equivalent annual cost (it is used to compare the costs of two projects with unequal lives)
- Payback period
- Discounted payback

3.4.2 Criteria for Debt Repayment

These are concerned with the calculations of paying back the loan taken for the project.

- Benefit/cost ratio of discounted cash flows (if this ratio is >1 then you are capable of returning the loan, also logically if benefit is greater than the cost only then can one return the loan).
- Debt service coverage ratio (used by most of the companies). Index of loan returning capability given by

$$\frac{\text{Actual cash flow}}{\text{Commitment to return the loan}}$$

- A company's reputation in terms of assets and liabilities and record of previous repayments is often considered by the financing institutions before disbursing a loan. (If the company has a good reputation, it gets the loan easily. Also if the loan is not returned, the project is overtaken by the loan giver.)

3.5 A SAMPLE PROJECT

Suppose a project has the following data:

- Initial investment (I) = Rs. 3,00,000
- Annual costs of operation = Rs. 20,000
- Expected annual revenues
  - Rs. 1,00,000 per annum for the first two years
  - Rs. 200,000 per annum for the next three years
- Planning horizon of five years

INVESTMENT, YEARLY COSTS & REVENUES
GROSS CASH FLOWS
UNDISCOUNTED CASH FLOWS BEFORE TAX

• Year	0	1	2	3	4	5
• Cash flow	–300	80	80	180	180	180
• Cumulative cash flow	–300	–220	–140	40	220	400

Net present value = 400 (in thousands)
Payback period = 2.78 years (interpolated as the year when cumulative cash flow becomes zero)

DISCOUNTED CASH FLOWS FOR INTEREST RATE = 10%

• Year	0	1	2	3	4	5
• Cash flows	–300	80	80	180	180	180
• Discount factor	1	0.909	0.826	0.751	0.683	0.621
• DCF	–300	72.72	66.08	135.18	122.94	111.78
• Cum DCF	–300	–227.28	–161.2	–26.02	96.92	208.70

- Net present value = 208.7 (in thousands)
- Payback period = 3.21 years

DISCOUNTED CASH FLOWS FOR INTEREST RATE = 20%

• Year	0	1	2	3	4	5
• Cash flows	–300	80	80	180	180	180
• Discount factor	1	0.833	0.694	0.579	0.482	0.402
• DCF	–300	66.64	55.52	104.22	86.76	72.36
• Cum DCF	–300	–233.36	–177.84	–73.62	13.14	85.50

- Net present value = 85.5 (in thousands)
- Payback period = 3.85 years

DISCOUNTED CASH FLOWS FOR INTEREST RATE = 30%

• Year	0	1	2	3	4	5
• Cash flows	–300	80	80	180	180	180
• Discount factor	1	0.769	0.592	0.455	0.350	0.269
• DCF	–300	61.52	47.46	81.90	63	48.42
• Cum DCF	–300	–238.48	–191.02	–101.92	–46.12	2.30

- Net present value = 2.30 (in thousands)
- Payback period = 5 years

NET AFTER TAX CASH FLOWS

• Year	0	1	2	3	4	5
• Depreciation (Straight line)		60	60	60	60	60

Year	1	2	3	4	5
Taxable income	20	20	120	120	120
Tax (30%)	6	6	36	36	36
After tax cash flows	74	74	144	144	144

NET CASH FLOWS (INTEREST = 0%)

Year	0	1	2	3	4	5
Net cash flow	–300	74	74	144	144	144
Cumulative net cash flow	–300	–226	–152	–8	136	280

- Net present value = 280 (in thousand Rs)
- Payback period = 3.06 years

NET DISCOUNTED CASH FLOWS (INTEREST RATE = 10%)

Year	0	1	2	3	4	5
Cash flows	–300	80	80	180	180	180
After tax cash flows	–300	74	74	144	144	144
Discount factor	1	0.909	0.826	0.751	0.683	0.621
DCF	–300	67.27	61.12	108.14	98.35	89.42
Cum DCF	–300	–232.73	–171.61	–63.47	34.88	124.30

- Net present value = 124.3 (in thousands)
- Payback period = 3.65 years

NET DISCOUNTED CASH FLOWS (INTEREST RATE = 20%)

Year	0	1	2	3	4	5
Cash flows	–300	80	80	180	180	180
After tax cash flows	–300	74	74	144	144	144
Discount factor	1	0.833	0.694	0.579	0.482	0.402
DCF	–300	61.64	51.36	83.38	69.41	57.89
Cum DCF	–300	–238.36	–187.00	–103.62	–34.21	23.68

- Net present value = 23.68 (in thousands)
- Payback period = 4.6 years

NET DISCOUNTED CASH FLOWS (INTEREST RATE = 30%)

Year	0	1	2	3	4	5
Cash flows	–300	80	80	180	180	180
After tax cash flows	–300	74	74	144	144	144
Discount factor	1	0.769	0.592	0.455	0.350	0.269
DCF	–300	56.91	43.81	65.52	50.40	38.74
Cum DCF	–300	–243.09	–199.28	–133.76	–83.36	–44.62

- Net present value = –44.62 (in thousands)
- Payback period >5 years

The Internal Rate of Return (IRR) is that value of the interest for which the NPV equal zero.

Before & After Tax Cash Flows for the sample project are summarized below for different rates of interest:

BEFORE TAX			*AFTER TAX*	
NPV	Payback	Interest	Payback	NPV
400	2.78	0%	3.06	280
208.7	3.21	10%	3.65	124.31
85.5	3.85	20%	4.6	23.67
2.2	4.95	30%	>5	–44.63

It can be seen that the before tax IRR is greater than 30% while the after tax IRR is 23.5% (by linear interpolation).

DEBT SERVICE COVERAGE RATIO

(A) Total Cash Accrual
- (i) Profit after tax
- (ii) Depreciation
- (iii) Interest on term loan

(B) Debt Service Requirements
- (i) Interest on term loan
- (ii) Repayment of term loan

Debt service coverage ratio equals

$$\frac{\text{Total cash accrual (A)}}{\text{Debt service requirements (B)}}$$

(Generally, a DSCR of 1.5–2 is considered satisfactory by financial institutions.

If it is < 1.5, loan of longer maturity is provided and

If it is > 2, maturity period may be shortened.)

Example

Year 1 2 3 4 5 6 7 8 9 10

(A) Total Cash Accrual (Rs. in million)

(i) Profit after tax	0.27	0.81	1.35	1.13	0.99	0.99	0.99	1.01	1.02	1.04
(ii) Depreciation	0.7	0.7	0.7	0.7	0.7	0.7	0.7	0.7	0.7	0.7
(iii) Interest on term loan	1.18	1.18	1.07	0.93	0.78	0.64	0.48	0.33	0.19	0.04
Total of A	2.25	2.69	3.12	2.76	2.47	2.33	2.17	2.04	1.91	1.78
Year	1	2	3	4	5	6	7	8	9	10

(B) Debt Service Requirements (Rs. in million)

(i) Interest on term loan

1.18	1.18	1.07	0.93	0.78	0.64	0.48	0.33	0.19	0.04

(ii) Repayment of term loan

–	0.4	0.8	0.8	0.8	0.8	0.8	0.8	0.8	0.4

Total of B

1.18	1.58	1.87	1.73	1.58	1.43	1.28	1.13	0.99	0.44

DSCR A/B (Average DSCR = 1.96)

1.82	**1.70**	**1.67**	**1.60**	**1.56**	**1.63**	**1.70**	**1.81**	**2.01**	**4.05**

3.6 SUMMARY AND CONCLUSIONS

- Vital role of financial appraisal in overall project evaluation
- Estimation of investment, yearly costs and revenues to obtain gross cash flows
- Depreciation and tax concepts to obtain net cash flows
- Computation of NPV, IRR, benefit/cost ratio and payback
- Debt service coverage ratio and its implications for financial institutions
- Role of financial appraisal of a project in conjunction with market, technical, economic and ecological analyses in producing the project feasibility report

PROBLEMS

1. What is the role of the following in project evaluation?
   (a) Market appraisal
   (b) Technical appraisal
   (c) Financial appraisal
   (d) Economic appraisal
2. An entrepreneur is considering investing in a project to manufacture a new brand of soap with an initial investment of Rs.10,00,000. Other relevant data is given below:

Year	1	2	3	4	5
Total sales expected (in lakhs of Rs.)	50	60	75	100	120
Likely market share (Percentage)	5	7	8	6	6

   Calculate the NPV, internal rate of return and discounted payback if the minimum expected rate of return is
   (a) 10% (b) 20%

3. Four alternative projects each requiring an investment of Rs. 20,000 yield the following benefits:

	Year			
	1	2	3	4
Alternative 1	8000	8000	8000	8000
Alternative 2	6000	8000	10,000	10,000
Alternative 3	4000	8000	10,000	10,000
Alternative 4	10,000	10,000	10,000	5000

Compare the project proposals on IRR, NPV and discounted payback assuming that the rate of interest is 10%.

4. Consider the following general project appraisal problem:
A project has an initial investment *I*.
The revenues from sales over the *n* year projected life of the project are $r_1, r_2, \ldots, r_n$.
The operating costs over the *n* years are $o_1, o_2, \ldots, o_n$.
The terminal salvage of the project at the end of *n* years is *S*.
The depreciation allowed for taxation purposes is *d*% (straight line, sum of digits or declining balance).
Tax rate applicable to the company is *T*%.
Compute (a) Before tax cash flows for the project.
(b) After tax cash flows for the project.
If a loan of *P*% of the initial investment of the project was to be taken at an interest rate of *I*%, what would be the loan instalment each year for *m* years ($m < n$)?
Compute the interest and principal component of the loan recovery each year.
With this information, compute the before and after tax rates of return. Compute the after tax NPV, IRR and payback. What is the debt service coverage ratio?

5. For various combinations of data, compute the following parameters: NPV, IRR, discounted payback, debt service coverage ratio (DSCR). Take the following data:

Year	0	1	2	3	4	5	6	
Revenues	–10	4	4	5	6	6	6	(in lakhs of Rs.)
Operating costs	0	1	1	1.5	1.5	1.5	1.5	(in lakhs of Rs.)
Terminal salvage							4	(in lakhs of Rs.)

Tax rate applicable 30%

For the following four cases, compute and compare NPV, IRR, undiscounted and discounted paybacks and the DSCR.

(a) Straight line depreciation over 4 years, no loan.
(b) Sum of digits depreciation over 4 years with 80% of investment as a loan with interest rate of 10% and recovery in 3 years.

(c) Sum of digits depreciation over 3 years with 80% of the investment as a loan with interest rate of 10% and recovery in 5 years.

(d) Depreciation over 5 years using declining balance and 50% of the investment as loan with interest rate of 10% and recovery over 3 years.

6. For the general situation described in Question 4, develop a computer package capable of handling arbitrary data inputs to generate the five crucial financial parameters NPV, IRR, discounted and undiscounted payback and the debt service coverage ratio.

   Use the package to verify your computations in Question 2.

CHAPTER

4

Project Selection with Multiple Criteria

4.1 INTRODUCTION

The appraisal of prospective projects results in information pertaining to their cost, revenues, NPV, risk, technical viability, environmental compatibility and other criteria of interest. Once these performance features of the candidate projects have been evaluated, comes the important decision of selecting the project to be chosen for implementation.

We are all faced with these kinds of decisions in our daily lives. For instance, if we have to purchase any article of personal consumption, such as a pair of shoes or a pair of trousers or a shirt, we may visit different shops and carry out an appraisal on the basis of quality, price and styling. A final choice is made considering all the above criteria. Notice that the final decision is subjective depending on the preferences given to various criteria by different individuals.

The nature of the project selection problem is also similar. However, since the decision involves greater investments, affects a larger number of people and generally involves penalties for wrong selection, it is important that the project selection be carried out systematically with due care.

The simplest decision from amongst alternative projects would be when a particular project outshines other projects on all the criteria. This would be very much like having a candidate in a class topping in all the individual subjects. There would then be no doubt in declaring him the winner irrespective of the weightages given to individual subjects. Similarly, if a project outperforms all the other projects on each of the various criteria, it is called a *dominant* project.

Dominance is an interesting property though it does not occur very frequently in project selection. A more common scenario is when certain projects are good on certain criteria and not so good on other criteria and there is no clear winning project. In a situation of this kind one can discover a set of *non-dominated projects* or *the Pareto-Optimal set* as it is often called. The selection of the best project out of the non-dominated set would involve trade-offs between performance on different attributes and clearly the choice would be based on the weightages assigned to the different criteria.

Since the weightages are so crucial to the project selection problem, considerable research has been devoted to methods for finding out the appropriate weightages to the various criteria. Some of the commonly used methods for assigning weights are

- Consensus between decision maker and his team
- Systematic procedure using pair-wise comparisons
- Use of the analytic hierarchy procedure (AHP) developed by Thomas L. Saaty (1977).

Each procedure may be used depending on the complexity of the problem and the preferences of the decision maker. Whilst the first two approaches are simple and give the participants a direct sense of involvement, the AHP approach is more rigorous and utilizes eigenvalues to give a rating of the inconsistency ratio for the relative weightages proposed by the decision maker.

Once the performance of different projects on the criteria of relevance is listed in a tabular form, known as the Decision Matrix, one can resort to a number of Multi-Attribute Decision Making Methods to rank these projects and select the best project. An excellent survey of techniques of Multi-Attribute Decision Making is available in Hwang and Yoon (1981). The two major problems in carrying out the comparisons are *incommensurate units* of different criteria (e.g. Rs. for investment and years for payback period) and the *intangible nature* of some of the evaluations (e.g. low, medium and high risk in an investment). Intangible units are generally converted to a convenient subjective scale (say from 0 to 10) so that they can be quantified and dealt with mathematically. The incommensurate nature of the evaluations is taken care of by normalization, which may be carried out in different ways. Figure 4.1 summarizes the nature of the attributes and the kinds of complexities involved in the evaluation process.

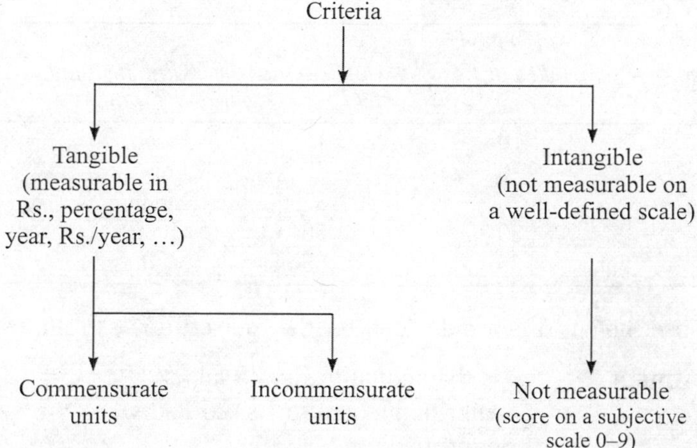

Fig. 4.1 The nature of criteria in projects.

In this chapter, we shall be discussing the following procedures:

- Simple additive weighting (SAW)
- Technique for order preference using similarity to ideal solution (TOPSIS)
- Analytic hierarchy procedure (AHP)

Finally, it may be noted that the solutions obtained from different methods need not be comparable. One can liken this to opinions given by different experts on a particular issue. Each method is based on a different logic and uses its scheme of normalization and evaluation of alternatives. Used intelligently, they would provide valuable guidelines to the decision maker in making a proper project selection.

4.2 PROJECT SHORTLISTING AND THE NOTION OF DOMINANCE

One of the simplest ways to consider alternative projects is to use a shortlisting procedure that would classify the set of projects in favourable and unfavourable categories. A commonly used approach is to define the cut-off values on each of the Performance criteria and determine the set of projects that satisfy the imposed cut-offs. The manner in which these cut-offs are imposed could reflect management preferences and expectations from the project. These are generally arrived at by mutual discussion and a consensus among the decision-making team.

EXAMPLE 4.1 Project shortlisting using cut-offs:

Suppose five projects have been reviewed and the performance on the four criteria considered relevant for the decision is summarized in Table 4.1.

Table 4.1 Project performance of different criteria

Criteria → ↓ *Project*	*Investment (lakhs of Rs.)*	*NPV (lakhs of Rs.)*	*Risk (low, medium, high)*	*Payback (years)*
P_1	10	15	Low	2
P_2	20	25	Low	3
P_3	25	35	Medium	5
P_4	30	50	High	5
P_5	35	55	Medium	6

Suppose the cut-offs are decided for the four criteria as follows:

Investment	Less than equal to Rs. 25 lakhs
NPV	Greater than equal to Rs. 25 lakhs
Risk	Low or medium
Payback	Less than equal to 5 years

The performance of the five projects on the four criteria is summarized in Table 4.2 in terms of (OK) when the criterion satisfies the cut-off and (reject) when the project fails to meet the cut-off. Finally, the shortlisted projects are the ones that satisfy all the criteria.

Table 4.2 Shortlisting based on different criteria

Criteria → ↓ *Project*	*Investment* (*lakhs of Rs.*)	*NPV* (*lakhs of Rs.*)	*Risk* (*low, medium, high*)	*Payback* (*years*)
P_1	10 (OK)	15 (reject)	Low (OK)	2 (OK)
P_2	20 (OK)	25 (OK)	Low (OK)	3 (OK)
P_3	25 (OK)	35 (OK)	Medium (OK)	5 (OK)
P_4	30 (reject)	50 (OK)	High (reject)	5 (OK)
P_5	35 (reject)	55 (OK)	Medium (OK)	6 (reject)

On the basis of the chosen cut-offs for the example only projects P_2 and P_3 qualify to be shortlisted on all the criteria (Table 4.2). It may be noted here that by making the cut-offs more lenient the number of shortlisted projects is likely to increase, whereas making the cut-offs more stringent is likely to reduce the number of shortlisted projects. The purpose of shortlisting is thus to focus on a set of feasible projects which could be examined in greater detail. A common example of the use of this procedure in practice is to invite a number of applications for a certain set of positions in the organization. These applications are examined and a shortlist is prepared on the basis of some relevant criteria. The shortlisted candidates are then called for a personal interview in which the most suitable ones are chosen. It is clear that shortlisting does not result in a ranking or selection of projects. It only reduces the number of alternatives to be rigourously evaluated.

If there is a unique project which excels all other projects on all the criteria, such a project is clearly the best and is referred to as the *Dominant Project.* Clearly in the example above, there is no dominant project. A dominant project, if one exists, is the best choice irrespective of the priorities given to the various criteria.

4.3 NON-DOMINATED SOLUTIONS (PARETO-OPTIMAL SET)

We now look at the concept of the non-dominated solution set. For simplicity, we consider only two relevant criteria, namely return and NPV in the project selection exercise. Figure 4.2 shows the performance for the eight prospective projects on these two criteria.

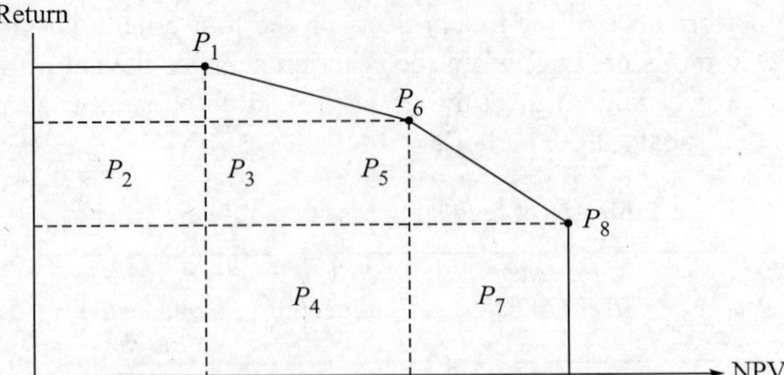

Fig. 4.2 Performance of candidate projects on NPV and return.

In the case of two criteria, it is obvious that a project like P_1 dominates all the projects in the quadrangle with P_1 at the north-east corner. Thus, P_1 is clearly better than P_2, a project which is lower than P_1 on both return and NPV. Similarly, P_6 is superior to P_2, P_3, P_4 and P_5. And P_8 is superior to P_4 and P_7. What emerges from this analysis is that P_1, P_6 and P_8 constitute the non-dominated set since these projects are not dominated by any project. It is not immediately clear as to which out of P_1, P_6 and P_8 is the best. Determination of the relative ranking amongst the non-dominated set would require trade-offs between the criteria. For instance, P_1 is the best project as far as the return is concerned. But P_6 is better than P_1 on NPV though it has sacrificed on the return front. The non-dominated set has so far not considered the weightages given to individual criteria. It can therefore be viewed as a shortlisting criterion in which the set of non-dominated solutions would be subjected to greater scrutiny to arrive at a ranking of the projects.

In this case P_1, P_6 and P_8 are the non-dominated solutions. All elements on the convex hull are non-dominated, but the opposite need not be true, that is there may be points which are non-dominated but do not lie on the convex hull.

4.3.1 Preferred Solution

The preferred solution would be the dominant solution if one exists, otherwise we chose from the **Pareto-Optimal** or **non-dominated solution set**. The selection out of these non-dominated solutions will involve *trade-offs*.

The trade-offs can be carried out more effectively by giving weightage to each criterion. The priorities or weights to the different criteria may be obtained by

- Mutual consultations or opinion polls
- Pair-wise comparison between criteria
- Establishing a hierarchy of priorities and using AHP (developed by Saaty)

For the case of pair-wise comparisons, we can visualize it as a case where we are asked to decide between the best among n dishes. Though we cannot outrightly say which one is the best, we can make comparison of two dishes at a time and say which one was remarkably better, slightly better, equally good (or bad), or worse. We will be making ${}^nC_2$ pairs and thus get a final weightage for each dish.

In the case of AHP, i.e. the analytic hierarchy process, the case is more or less the same except that we have well-defined scheme for inconsistencies using eigenvalues and vectors.

4.4 THE DECISION MATRIX

In order to make a decision based on these criteria, we make a decision matrix, in which, we have the projects on one hand, the criteria on the other, and then we evaluate the project for each criterion, and later add up the scores to get the total score of that project.

In the decision matrix of Table 4.3, C_j are the criteria, P_i are the projects and x_{ij} are scores for the project i on criteria j. S_i is the total score for each project i.

Table 4.3 The structure of a decision matrix

Criteria → ↓ *Projects*	C_1	C_2	C_3. .	C_n	
P_1	x_{11}	x_{12}	x_{13}	x_{1n}	S_1
P_2	x_{21}	x_{22}	x_{23}	x_{2n}	S_2
P_m	x_{m1}	x_{m2}	x_{m3}	x_{mn}	S_m

EXAMPLE 4.2 A decision matrix with four projects and six attributes

Suppose there are four projects to be evaluated on six criteria.

X_1: Internal rate of return
X_2: NPV in thousands of rupees with cash flows discounted at a rate of 8%
X_3: Prospective customer reach
X_4: Payback period in years
X_5: Market risk [subjective scale 0 (max risk) and 9 (min risk)]
X_6: Projected market growth [subjective scale 0 (worst) and 9 (best)]

The manner in which these criteria have been defined is as follows: all except X_4 are benefit criteria, while X_4 is a cost criterion. A benefit criterion is one which the decision maker would like to maximize (e.g. profit, NPV, customer reach), whereas a cost criterion is one which the decision maker would like to minimize (e.g. cost, payback, pollution).

Step 1 Obtain the decision matrix after using a numerical scale for intangibles. In this example, there are two intangible attributes—market risk and projected market growth, both of which are evaluated on the subjective scale shown in Table 4.4.

Table 4.4 Subjective scale for cost and benefit criteria

Very low	*Low*	*Medium*	*Good*	*Very good*	
1	3	5	7	9	(for benefit criteria)
9	7	5	3	1	(for cost criteria)

Using this scheme numerical values can be assigned to each of the attributes for the four alternative projects. This decision matrix is generally the starting point for the use of multi-criteria decision making methodologies.

By using the numerical scale for intangibles suggested in Table 4.4, the initial decision matrix of Table 4.5 may be modified to get the matrix of Table 4.6.

Table 4.5 The initial decision matrix

	X_1	X_2	X_3	X_4	X_5	X_6
A_1	2.0	1500	20,000	5.5	medium risk	very good growth
A_2	2.5	2700	18,000	6.5	high risk	medium growth
A_3	1.8	2000	21,000	4.5	low risk	good growth
A_4	2.2	1800	20,000	5.5	medium risk	medium growth

Table 4.6 Modified matrix with numerical scores for intangibles

	X_1	X_2	X_3	X_4	X_5	X_6
A_1	2.0	1500	20,000	5.5	5	9
A_2	2.5	2700	18,000	6.5	3	5
A_3	1.8	2000	21,000	4.5	7	7
A_4	2.2	1800	20,000	5.5	5	5

The next difficulty with using the above decision matrix (Table 4.6) directly is that the units for the various attributes are inconsistent. For instance, the first attribute is the internal rate of return in percentage, whereas the second attribute is the NPV measured in thousands of rupees. It would not be possible to perform mathematical operations on two distinct commodities. The way out of this difficulty is to resort to *normalization* so that each quantity under a particular attribute is dimensionless. Different procedures follow their respective methods of normalization as we shall see when we discuss the various procedures.

4.5 ANALYTIC HIERARCHY PROCEDURE (AHP)

The analytic hierarchy procedure was developed by Saaty (1977) as a mathematical procedure to assign weights to n entities using a scheme of pair-wise comparisons. The elements of this procedure are described as follows:

Pair-wise Comparisons in AHP

Let C_1, C_2, ..., C_n be the set of activities. The quantified judgments on a pair of activities (C_i, C_j) are represented by the ($n \times n$) matrix **A**, with the element in the ith row and the jth column denoted by $a_{ij} = w_i/w_j$, the ratio of weights or importance given to the ith activity as a fraction of the importance given to the jth activity in the square matrix $\mathbf{A} = (a_{ij})$ $(i, j = 1, \ldots n)$. These ratios are assumed to satisfy the following conditions:

- Positive ($a_{ij} > 0$)
- Reciprocal ($a_{ij} = 1/a_{ji}$)
- Unit diagonal ($a_{ii} = 1$)
- Consistent ($a_{ik} = a_{ij} \cdot a_{jk}$, $i,j,k = 1, \ldots, n$)

Step 1 in determining weights

Assuming the ideal case of exact measurements, with the above definition of a_{ij} the **A** matrix may be written in terms of the ratio of weights w_1, w_2, ..., w_n as given below

$$\mathbf{A} = \begin{matrix} w_1/w_1 & w_1/w_2 \ldots w_1/w_n \\ w_2/w_1 & w_2/w_2 \ldots w_2/w_n \\ \ldots & \\ w_n/w_1 & w_n/w_2 \ldots w_n/w_n \end{matrix}$$

If in the ith row we multiply the 1st entry by w_1, 2nd by w_2, and nth by w_n, we would obtain w_i in each case. In matrix notation, this means that $\mathbf{Aw} = n\mathbf{w}$, where **w** is a column vector of the weights. For each element a_{ij} in the matrix **A**, we note that

$$w_i = w_j \times a_{ij} \; (i, j = 1, \ldots, n) \tag{1}$$

Step 2 in determining weights

Make allowance for deviations in a_{ij}.

Multiplication of the ith row of **A** by corresponding weights yields a statistical scattering around w_i and it is reasonable to require that w_i should be the average of these values.

$$w_i = \sum_{j=1}^{n} (a_{ij} \times w_j)/n \;\; (i = 1, \ldots, n) \tag{2}$$

Step 3 in determining weightages

Good estimates of a_{ij} tend to be close to w_i/w_j.

a_{ij} is a small perturbation to this ratio w_i/w_j. If a_{ij} changes, there would be a corresponding solution of Eqn (2), if n were also to change. We denote this value of n by λ_{max}. Thus,

$$w_i = \sum_{j=1}^{n} (a_{ij} \times w_j)/\lambda_{max} \; (i = 1, \ldots, n) \tag{3}$$

Eigenvalue Problem

Paradigm case (A as a consistent matrix)

$$\mathbf{Aw} = n\mathbf{w}$$

Reciprocal matrix **A*** which is a perturbation of **A** elicited from pair-wise comparisons w^* is governed by the relation:

$$\mathbf{A^*w^*} = \lambda_{max}\,\mathbf{w^*};\ \text{or}$$
$$(\mathbf{A^*} - \lambda_{max}\,\mathbf{I})\mathbf{w^*} = 0$$

where **I** is the unit identity matrix of size $(n \times n)$ with 1s on the diagonal and 0s elsewhere.

This is a set of n homogeneous equations with a trivial solution ($\mathbf{w^*} = 0$). For the non-trivial solution, we solve the determinant of $(\mathbf{A^*} - \lambda_{max}\,\mathbf{I}) = 0$, the characteristic equation, which has n roots and obtain the largest root for λ as λ_{max}. Eigenvalues and eigenvectors λ

For non-trivial solution, $(\mathbf{A^*} - \lambda_{max}\,\mathbf{I})$ must be singular. That is,

$\det(\mathbf{A^*} - \lambda_{max}\,\mathbf{I}) = 0$ (characteristic eqn).

This nth degree polynomial yields n roots.

The largest root is the *eigenvalue* chosen for λ_{max}.

In terms of the largest root, the solution to the equation $(\mathbf{A^*} - \lambda_{max}\,\mathbf{I})$ $\mathbf{w^*} = 0$ yields the values of $\mathbf{w^*}$, the *eigenvector*, which determines the weights to the n activities.

Example

$$\mathbf{A} = \begin{bmatrix} 1 & 2 \\ 3 & 4 \end{bmatrix},\ \mathbf{I} = \begin{bmatrix} 1 & 0 \\ 0 & 1 \end{bmatrix},\ \lambda\mathbf{I} = \begin{bmatrix} \lambda & 0 \\ 0 & \lambda \end{bmatrix}$$

$$(\mathbf{A} - \lambda\mathbf{I}) = \begin{bmatrix} 1-\lambda & 2 \\ 3 & 4-\lambda \end{bmatrix}$$

$$|\mathbf{A} - \lambda\mathbf{I}| = (1-\lambda)(4-\lambda) - 6 = \lambda^2 - 5\lambda - 2 = 0$$

$$\lambda_1 = \frac{5+\sqrt{33}}{2}$$

$$\lambda_2 = \frac{5-\sqrt{33}}{2}$$

$$\begin{bmatrix} 1 & 2 \\ 3 & 4 \end{bmatrix}\begin{bmatrix} w_1 \\ w_2 \end{bmatrix} = \lambda_1\begin{bmatrix} w_1 \\ w_2 \end{bmatrix}$$

$$w_1 + 2w_2 = \lambda_1 w_1$$

$$w_1 = -\frac{2}{1-\lambda}\,w_2$$

Assigning an arbitrary value to w_2 (say 1) and calculating w_1 from the above relation, we have

$$\mathbf{w} = \left[\frac{2}{\lambda_1 - 1}, 1\right]$$

Normalizing (i.e. noticing that $w_1 + w_2 = 1$), we obtain

$$= \left[\frac{2}{\lambda_1 + 1}, \frac{\lambda_1 - 1}{\lambda_1 + 1}\right]$$

Analytic Hierarchy Procedure

The analytic hierarchy procedure (AHP) was proposed by Thomas L. Saaty (1977). It uses the notion of hierarchical structures and sets up the multi-criteria problem as a tree with a node at the top or 1st level followed by the attributes at the 2nd level and the options or alternatives to be evaluated at the 3rd level. The weights for each of the attributes are then evaluated, using the procedure of the eigenvalues and square matrices discussed above. One progressively proceeds from level to level till the weights and the rankings of the alternatives are obtained.

- 1st level (overall objective): Priority unity
- 2nd level (n attributes): Weights derived by pair-wise comparisons of n by n matrix
- 3rd level (m alternatives): Weights derived by pair-wise comparisons of every one of n attributes for each m by m matrix of alternatives

In general, there could be h ($\geqslant 3$) levels in the hierarchy, but in most situations the indicated three levels suffice. It may be mentioned here that no interactions horizontally or diagonally are permitted in the conventional treatment of AHP. However, in a later development, Saaty extended the concept when interactions between elements at a level are also present and this revised procedure is referred to as the Analytic Network Process (ANP).

The AHP procedure adopted will be illustrated through the examples below.

EXAMPLE 4.3 Hierarchy for Fighter Aircraft Problem

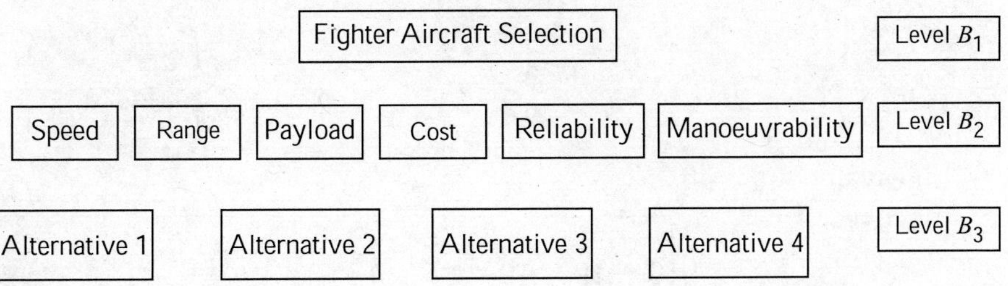

Priorities derived from decision matrix, B_3

	X_1	X_2	X_3	X_4	X_5	X_6
A_1	.2353	.1875	.2532	.2399	.25	.3462
A_2	.2941	.3375	.2278	.2030	.15	.1923
A_3	.2118	.25	.2658	.2932	.35	.2692
A_4	.2588	.2250	.2532	.2639	.25	.1923

$$[k_j = x_{ij}/\Sigma x_{ij}, \text{ for benefit criteria}$$
$$= 1/x_{ij}/\Sigma(1/x_{ij}), \text{ for cost criteria}]$$

Weights of six attributes, B_2

$$B_2 = [.2 \quad .1 \quad .1 \quad .1 \quad .2 \quad .3]^T$$

The composite vector for the hierarchy of mission effectiveness is given by

$\mathbf{W} = \mathbf{B_3} * \mathbf{B_2} * \mathbf{W'}$ ($\mathbf{W'}$ is 1 because of single element in level 1)

$= A_1$ .269

A_2 .223

A_3 .274

A_4 .234

Ranking order: $A_3 > A_1 > A_4 > A_2$

EXAMPLE 4.4 Choosing a Job

	Choosing a Job Research (RS)	Growth (G)	Benefits (B)	Colleagues (C)	Location (L)	Reputation (RP)
RS	1	1	1	4	1	$\frac{1}{2}$
G	1	1	2	4	1	$\frac{1}{2}$
B	1	$\frac{1}{2}$	1	5	3	$\frac{1}{2}$
C	$\frac{1}{4}$	$\frac{1}{4}$	$\frac{1}{5}$	1	$\frac{1}{3}$	$\frac{1}{3}$
L	1	1	$\frac{1}{3}$	3	1	1
RP	2	2	2	3	1	1

Eigenvalue $\lambda_{max} = 6.35$
Eigenvector is:

$$[.16 \quad .19 \quad .19 \quad .05 \quad .12 \quad .30]$$

Comparison of jobs *A*, *B* and *C* with respect to six attributes

Research (RS)

$$\begin{array}{cccc} & A & B & C \\ A & 1 & \frac{1}{4} & \frac{1}{2} \\ B & 4 & 1 & 3 \\ C & 2 & \frac{1}{3} & 1 \end{array}$$

Growth (G)

$$\begin{array}{cccc} & A & B & C \\ A & 1 & \frac{1}{4} & \frac{1}{5} \\ B & 4 & 1 & \frac{1}{2} \\ C & 5 & 2 & 1 \end{array}$$

Benefits (B)

$$\begin{array}{cccc} & A & B & C \\ A & 1 & 3 & \frac{1}{3} \\ B & \frac{1}{3} & 1 & 1 \\ C & 3 & 1 & 1 \end{array}$$

Colleagues (C)

$$\begin{array}{cccc} & A & B & C \\ A & 1 & \frac{1}{3} & 5 \\ B & 3 & 1 & 7 \\ C & \frac{1}{5} & \frac{1}{7} & 1 \end{array}$$

Location (L)

$$\begin{array}{cccc} & A & B & C \\ A & 1 & 1 & 7 \\ B & 1 & 1 & 7 \\ C & \frac{1}{7} & \frac{1}{7} & 1 \end{array}$$

Reputation (RP)

$$\begin{array}{cccc} & A & B & C \\ A & 1 & 7 & 9 \\ B & \frac{1}{7} & 1 & 5 \\ C & \frac{1}{9} & \frac{1}{5} & 1 \end{array}$$

Eigenvalues and eigenvectors of six comparison matrices
Eigenvalues λ_{max}: 3.02 3.02 3.56 3.05 3.00 3.21
And the eigenvectors of the six matrices are given below:

$$B_3 = \begin{array}{ccccccc} & \textbf{RS} & \textbf{G} & \textbf{B} & \textbf{C} & \textbf{L} & \textbf{RP} \\ \textbf{A} & .14 & .10 & .32 & .28 & .47 & .77 \\ \textbf{B} & .63 & .33 & .22 & .65 & .47 & .17 \\ \textbf{C} & .24 & .57 & .46 & .07 & .07 & .05 \end{array}$$

The composite vector for the job with $h = 3$ is given by

$$\mathbf{W} = \mathbf{B}_3 * \mathbf{B}_2 * \mathbf{W}' = \begin{array}{l} A\ 0.40 \\ B\ 0.34 \\ C\ 0.26 \end{array}$$

Thus, $A > B > C$.
Using pair-wise comparisons to obtain weights

A	B	C
–2.0536	$\frac{1}{3}$	$\frac{1}{2}$
3	–2.0536	3
2	$\frac{1}{3}$	–2.0536

(The largest eigenvalue of A is $\lambda_{max} = 3.0536$.)
The solution of the homogeneous system of linear equations gives $w_T = \{0.1571, 0.5936, 0.2493\}$. Notice that $\Sigma w = 1$.
This gives the final ranking of the jobs as $A_2 > A_3 > A_1$.

4.6 SIMPLE ADDITIVE WEIGHTING (SAW)

Step 1 Obtain the decision matrix after converting intangibles to numbers

	X_1	X_2	X_3	X_4	X_5	X_6
A_1	2.0	1500	20,000	5.5	5	[9]
A_2	[2.5]	[2700]	18,000	6.5	3	5
A_3	1.8	2000	[21,000]	[4.5]	[7]	7
A_4	2.2	1800	20,000	5.5	5	5

Normalization

Step 2 Obtain the normalized decision matrix **R** (r_{ij}, $i = 1,..., m$; $j = 1, ..., n$) using $r_{ij} = x_{ij}/x_j^*$, if the jth criterion is a benefit criterion, and $r_{ij} = x_j^*/x_{ij}$, if the jth criterion is a cost criterion. Here x_j^* is the column maximum for a benefit criterion and the minimum for a cost criterion. (X_4 in the above example).

Final scores

Step 3 Using the weights for the different criteria obtain the weighted score for each alternative using the normalized decision matrix.

Step 4 Based on the final scores, rank the alternatives for a decision by the decision maker.

Normalized decision matrix

							Score
A_1	0.80	0.56	0.95	0.82	0.71	1.00	0.835
A_2	1.00	1.00	0.86	0.69	0.43	0.56	0.709
A_3	0.72	0.74	1.00	1.00	1.00	0.78	0.852
A_4	0.88	0.67	0.95	0.90	0.71	0.36	0.738
W	(0.2	0.1	0.1	0.1	0.2	0.3)	

Ranking of alternatives with SAW:

$$A_3, A_1, A_4, A_2$$

4.7 TECHNIQUE FOR ORDER PREFERENCE USING SIMILARITY TO IDEAL SOLUTION (TOPSIS)

Step 1 Obtain the decision matrix after using a numerical scale for intangibles.

	X_1	X_2	X_3	X_4	X_5	X_6
A_1	2.0	1500	20,000	5.5	5	9
A_2	2.5	2700	18,000	6.5	3	5
A_3	1.8	2000	21,000	4.5	7	7
A_4	2.2	1800	20,000	5.5	5	5

Normalized decision matrix

Step 2 Obtain the normalized decision matrix, **R**, using the relationship

$$r_{ij} = x_{ij}/\sqrt{\Sigma x_{ij}^2}\,;\ i = 1, \ldots, m$$

$$\begin{matrix} 0.4671 & 0.3662 & 0.5056 & 0.5063 & 0.4811 & 0.6708 \\ 0.5839 & 0.6591 & 0.4550 & 0.5983 & 0.2887 & 0.3727 \\ 0.4204 & 0.4882 & 0.5308 & 0.4143 & 0.6736 & 0.5217 \\ 0.5139 & 0.4392 & 0.5056 & 0.4603 & 0.4811 & 0.3727 \end{matrix}$$

Weighted decision matrix

Step 3 Obtain the weighted decision matrix **V** (v_{ij}, $i = 1, \ldots, m, j = 1, \ldots, n$) by multiplying each column of **R** by the corresponding weight.

$$W = (0.2, 0.1, 0.1, 0.1, 0.2, 0.3)$$

$$\begin{matrix} 0.0934 & 0.0366 & 0.0506 & 0.0506 & 0.0962 & \boxed{0.2012} \\ \boxed{0.1168} & \boxed{0.0659} & 0.0455 & 0.0598 & 0.0577 & 0.1118 \\ 0.0841 & 0.0488 & \boxed{0.0531} & \boxed{0.0414} & \boxed{0.1347} & 0.156 \\ 0.1028 & 0.0439 & 0.0506 & 0.0460 & 0.0962 & 0.1118 \end{matrix}$$

Ideal and negative ideal solutions

Step 4 Obtain the ideal (A^*) and the negative ideal (A^-) solutions from the weighted decision matrix V by identifying the best and worst options denoted by v_j^* and v_j^- in the jth column ($j = 1, \ldots, n$).

$$A^* = (0.1168, 0.0659, 0.0531, 0.0414, 0.1347, 0.2012)$$
$$A^- = (0.0841, 0.0366, 0.0455, 0.0598, 0.0577, 0.1118)$$

Separation measures

Step 5 Compute the separation measures from the ideal (S_i^*) and the negative ideal (S_i^-) solutions for all alternatives, $i = 1, \ldots, m$.

$$S_i^* = \sqrt{\Sigma(v_{ij} - v_j^*)^2}\,;\ j = 1, \ldots, n$$
$$S_i^- = \sqrt{\Sigma(v_{ij} - v_j^-)^2}\,;\ j = 1, \ldots, n$$

Values of separation measures

Separation measures from:

Ideal solution	Negative ideal solution
$S_1^* = 0.0545$	$S_1^- = 0.0983$
$S_2^* = 0.1197$	$S_2^- = 0.0439$
$S_3^* = 0.0580$	$S_3^- = 0.0920$
$S_4^* = 0.1009$	$S_4^- = 0.0458$

Relative closeness to ideal solution

Step 6 For each alternative, determine the relative closeness to the ideal solution (C_i^*, $i = 1, \ldots, m$) as

$$C_i^* = S_i^-/(S_i^* + S_i^-)$$

Relative closeness values

$$C_1^* = 0.643$$
$$C_2^* = 0.268$$
$$C_3^* = 0.613$$
$$C_4^* = 0.312$$

(Notice that the closeness rating is a number between 0 and 1, with 0 being the worst possible and 1 the best possible solution.)

Rank the preference order

Step 7 Determine the preference order by arranging the alternatives in the descending order of C_i^*, $i = 1,..., m$.

Thus, the ranks for the alternatives in the fighter aircraft selection problem using TOPSIS emerge as

$$A_1, A_3, A_4, A_2.$$

SAW and TOPSIS (a Comparison)

Now let us compare the two methods used for project selection.

Rankings obtained using two multi-attribute decision-making techniques need not be identical.

For the Fighter Aircraft Selection Project:

SAW gave a ranking A_3, A_1, A_4 and A_2.

TOPSIS gave a ranking A_1, A_3, A_4 and A_2.

4.8 SUMMARY AND CONCLUSIONS

Finally, we see that project selection involves consideration of multiple, often conflicting criteria among alternatives and the task is made more difficult because project appraisal leads to evaluations which may be tangible, incommensurate or intangible. The incommensurate evaluations are handled through appropriate normalization, whilst the intangibles are evaluated on a numerical subjective scale. This leads to a decision matrix wherein the alternative projects are scored on the multiplicity of criteria. Among the various methods for project selection treated in this chapter are

(i) Shortlisting based on a cut-off for performance level of each criterion
(ii) Notion of a dominant project (if one exists)
(iii) The determination of the non-dominated solution set or the Pareto Optimal frontier

The three procedures above do not require determination of the weightages to different criteria. However, when none of the above suffices, suitable weightages may be given to the different criteria for project selection and a ranking to the projects may be obtained. The methods treated under this category differ in the manner the weightages are assigned and the normalization procedure of the decision matrix. In this chapter, the following three multi-attribute selection procedures have been discussed and illustrated with suitable examples:

(i) AHP or the analytic hierarchy procedure
(ii) SAW or simple additive weighting
(iii) TOPSIS or technique for order preference using similarity to ideal solution

The results obtained by these procedures need not be similar, but may be treated as educated estimates of the worthwhileness of different expert groups on a set of projects. The final decision on selection is the prerogative of the decision maker, but these techniques serve to provide valuable clues in making a rational choice.

PROBLEMS

1. Seven projects (P1–P7) have the following NPV and payback periods:

Project	1	2	3	4	5	6	7
NPV (*lakhs of Rs.*)	45	30	35	45	45	38	25
Payback (years)	1	1	3	3	5	5	5

   (a) Represent the projects on a two-dimentsional criteria graph.
   (b) Determine the Pareto Optimal set of projects.
   (c) For each project on the efficient frontier, determine the set of projects that it dominates.
   (d) If you were to choose one project from the Pareto Optimal set, which one would you choose?
      (i) If NPV had 80% weightage and payback 20%?
      (ii) If NPV had 20% weightage and payback 80%?
      (iii) If both NPV and payback had 50% weightage each?

      Assume normalization using the SAW procedure.
   (e) Answer part (d) by using the normalization procedure of TOPSIS.

2. The performance of 15 projects on two attributes x and y is summed up as the following:

Project k (xk, yk)		*Project k (xk, yk)*		*Project k (xk, yk)*	
P_1	(5, 35)	P_2	(5, 45)	P_3	(10, 30)
P_4	(10, 40)	P_5	(10, 48)	P_6	(12, 50)
P_7	(15, 30)	P_8	(15, 45)	P_9	(20, 20)
P_{10}	(20, 35)	P_{11}	(20, 45)	P_{12}	(20, 50)
P_{13}	(30, 30)	P_{14}	(30, 35)	P_{15}	(30, 45)

Determine the set of non-dominated solutions if the (x, y) pair is

(a) Investment and risk
(b) Investment and return
(c) NPV and risk
(d) NPV and return

3. For a set of projects the following set of attributes is considered for selection:

X_1 = Investment (in lakhs of Rs.)
X_2 = Payback period (in years)
X_3 = NPV (present worth in lakhs of Rs.)
X_4 = Annual profit (in lakhs of Rs.)
X_5 = Risk (as a probability of losing the initial investment)
X_6 = Future competitive position (poor, good, very good, excellent)

Construct a plausible decision matrix for five possible projects, assign suitable weights and determine the ranking for the five projects by using

(a) TOPSIS (b) SAW (c) AHP

4. Develop a computer program for SAW, TOPSIS and AHP and use it to compute the ranking for projects in Question 3 above.
5. Five projects evaluated on six criteria yield the decision matrix shown below:

Project/ Criterion	*Investment (lakhs of Rs.)*	NPV *(lakhs of Rs.)*	IRR	*Risk*	*Growth*	*Payback*
P_1	10	40	10%	Low	V. good	6 years
P_2	6	30	12%	Low	Good	4 years
P_3	15	50	15%	High	Excellent	3 years
P_4	20	60	20%	Medium	Poor	5 years
P_5	12	20	12%	Medium	Good	6 years

(a) In determining the non-dominated set of projects, what is the upper bound on the number of project comparisons?
(b) Is there a dominant project in the above table? Determine the set of non-dominated projects.

6. For the project selection problem in Question 5 above, determine the rankings using SAW.
7. For the project selection problem in Question 5 above, determine the rankings using TOPSIS.
8. In using AHP, the pair-wise importance of some criteria is indicated in the table below:

Criteria	NPV	*Payback*	*Growth*	*Flexibility*	*Liquidity*
NPV	1	4	2	0.5	1
Payback		1			
Growth			1		
Flexibility				1	
Liquidity					1

(a) Complete the table of pair-wise comparisons such that the reciprocal and transitive properties are satisfied.
(b) Determine the weights for the criteria using AHP.
(c) If there are three projects P1, P2 and P3 whose performance on these criteria is summarized below, determine the project ranks under AHP.

Criteria/ Project	NPV	*Payback*	*Growth*	*Flexibility*	*Liquidity*
P_1	20	5	Good	V. good	Good
P_2	40	6	V. good	Good	Good
P_3	60	4	Poor	Good	V. good

9. In Question 8 above, a committee estimates the pair-wise comparisons as given in the table below:

	NPV	*Payback*	*Growth*	*Flexibility*	*Liquidity*
NPV	1	4	2	0.5	1
Payback	4	1	0.4	0.13	0.25
Growth	2	0.4	1	0.25	0.6
Flexibility	0.5	0.13	0.25	1	2
Liquidity	1	0.25	0.6	2	1

(a) Calculate the principal eigenvalue (λ_{max}).
(b) Determine the eigenvector.
(c) What are the values of the consistency index and the consistency ratio? Comment on these values.
(d) What would be your ranking of projects P_1, P_2 and P_3 in Question 8(c) above under these circumstances?

CHAPTER

5

Project Representation and Preliminary Manipulations

5.1 INTRODUCTION

As we have already seen in Chapter 1, a project is a collection of jobs required to accomplish an objective. There could thus be many ways of representing a project.

(i) By a name (which could be a reminder of the purpose, people or places involved in the project), e.g. Operation Desert Storm, Sarpavinashak, Operation Blackboard, etc.

(ii) By the set of constituent jobs of the project. This is not a convenient form for project representation since the number of jobs in the project could be very large. Nevertheless for smaller projects this is quite a common representation. When, for instance, we carry a shopping list to perform a number of tasks, we are in fact doing this. The disadvantage with this representation is that it does not give the precedence relations among jobs and nor does it specify the sequence in which all the jobs are to be carried out.

(iii) A project schedule in the form of a Gantt chart shows the various activities and the time when each job is to be done. However, the disadvantage is that precedence relations are generally not available on the Gantt chart and the impact of shift of one job on the others may not be easy to see.

(iv) A project could easily be represented as a network of nodes and arcs. This is the most popularly used representation for a project since it gives the activities as well as their precedence relationships. All planning for the project, development of schedule, implementation and control and project audit could all be easily done using the network framework. In this chapter, we shall investigate how to represent projects as networks and what kinds of preliminary manipulations are needed before one obtains a valid and representative network.

5.2 PROJECT REPRESENTATION AS A NETWORK

There are two commonly used methods of representing projects as networks—the A-O-A (activity on arc) mode and the A-O-N (activity on node) mode. Both these modes require that a breakdown of the project into its constituent tasks be done and the precedence relationships among these jobs be established before a proper project network can be drawn. Suppose for illustrative purposes we consider the project of designing a house, carrying out the construction and shifting into the new house. A feasible work breakdown structure for the project is given below:

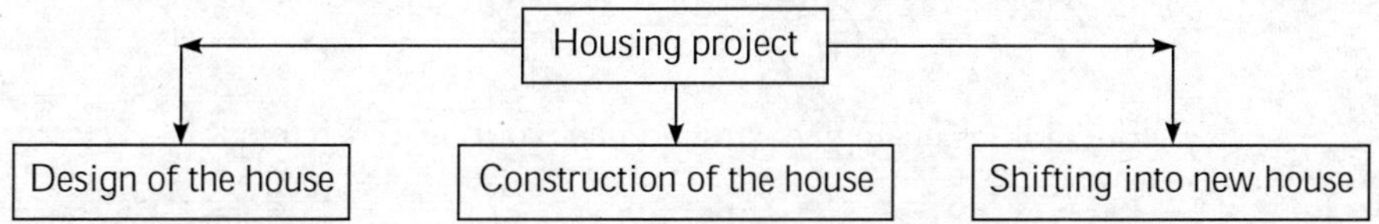

(a) Review houses
(b) Finalize requirements
(c) Engage Architect
(d) Evaluate alternative designs on cost, space and aesthetics
(e) Finalize contractor
(f) Foundations
(g) Brickwork
(h) RCC
(i) Plumbing
(j) Woodwork and Finishing
(k) Organize party
(l) Shift luggage
(m) Settling in new house

For the above activities [defined above from (a) to (m)], the following precedence requirements can be developed:

Job	*a*	*b*	*c*	*d*	*e*	*f*	*g*	*h*	*i*	*j*	*k*	*l*	*m*
Predecessors	–	–	*a, b*	*a, c*	*d*	*d, e*	*f*	*g*	*g, h*	*i*	*j*	*k*	*l*

This is shown as an A-O-A network in Fig. 5.1.

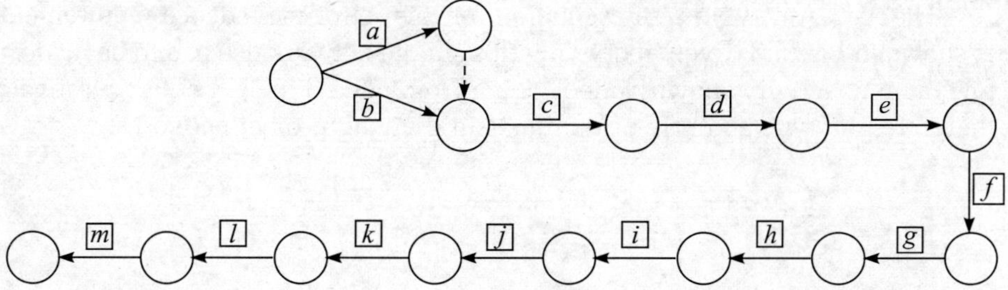

Fig. 5.1 A housing project.

With the same set of precedence relations it is possible to draw an A-O-N network. An A-O-N network is one in which the activities are represented on the nodes or junctions and the arrows represent the precedence relations. Both the types of networks essentially give the same information about the jobs in the project and the implied precedence relations. The A-O-N network for the above data is drawn in Fig. 5.2 below.

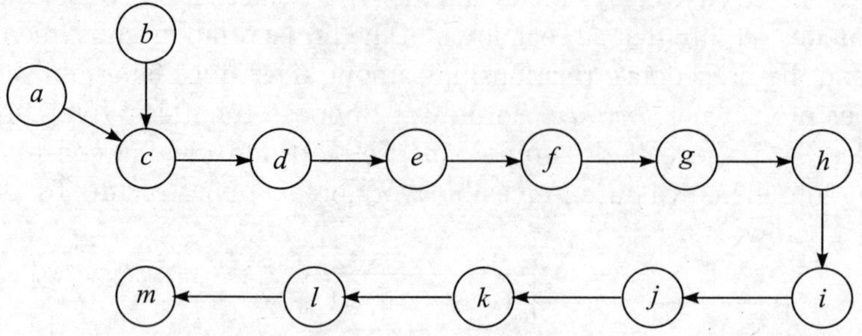

Fig. 5.2 Housing construction network in A-O-N mode.

5.3 ROLE OF DUMMIES IN DEVELOPING NETWORKS

As seen in the previous section, dummy jobs (jobs with zero cost and duration) have often to be inserted in the network to represent the correct logical sequence of jobs as specified in the precedence relations. Suppose the precedence specified for a set of five jobs *A*, *B*, *C*, *D* and *E* is given in Table 5.1.

Table 5.1 Immediate predecessor list for a sample project

Job	*Immediate predecessors*
A	—
B	—
C	*A*
D	*A*, *B*
E	*C*, *D*

The A-O-A network representation for this set of precedence requirements is shown in Fig. 5.3. Even in drawing this simple network use had to be made of one dummy activity shown dotted (going from node 3 to 4). Let us investigate, therefore, the type and role of dummies in drawing project networks.

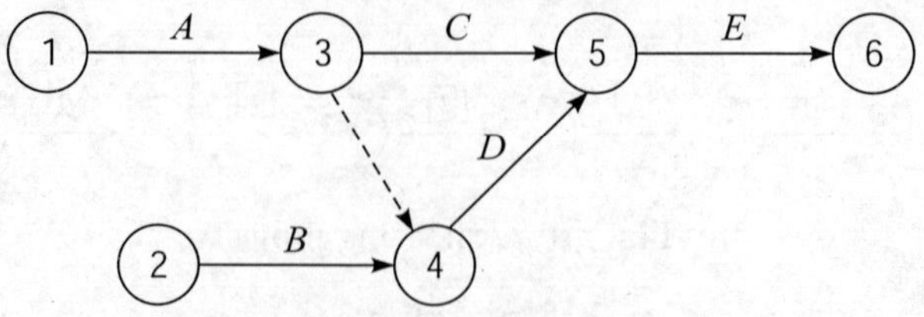

Fig. 5.3 A sample project network (A-O-A).

5.3.1 Three Types of Dummies in Projects

It may be noticed from Table 5.1 of predecessor relationships of the sample project that activity *C* has only *A* as its predecessor, whereas activity *D* has both *A* and *B* as predecessors. This requirement can be met only if we insert a dummy activity from node 3 to node 4 in the project network of Fig. 5.3. The dummy from 3 to 4 is known as a *logical dummy* and is necessary for representing the correct precedence logic implied by the structure of the project. In general, logical dummies need to be inserted in the project network when the predecessor sets of some of the activities are proper subsets of the predecessor sets of some other activities.

Apart from logical dummies one may be faced with situations where two or more activities have identical sets of predecessors and successors. In this situation, the activities can be done in parallel or concurrently and their unique identification by referring to node numbers is not possible. In such a situation (Fig. 5.4), *k* parallel activities are modelled using *k*–1 dummies. The dummies so inserted are not logical dummies, but perform the function of *dummies for unique representation.* We can consider them to be a special class of dummies in that they consume no time or resources and do not violate the precedence relations among the jobs.

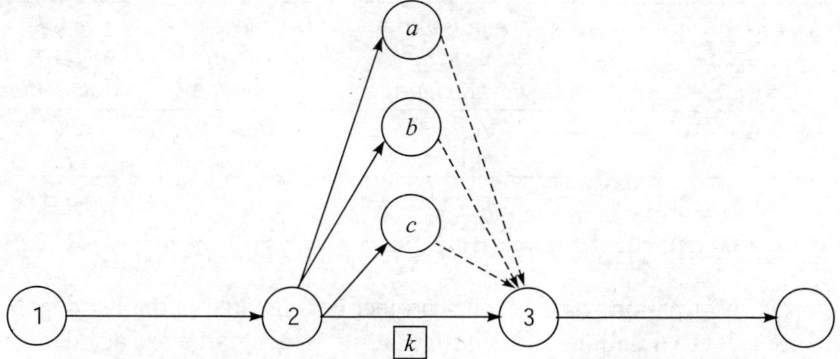

Fig. 5.4 Dummies for unique representation of parallel activities.

Another use of dummies is for creating a *single source* or *single sink* in a network which has multiple sources and/or sinks. In such situations, all the sources may be assumed to be hung from a common node which acts as the single source and all the sinks may be combined into a single node which may be viewed as a sink. In many computer representations, it may be worthwhile to use single source–single sink networks. An example of this usage of dummies for the generation of single source sink representations is shown in Fig. 5.5.

It may be noticed that if we use the A-O-N mode of representation where each activity is represented as a node, there is no need of adding any dummy activities to represent precedence or parallelism in activities since each activity would be well taken care of with suitable predecessors. However, dummies may be needed only for the creation of a single source–single sink network in situations where multiple sources and sinks are present as shown in Fig. 5.5.

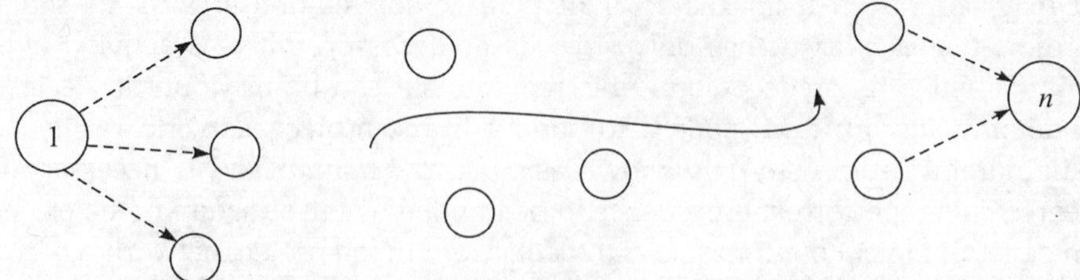

Fig. 5.5 Dummies added for the creation of single source and sink.

There is thus an advantage of using the A-O-N representation vis-à-vis the A-O-A representation in that no dummies are needed. However, the interpretation of milestones or activities as progression of activities on an arc is not available in A-O-N networks. However, both representations are equivalent and any one can be used to represent the correct network logic.

A comparison of the various types of dummies in both types of networks is summarized in Table 5.2.

Table 5.2 Purpose and usage of dummies in different network representations

Network/Dummy usage	*To represent correct logic (logical dummy)*	*Uniqueness of activity designation*	*Single source and destination*
A-O-A	Yes	Yes	Yes
A-O-N	No	No	Yes

5.4 CONSISTENCY IN PROJECT NETWORKS

The basic information from which a project is generated is the list of jobs and their precedence relations. This information is generally extracted from the experts in the field who have experience of similar projects. It is likely that the information is not correct or lacks some important elements which may lead to either erroneous networks or a situation where the network is not possible to be drawn. Consistency in project networks refers to the feasibility of generating a proper network from the given precedence relations. We discuss below the following three simple procedures to check for inconsistency in project networks.

Now let us consider the precedence relations given in Table 5.3 and try to develop a project network.

Table 5.3 Predecessor list for a sample project

Job	*A*	*B*	*C*	*D*	*E*
Immediate predecessor(s)	*B*	*C*	*A*	*A*	*C*

A project network should not contain any cycles.

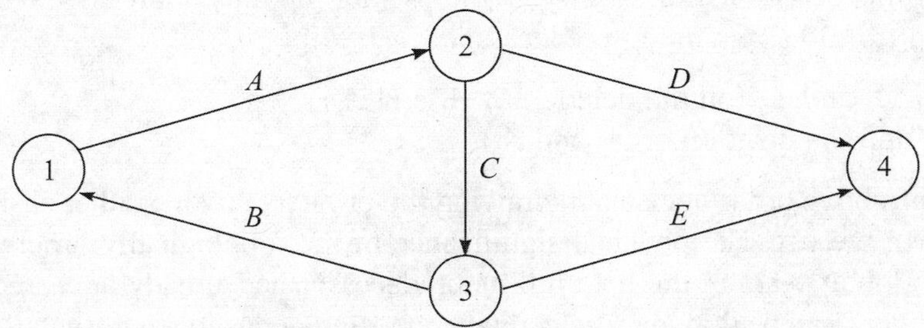

Fig. 5.6 An example of a loop (A-C-B) in a network.

The network shown in Fig. 5.6, however, is inconsistent because of the presence of a cycle or a loop, which is an inconsistency. Project networks must be consistent because a loop implies by transitivity (if $A < C$ and $C < B$ and $B < A$ implies $A < A$), which is a logical inconsistency that a job would have to be done before it is undertaken, which is not possible. The checking for cycles or loops may be simple in small networks of the kind shown in Fig. 5.6, but systematic procedures are needed for large networks. Depending on whether we are dealing with job lists, networks or adjacency matrices for the project, different procedures are highlighted below for checking of consistency.

5.4.1 Topological Ordering of Jobs

Suppose we are given the following list (Table 5.4) of jobs and predecessors:

Table 5.4 Predecessor list

S. No.	*Job*	*Predecessors*
1	A_1	—
2	A_3	A_1, A_2
3	A_5	A_1
4	A_6	A_3, A_5
5	A_2	—
6	A_4	A_1

It is easy to draw the project network for this simple case by simply going through the list of jobs. However, to proceed systematically, we first topologically order the jobs by applying the following rules:

(i) List the job(s) with no predecessors (sources).
(ii) Delete such jobs from the predecessor list of all the remaining jobs.
(iii) Return to step (i) till either of the following happens:
 (a) No job remains to be placed on the list, in which case we have a consistent network.
 (b) No sources are generated and all the jobs cannot be placed on the list, in which case an inconsistency is detected.

Let us apply this procedure to the table above. The topologically ordered list for this case is as follows: A_1, A_2 (these are the only sources which can be deleted from the remaining predecessors)

A_3, A_4 and A_5 (on the deletion of A_1 and A_2)
A_6 (on the deletion of A_3 and A_5)

The above order helps us in drawing the project network rather easily if we go down the list. The physical significance of the topologically ordered list is that no job appears in the list until its predecessor has already appeared. Thus, the network can be drawn by selectively choosing nodes for representation from left to right in an orderly fashion.

For the example above, the A-O-N network is given in Fig. 5.7. It is also easy to represent this network in A-O-A mode if one desires.

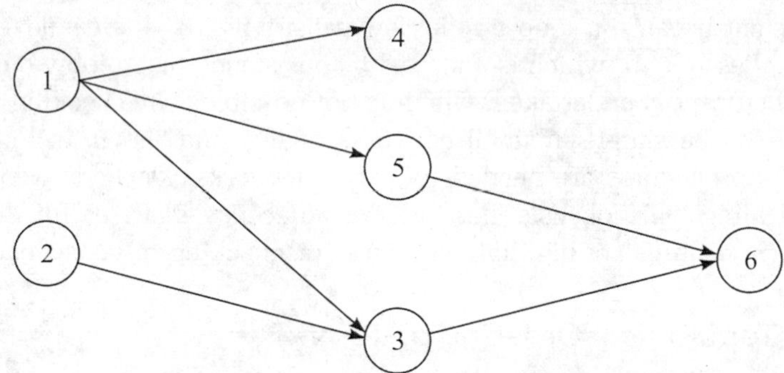

Fig. 5.7 A-O-N representation of the sample network.

Now let us consider an example with the following predecessor list of jobs:

Job	*A*	*B*	*C*	*D*	*E*	*F*	*G*
Predecessors	—	—	*A, B*	*C, F*	*D*	*C, G*	*E*

Topologically ordering yields the following list:

A, B
C

At this stage all the rest of the nodes (*D, E, F* and *G*) are remaining to be placed but none of them is a source node after the deletion of the above list. Thus, the list terminates prematurely indicating that there is an inconsistency or a loop in the network. As the representation of this network shows, in Fig. 5.8 there is a loop *D-E-G-F-D* in the network which has to be corrected before a valid network can be drawn. On examination it turned out that the predecessors of *D* should be *C* alone and that of *F* should be *C, D* and *G* to reverse the arrow from *D* to *F* and result in a consistent network.

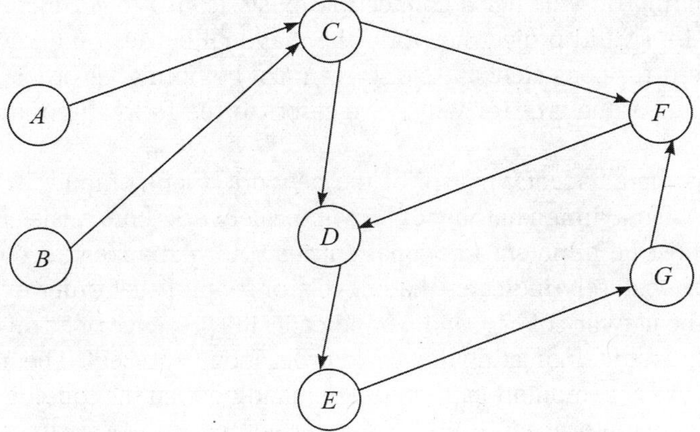

Fig. 5.8 An inconsistent network (loop *D-E-G-F-D*).

5.4.2 Fulkerson's Numbering Rule for Node Numbering

If each arc of an A-O-A or an A-O-N network can be numbered such that for every arc (ij) the value of i is less than the value of j, the network is consistent. This would lead to a simple procedure for checking the consistency of networks with unnumbered or randomly numbered nodes. The following procedure is referred to as numbering by Fulkerson's rule:

(i) Identify source nodes (those nodes without predecessors) and number them sequentially in any order as 1, 2, ...
(ii) Delete the arcs emanating from the sources identified in step (i) and identify the new sources so generated.
(iii) Go back to step (i) till one of the following happens:
 (a) All nodes are numbered leading to a consistent network.
 (b) Numbering cannot be completed for lack of sources, yet some nodes are left unnumbered.

On application of this rule to the network of Fig. 5.8 the two sources A and B can be numbered 1 or 2 in any order. After deleting the arcs AC and BC, C emerges as the new source which is numbered as node 3. However, after deleting the arcs from C no new sources are generated and the numbering terminates prematurely, indicating an inconsistency. It is easy to see that the loop or cycle lies in the unnumbered portion which in this case constitutes nodes D, E, G and F.

Fulkerson's numbering rule may be interpreted as the network equivalent of topologically ordering on job lists and is useful when the initially drawn network is available and consistency is to be checked.

5.4.3 Matrix Multiplication Procedures for Adjacency Matrices

As we had indicated, the project network can be represented as a square matrix (the adjacency matrix) wherein the entries corresponding to cell (i, j) can be 0 or 1 depending on whether a connection exists from *i* to *j*. Since there are no self loops in a valid project network, the diagonal entries on all such matrices must be zero for consistency. Also, there must be no higher order loops (loops with more than one arc) for which we resort to the following matrix squaring procedure.

If *M* is the adjacency matrix of the network, then compute M^2, M^3, M^{k-1}, where *k* is the maximum number of arcs in the network. For consistency, all these matrices must be nilpotent (diagonal entries = 0). An appearance of 1s on the diagonal prematurely indicates that a cycle or loop of that order exists. For example, in the network of Fig. 5.9, M^3 indicates the presence of 1s on the diagonal of nodes 2, 4 and 5 indicating that a 3rd order loop is present. The matrix squaring procedure is computationally more demanding than the topologically ordering and Fulkerson procedures discussed earlier and is resorted to only when we want to operate on the adjacency matrix rather than the list or network directly.

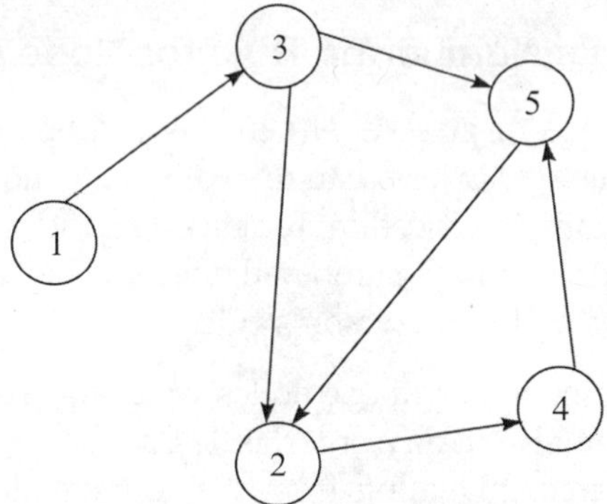

Fig. 5.9 A sample network along with its adjacency matrix *M*.

The adjacency matrix *M* is shown below.

From node i to node j	1	2	3	4	5
1	0	0	1	0	0
2	0	0	0	1	0
3	0	1	0	0	1
4	0	0	0	0	1
5	0	1	0	0	0

M^2 can be computed as under:

From node i to node j	1	2	3	4	5
1	0	1	0	0	1
2	0	0	0	0	1
3	0	1	0	1	0
4	0	1	0	0	0
5	0	0	0	1	0

Since M^2 has all 0s on the diagonal, we continue the process and compute M^3 as under:

From node i to node j	1	2	3	4	5
1	0	1	0	1	0
2	0	1	0	0	0
3	0	0	0	1	1
4	0	0	0	1	0
5	0	0	0	0	1

The appearance of 1s corresponding to the diagonal elements of nodes 2, 4 and 5 indicates the presence of a loop and an inconsistency in the network. The interpretation of the 1 in each of these nodes is the presence of the 3rd order path (involving 3 arcs) connecting the node to itself. Thus, the loop (2, 4, 5) in Fig. 5.9 is also identified in this procedure owing to the appearance of 1s on the corresponding diagonal in M^3.

5.5 REDUNDANCY IN PROJECT NETWORKS

In any given list of project predecessors, sometimes the predecessors are over-specified and may be pruned to yield a more compact network. There is unnecessary additional information which only adds clutter to the network. It is thus useful to check for any redundancies after the topological ordering of activities has been performed. As an example, take the following predecessor relations and let us illustrate the procedure of checking for redundancies on this list:

Job	*A*	*B*	*C*	*D*	*E*	*F*	*G*	*H*
Predecessors	—	—	*A*	*A, C*	*B, D*	*D, E*	*C*	*G, F*

Arranging the jobs in topological order a list is prepared indicating the immediate predecessors as depicted in the given list or network. This table is shown below:

Job/immediate predecessors	*A*	*B*	*C*	*D*	*E*	*F*	*G*	*H*
A								
B								
C	x							
D	x 0		x					
E	0	x	0	x				
F	0	0	0	x 0	x			
G	0		x					
H	0	0	0	0	0	x	x	

In this table the x values show the immediate predecessors in the list and the 0's indicate the implied predecessors. The procedure for detecting the redundancies is summarized below.

Arrange jobs in topological order (in the above case jobs are already in topological order). Scan the predecessor list of jobs from top to bottom and mark predecessors of each job with a zero (0). Each cell may land up in one of the four possible states:

(i) empty, indicating no predecessor–successor relationship.
(ii) x, indicating that job j is an immediate predecessor of job i.
(iii) 0, indicating that job j is an implied or distant predecessor of job i.
(iv) x0, indicating a redundancy, as job j is an implied predecessor of job i.

The matrix so generated may be called the *all predecessor–successor matrix*. The marked rows give all the predecessors (immediate and distant) of a job. Similarly, all the successors can be obtained from the columns of this matrix. One can see from the network of this project that arcs from A to D and D to F are in fact redundant and can be eliminated, resulting in a well-pruned network. Redundancies in the example project network have been shown as dotted lines in Fig. 5.10.

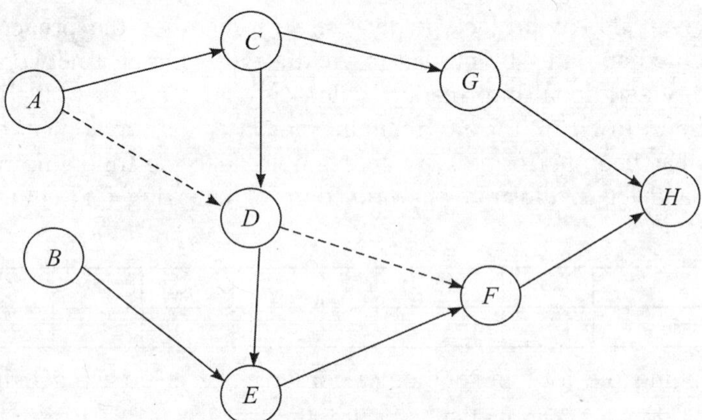

Fig. 5.10 Redundancies in a project network.

5.6 SUMMARY AND CONCLUSIONS

In this chapter, we have looked at the process of developing project networks from given precedence relationships. The role of dummies in the correct and compact representation of networks has been highlighted. Dummies perform three kinds of roles—the representation of correct logic, for uniqueness of representation, and creating single source and sink in networks. As is generally the case both A-O-A and A-O-N networks can be used to represent the required logic. However, A-O-N networks are easier to draw and do not require dummies except for creation of single source and sink in case of multi-sources and sinks.

The network can be developed only if the precedence relations are consistent. Consistency or the absence of loops or cycles can be detected by topologically ordering on precedence lists, Fulkerson's numbering on networks and by matrix squaring on adjacency matrices. Each of these procedures has been illustrated through examples.

Then, a redundancy check procedure to develop the all predecessor–successor matrix has been discussed so that a well-pruned network without unnecessary arcs is obtained. It may be indicated that whilst consistency in a network is necessary, it is desirable to remove redundancy.

Finally, as a consequence of these procedures, a proper project network is drawn which is the foundation of all computations of schedules, costs and resources to be discussed in later chapters.

PROBLEMS

1. Show through sample network constructions in A-O-A and A-O-N modes how a dummy could be used to
   (a) Generate a single source and sink in the network.
   (b) Permit uniqueness of activity representation.
   (c) Represent correct network logic.
   (d) Represent a redundancy.
2. A project of 10 jobs has the following precedence relations:

Job	*Predecessors*
a	*c, e, f*
b	*d, g*
c	*d, g*
d	*h, i*
e	*h, i*
f	*j*
g	*j*
h	*j*
i	—
j	—

Draw (i) An A-O-A network.
(ii) An A-O-N network.
(iii) An adjacency matrix.
(iv) A node arc incidence matrix for the project.
(v) The fundamental loop and cut set matrices for any chosen tree.

Is there a redundancy in the above predecessor list?

If all jobs are of equal duration, determine the critical path and the four floats for all jobs.

3. A project consists of 12 activities, labelled *A* to *L*. When the work manager was asked to specify the order in which jobs have to be done, he answered as follows: Job *A* comes first and precedes *B*, *C* and *D*. Both *B* and *C* must be done before *E* starts, and *C* and *D* must precede *F*, but *G* and *H* can start as soon as *D* is completed. Job *I* succeeds *D*, *E*, *F* and *G*, and jobs *J* and *K* can start when *G*, *H* and *I* are all completed. Job *L* comes after *J* and *K*.
   (a) Using a precedence matrix, assist the work manager to eliminate redundancy in his list of precedence relationships. List the immediate predecessors for each job.
   (b) Draw an A-O-N diagram, using as few precedence arrows as necessary to show correct precedence relationships.
   (c) Draw an arrow-diagram representation of the same project, using as few dummy jobs as necessary to show correct precedence relationships and unique node identification of activities.
4. Arun Sharma, project manager, was interested in developing a network for a 20-job project under his responsibility. He labelled the jobs A to T and for each job listed all its predecessors as best as he could determine.

Job	*Immediate predecessors*	*Job*	*Immediate predecessors*
A	—	*K*	*G*
B	—	*L*	*F, G, K*
C	—	*M*	*H, I*
D	*A, B*	*N*	*H, I, J, L*
E	*A, B, C*	*O*	*J, K, L*
F	*A, B, C*	*P*	*M, N*
G	*C*	*Q*	*O, P*
H	*D, E*	*R*	*J, K, L, O*
I	*D, E, F*	*S*	*N, Q, R*
J	*F, G*	*T*	*O, S*

   Arun suspected that some predecessors he listed were redundant, and he was not sure how to develop a network from his list of jobs and predecessors.
   (a) Which (if any) predecessors shown could be eliminated without affecting the network logic?
   (b) Assist Mr. Sharma by drawing an arrow diagram for this project, using as few dummies as possible.
   (c) Draw an A-O-N diagram from the original project list (including redundant predecessors) and determine to your satisfaction that the redundant predecessor arrows could be removed without changing the network logic.

5. In the table below, each activity of a project is listed in the first column, and those activities which must follow the given job are listed in the second column. From this information draw both the A-O-A and the A-O-N networks for the project.

Activity	*Must follow*
A	*P, N, M*
B	*P*
C	*A, B*
D	*I, J, C*
E	*I, J, C*
F	*D, E*
G	—
H	*G*
I	*H*
J	*H, B, A*
K	*G*
L	*G*
M	*L*
N	*K, O*
O	*L*
P	*Q, O*
Q	*K*

6. To any directed graph whether cyclic or acyclic, there correspond three basic matrices:

   (a) The adjacency matrix: both row and column headings are the nodes 1 to n, and an entry +1 in position ij means that an arc leads from node i to node j; otherwise there is a zero entry.
   (b) The incidence (or vertex) matrix, g: the row headings are the nodes 1 to n, and the column headings are the arcs of the graph; the entry is +1 if the arrow is incident from that node, it is –1 if the arrow is incident on that node, and it is zero otherwise.
   (c) The circuit matrix, h: the row headings are the circuits (independent of arrow direction), and the column headings are the arcs of the graph. An entry is +1 if the direction of the arrow coincides with the orientation of the circuit (which is arbitrary); it is –1 if it is opposite to orientation, and it is 0 if the arrow does not lie on the circuit.

   You are asked to construct all the three matrices for the following activity network and to verify the following properties:

   (i) The rank of the adjacency and incidence matrices is $N-1$, where N is the number of nodes.

(ii) If T is a tree of a connected directed graph G then $N-1$ columns of the incidence matrix corresponding to T constitute a nonsingular sub-matrix of the incidence matrix of G.

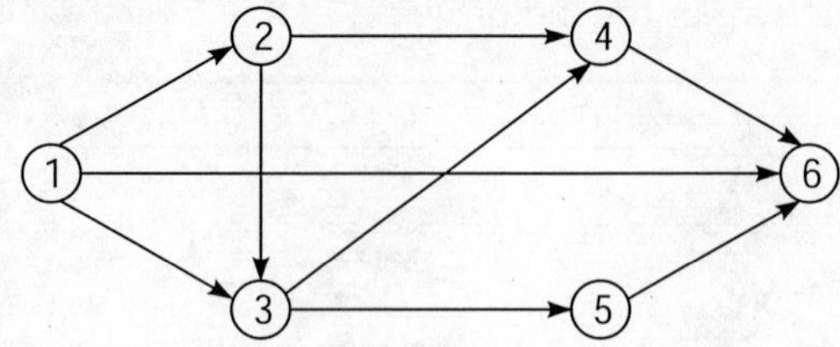

(iii) The rank of the circuit matrix of a connected directed graph G of A arcs and N nodes is $A - N + 1$.

(iv) If the columns of the incidence matrix and the circuit matrix are arranged in the same arc order, $[g][h]' = 0$, where the prime denotes transpose.

7. What are the methods available to check the consistency of a project network? Use all these methods to check the consistency of the following network:

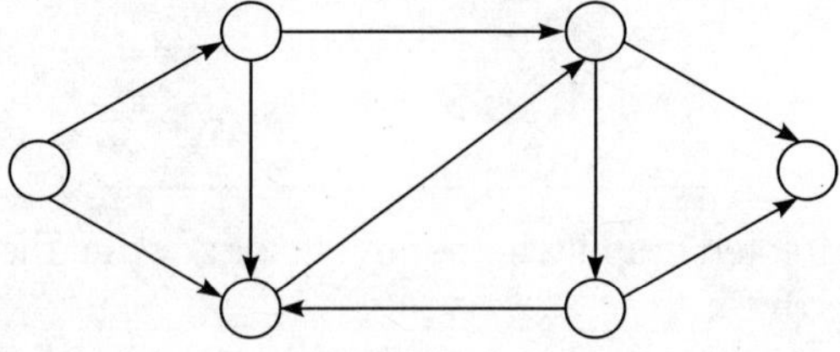

Comment on the computational complexity of each procedure.

8. You are in charge for organizing an international conference on project management some time two years hence.
   (i) Develop the proper work breakdown structure for jobs to be done, with proper allocation of responsibility.
   (ii) Develop the precedence relations for jobs.
   (iii) Draw the project network in A-O-A mode.
   (iv) Make estimates of time for various activities and determine the critical path and schedule of activities.
   (v) Outline your planning, scheduling, monitoring and control actions in implementing the project.

CHAPTER

6

Basic Scheduling Concepts

6.1 INTRODUCTION

Once the project network has been drawn (in either the A-O-A or the A-O-N mode), it is necessary to obtain estimates of the task times that are conceived in the project. Two popular schemes are in vogue, as depicted below in Table 6.1.

Table 6.1 Common schemes for task times

CPM (*critical path method*) (*for deterministic durations*)	PERT (*program evaluation and review technique*) (*for probabilistic durations*)
Here each activity is given a fixed duration (generally based on past experience, e.g. construction or other repetitive jobs).	Each activity is assumed to follow a logical probability distribution. The originators of PERT chose a beta distribution for its apparent simplicity, where *a*, *m* and *b* were likened to the optimistic, most likely and the pessimistic times, respectively.

It may be noted that any probability distribution, e.g. one of the following illustrated in Fig. 6.1, may be utilized in probabilistic scheduling similar to that in PERT.

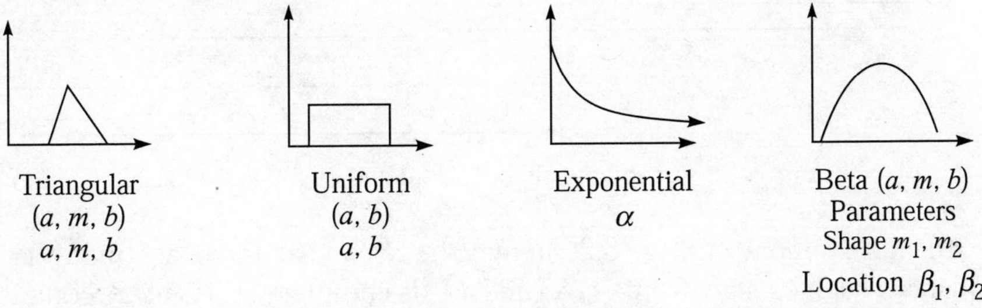

Fig. 6.1 Variety of probability distributions.

For the chosen distribution, the activity mean (μ) and the variance (σ^2) may be used to perform the computations. In conventional scheduling (both PERT and CPM), the longest expected path (this is the longest path in CPM since activities have no flexibility whatsoever) is determined which has the implication of the shortest possible time in which the project can be done. Of course the notion of floats for activities and slacks in various paths is easy to comprehend.

Some of the commonly used procedures for determining the critical path are

- Path enumeration using tree search (generally time consuming)
- Forward and backward pass procedures with expected job durations

Once these procedures are completed, the floats/slacks for each activity are determined and the critical path and the schedule of activities with their early and late start and finish times can be established. Owing to the fact that the non-critical activities have positive floats, they could be interrupted at will between the imposed limits if no adverse effects are envisaged and the project as a whole is benefitted. This requires a holistic view of the project which can be investigated by a discriminative project leader.

An interesting observation pointed out by Elmaghraby, et al. in a paper published in 2003 in the *International Journal of Project Management* brought out beautifully the distinction betweeen display devices and scheduling algorithms. It may be mentioned that the existing popular software packages available, such as Primavera or MS Project, are essentially display devices. Even the case when precedence networks with the four kinds of lead-lag relations *SS*, *SF*, *FS* and *FF* are utilized, the Gantt chart displayed is only a convenient device to represent the constraints imposed by the schedule, though of course a systematic procedure has been adopted to accomplish the same. It is more like some activity starts here and is likely to finish here depending on the constraints that the problem imposes.

A project schedule of this nature is depicted in Fig. 6.2.

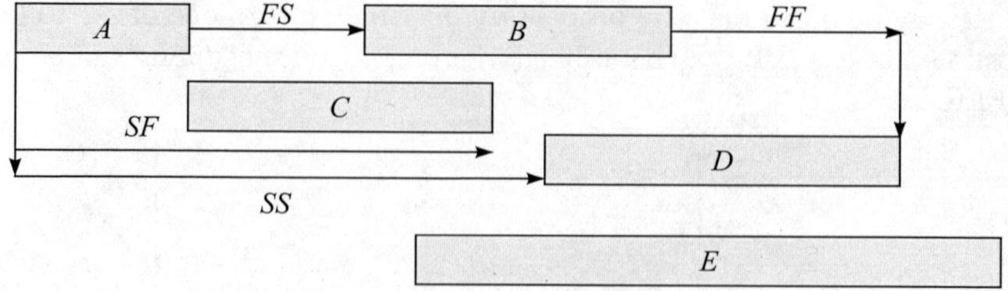

Fig. 6.2 A project schedule depicted as a Gantt chart.

In the example of Fig. 6.2, it may be seen that there are many critical sequences such as start from *A*, *SS* and *D*, or complete *A*, *FS* to *B*, complete *B* and wait for *D* to finish, which would both consume the same amount of time. However, the point to be noted is that an activity like *E* has no predecessors or successors and could be accommodated by sliding it anywhere in between the project start and finish. Thus, the minimum project duration for this illustrative project is the length of any one of the critical sequences though the schedules could be different in each case.

No doubt, such information can be updated very frequently and is thus useful for both periodic and online project monitoring. Goldratt (1997) has introduced the notion of the critical chain which is an improvement over the traditional concept of the critical path. The critical chain is determined by both the durations and the resources available for an activity.

6.2 DETERMINISTIC PROJECT SCHEDULING

Once a project is identified, estimates of individual activity times are obtained. These are usually obtained from experts in the field who have had experience with handling similar projects in the past. Once the times for activities are obtained deterministically, the next task is obtaining the schedule of carrying out the various tasks in the project and developing the project duration. This is the essential process involved in deterministic project scheduling.

The project network contains a number of paths from origin to terminal. It is intuitively clear that the project will be complete only when all the tasks are complete. This can happen when the longest path in the project network is completed. This longest path is commonly known as the *critical path* in the project. The critical path represents a lower bound on the project completion time and any delay in a critical activity (an activity on the critical path) would lead to a delay in the total project completion time.

In this chapter, various procedures are outlined for the determination of the critical path. Among these, the brute force approach is to determine all the paths by enumeration and discover the longest. This is discussed in Section 6.3 where a tree algorithm for path enumeration is presented. This is, however, an inefficient approach but has the advantage of obtaining all the paths which may be useful in a number of situations, such as project crashing or selective reduction in duration of the project.

The most commonly used procedures for determination of the project schedule include a forward and backward pass on the project network. This can be done easily for both A-O-A and A-O-N representations of the project which are described in Sections 6.4 and 6.5, respectively.

Activities or jobs on the critical path are called critical jobs and any delay in them causes the project to be delayed. However, for the other non-critical activities some cushion is available which is referred to as the float. It is shown in Section 6.6 that there are four kinds of float, such as total, safety, free and independent, which measure this cushion under varying circumstances. Floats help the manager by providing flexibility in scheduling and guarding against uncertainties.

6.3 CRITICAL PATH DETERMINATION BY ENUMERATION

Perhaps the simplest approach in concept is to enumerate all the paths in a project network along with their lengths. Then it is easy to compute the longest path or the critical path which signifies the minimum project duration. Take, for instance, the network shown in Fig. 6.3.

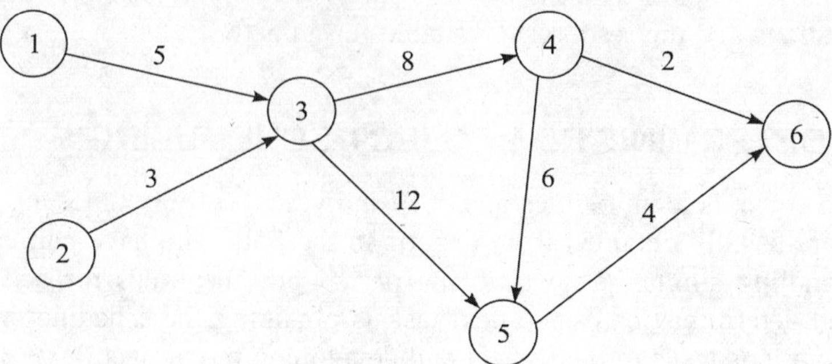

Fig. 6.3 Sample project network (A-O-A) with indicated activity durations in days.

For the project in Fig. 6.3, it is easy to enumerate all paths from source(s) to sink(s) as follows:

1-3-4-6 length 15
1-3-5-6 length 21
1-3-4-5-6 length 23
2-3-5-6 length 19
2-3-4-6 length 13
2-3-4-5-6 length 21

In this example, the critical path is 1-3-4-5-6 with a length 23 days. A more systematic procedure for the enumeration of all the paths is a tree search as outlined below:

Step 1 In the case of multiple sources, create a dummy single source as the starting source (in the above example of Fig. 6.3 imagine a node 0 with arcs going to nodes 1 and 2) and treat it as the beginning node at level 1.

Step 2 For each level k examine the nodes and for each node determine the successor arcs in the network placing them in level $k + 1$.

Step 3 Continue the process in step 2 till all paths terminate in the final node.

This process applied to network in Fig. 6.3 yields the tree of Fig. 6.4.

It is seen from the tree that there are four paths terminating at level 4 and two at level 2. These can be traced from the tree along with their lengths as indicated below:

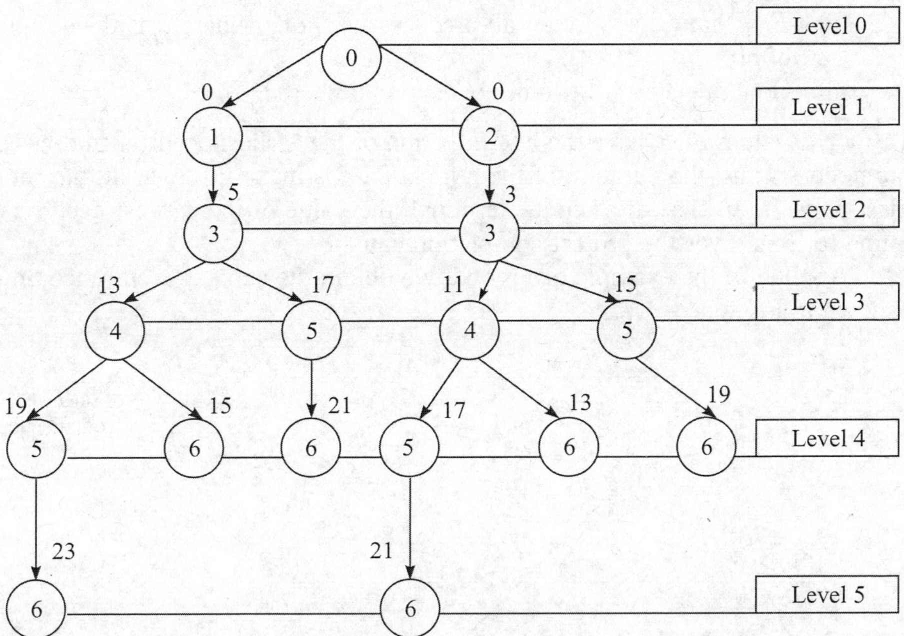

Fig. 6.4 Tree representation for the network of Fig. 6.3.

0-1-3-4-5-6	Length 23	Level 5
0-1-3-4-6	Length 15	Level 4
0-1-3-5-6	Length 21	Level 4
0-2-3-4-5-6	Length 21	Level 5
0-2-3-4-6	Length 13	Level 4
0-2-3-5-6	Length 19	Level 4

The nomenclature in the tree indicates the level number which is the number of arcs in a particular path starting from the origin node. Thus, in the example above there are four paths containing four arcs and two paths containing five arcs.

6.4 EVENT ORIENTED ALGORITHMS FOR A-O-A NETWORKS

The enumeration algorithm is not a practical method of computing the critical path. A more practical approach is a procedure based on the forward and backward pass computation. This involves scanning the network from source to sink and then from sink to source in topological order and assigning the event times. The algorithm to determine the *earliest occurrence times* consists of the following steps:

(i) For all starting nodes i, assign $E_i = 0$, or S, the project start date.

(ii) $E_j = \text{Max}\{E_i + t_{ij}\}$ over all predecessors *i* of *j*, where t_{ij} is the duration of arc (*ij*).

(iii) Continue step (ii) till all nodes are numbered.

The values of E_i have the interpretation of the earliest occurrence times up to node *i*. Thus, the duration of the critical path is max (E_k), over all the set of last nodes *k*. In case of a unique terminal, the value of the earliest occurrence time for this gives the project completion date.

Applied to the example of Fig. 6.3 we obtain the earliest occurrence times shown in Fig. 6.5.

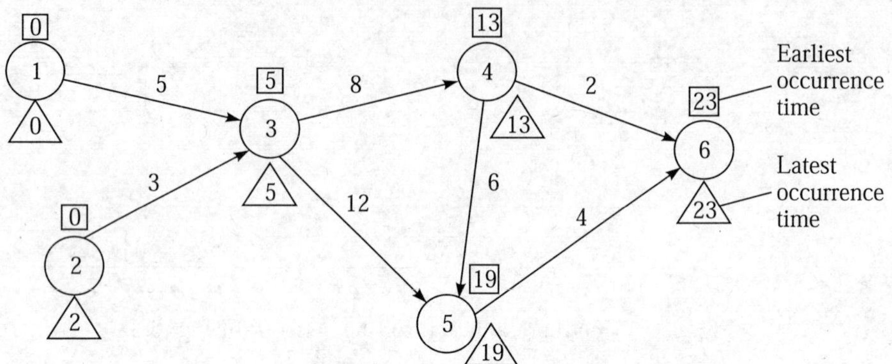

Fig. 6.5 Sample network with earliest and latest occurrence times.

Notice that the earliest occurrence times for nodes 1 and 2 are 0, for node 3 is the max of {0 + 5; 0 + 3} that is 5, that of node 4 is {5 + 8}, that is 13, that of node 5 is max of {5 + 12; 13 + 6}, that is 19 and that of node 6 is max of {13 + 2; 19 + 4}, that is 23 which is the length of the critical path.

Once the forward pass is done to obtain the earliest occurrence times, *a backward pass* is done to generate the latest occurrence times of all nodes. This procedure starts from the last node(s) and proceeds in reverse order to the initial node(s).

The backward pass may be stated as follows:

(i) The latest occurrence time of the last nodes, L_n = length of critical path.

(ii) $L_i = \min\{L_j - t_{ij}\}$ for all successors *j* of node *i*.

(iii) Continue step (ii) till all nodes are numbered.

The L_i values so computed have the interpretation of the latest occurrence of all the nodes.

In the example of Fig. 6.3 the latest times are computed below:

Node	6	5	4	3	2	1
i	23 (critical path length)	[23 – 4] = 19	Min[23 – 2; 19 – 6] = 13	Min[13 – 8; 19 – 12] = 5	[5 – 3] = 2	[5 – 5] = 0

The earliest and the latest occurrence times can be related to the early and late start and finish of the activities as indicated in Fig. 6.6.

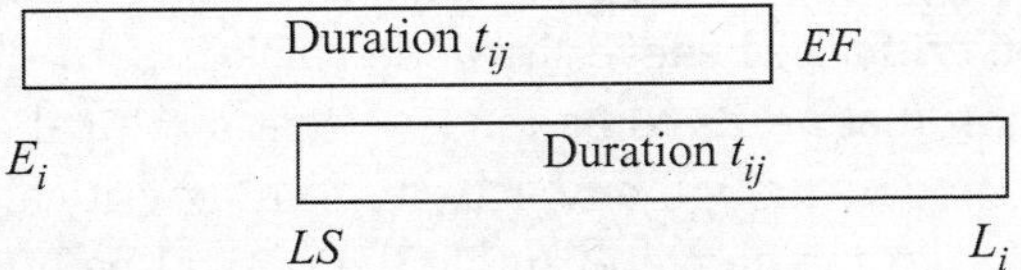

Fig. 6.6 The early the and late finish of an activity.

It can be seen from Fig. 6.6 that

Early Start (*ES*) of an activity = E_i (the earliest occurrence time of its predecessor node)

Latest Finish (*LF*) of an activity = L_j (the latest occurrence time of its successor node)

Once these two quantities are determined, the early finish (*EF*) and late start (*LS*) of the activity can be obtained by using the following relationships:

$$EF = ES + t_{ij}$$
$$LS = LF - t_{ij}$$

These computations are summarized in Tables 6.2 and 6.3.

Table 6.2 Earliest and latest occurrence times of nodes in A-O-A network

Node	1	2	3	4	5	6
Earliest time	0	0	5	13	19	23
Latest time	0	2	5	13	19	23

Table 6.3 Earliest and latest start and finish times of activities

Activity	*Duration* t_{ij} (*A*)	*Early Start* = E_i (*B*)	*Early finish* $E_i + t_{ij}$ (*C*)	*Late start* $L_j - t_{ij}$ (*D*)	*Late finish* $= L_j$ (*E*)	*Total float* (*F*)	*Remarks*
(1, 3)	5	0	5	0	5	0	Critical
(2, 3)	3	0	3	2	5	2	
(3, 4)	8	5	13	5	13	0	Critical
(3, 5)	12	5	17	7	19	2	
(4, 5)	6	13	19	13	19	0	Critical
(4, 6)	2	13	15	21	23	8	
(5, 6)	4	19	23	19	23	0	Critical

Those activities for which $ES = LS$ or $EF = LF$ are termed *critical* and determine the critical path. The quantity $LS - ES$ or $LF - EF$ is termed the *total float* of the activity and denotes the amount of cushion available in that activity for accomplishing the project in the critical duration. In the A-O-A representation we can term the activity $(L_i - E_i)$ as the *node slack* for node *i*. A node is said to be critical whenever its node slack is zero.

An observation that needs to be made is that a critical activity necessarily joins two critical nodes, though any activity joining critical nodes may not be critical. Notice that in the above example the critical path is 1-3-4-5-6, which has only four critical activities but all the nodes except node 2 are critical. Activities (3, 5) and (4, 6) though joining critical nodes are not critical. This is the reason to follow a systematic search procedure outlined above to identify the critical path and the total floats.

6.5 ACTIVITY ORIENTED ALGORITHMS FOR A-O-N NETWORKS

The forward and backward pass computations can alternatively be done for A-O-N networks along the lines indicated in Section 6.4 for A-O-A networks. Since no event times are involved, we work directly with *ES*, *EF*, *LS* and *LF* of activities and the forward and backward passes are modified as shown below: The forward pass would involve the following:

(1) *ES* (all beginning jobs) = 0 or project start date, *S* (initialization)
(2) $EF = ES$ + duration
(3) *ES* (successor) = Max {*EF* all predecessors}
(4) Continue step 2 till *EF* is computed for all jobs
(5) Project duration T = Max{*EF* all jobs}

Notice that in the last equation the maximum needs to be taken only over the terminal jobs.

Similarly the backward pass would involve the computation of the latest schedule for the activities as indicated below:

(1) *LF* (ending jobs) = Project duration *T* (initialization)
(2) $LS = LF$ – duration
(3) *LF* (predecessor) = Min {*LS* of successors}
(4) Continue step 2 till *LS* is computed for all jobs

Once again, the total floats for all the activities can be computed by

$$TF = LS - ES = LF - EF$$

The computations may be performed on the network or predecessor successor lists as indicated in Table 6.4 for the network of Fig. 6.3.

Table 6.4 Forward pass on a list of jobs

Activity	*Duration t* (*A*)	*Immediate predecessors* (*B*)	*Early start, ES* (*C*)	*Early finish, EF = max{ES + duration of predecessors}* (*D*)
(1, 3) *a*	5	—	0	5
(2, 3) *b*	3	—	0	3
(3, 4) *c*	8	*a, b*	5	13
(3, 5) *d*	12	*a, b*	5	17
(4, 5) *e*	6	*c*	13	19
(4, 6) *f*	2	*c*	15	15
(5, 6) *g*	4	*d, e*	19	23

6.6 FLOATS AND THEIR SIGNIFICANCE

Apart from the total float defined previously, there are a total of four kinds of float that can be defined on a job. Referring to Fig. 6.7 it can be seen that once an activity is scheduled it has both predecessors and successors which can be played with.

If E_i, and L_i refer to the earliest and latest occurrence time of node i and E_j and L_j refer to the earliest and latest occurrence times of node j in an A-O-A network, then four kinds of floats may be defined for the activity (i_j) as indicated below:

$$\text{Total float} = L_j - E_i - t_{ij}$$
$$\text{Safety float} = L_j - L_i - t_{ij}$$
$$\text{Free float} = E_j - E_i - t_{ij}$$
$$\text{Independent float} = \text{Max}\{0,\ E_j - L_i - t_{ij}\}$$

For ease of computation in the A-O-A mode, the computations may be made from the activity floats and node slacks as given below:

Safety float = Total float – slack on preceding node i
Free float = Total float – slack on succeeding node j

Independent float = Max{0, Total float – Slack on preceding and succeeding nodes}

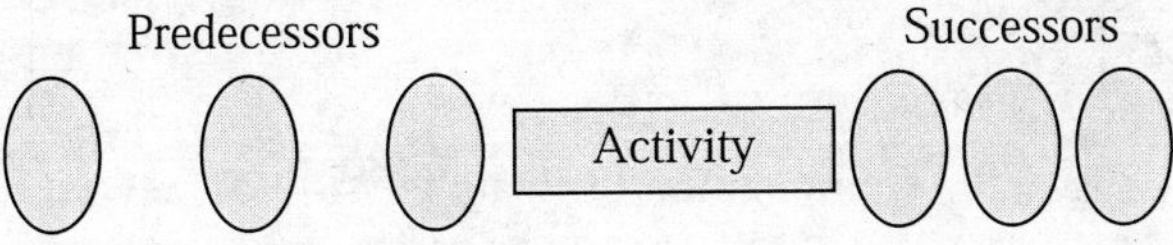

Fig. 6.7 An activity sandwiched between predecessors and successors.

The significance of the four kinds of float as defined above is depicted graphically in Fig. 6.8, as the relative placement of predecessors and successors of an activity.

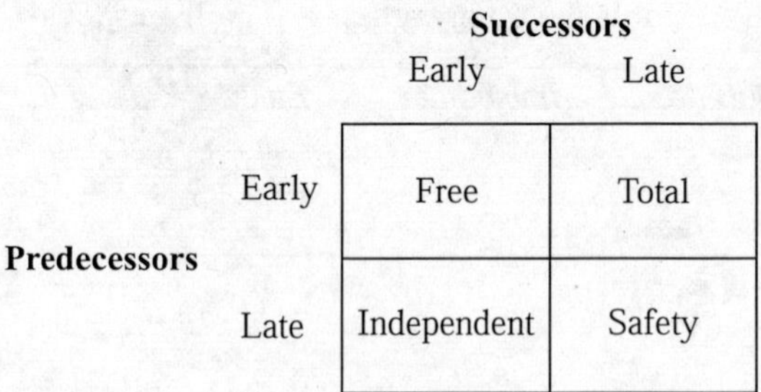

Fig. 6.8 Significance of the four activity floats.

The four floats arise depending on the placement of predecessors and successors as shown in Fig. 6.8. The total float is the largest and the independent float, in general, would be the shortest whilst the relative ranking of the other two could be any.

A procedure for direct calculation of floats without drawing the A-O-A network for a given A-O-N network can be illustrated in the following diagrammatic form (Fig. 6.9) after the forward and backward pass has been conducted and the *ES*, *EF*, *LS* and *LF* for all the jobs are available.

E_i (of n in A-O-A mode) = *ES* of n
L_i (of n in A-O-A mode) = max (*LF* of all predecessors)
E_j (of n in A-O-A mode) = max (*ES* of all successors of n)
L_j (of n in A-O-A mode) = *LF* of n.

With this we can compute all the floats and slacks in the A-O-N network.

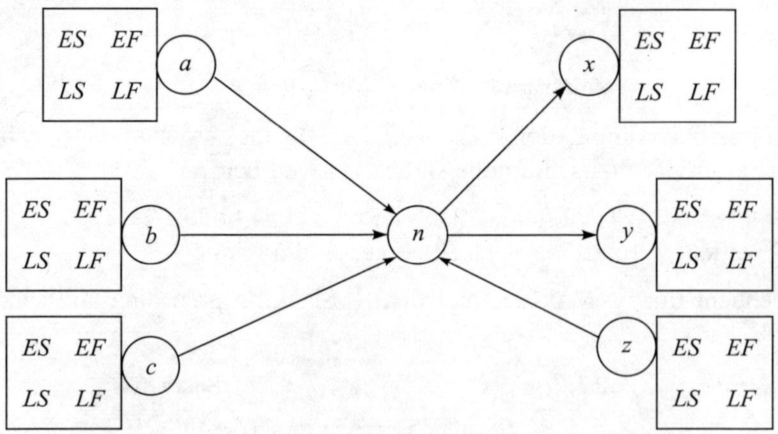

Fig. 6.9 Computation of floats for A-O-N networks.

6.7 SCHEDULING WITH UNCERTAIN ACTIVITY TIMES

There are a large number of projects which are undertaken for the first time and no experience is available on the estimates of time the project is likely to take. In such cases, it may be assumed that the project will lie between some optimistic (a) or pessimistic time (b) and a probability distribution may be assumed for the same.

Conventional PERT assumes a beta distribution for the activity times which is mathematically given by the following formula:

$$f(t) = K(t - a)^c(b - t)^d, \ (a \leq t \leq b) = 0, \text{ otherwise}$$

This is a four parameter distribution in which *a* and *b* are called the location parameters and *c* and *d* are referred to as the shape parameters.

This distribution looks as shown in Fig. 6.10.

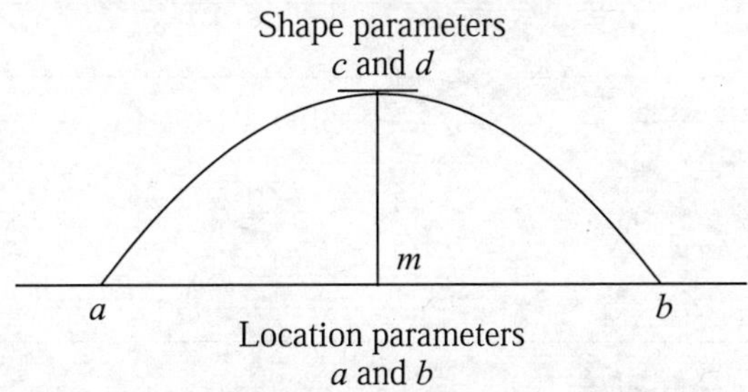

Fig. 6.10 The beta distribution.

Features of the beta distribution are summarized below:

(i) It is a four parameter distribution (since *K* can be computed by equating the total area under the curve equal to 1).
(ii) It has a single mode *m* which can be given the interpretation of the most likely time.
(iii) The shape of the distribution can be changed by changing the shape parameters *c* and *d*. However, by making the assumption that $(b - a) = 6\sigma$ and the mean $= (a + 4m + b)/6$, there is no real flexibility about shape.
(iv) It is bounded by the optimistic time *a* and the pessimistic time *b*.
(v) The beta distribution otherwise appeals to common sense, though it may not be the real distribution representing the activity completion time.
(vi) The originators of PERT, however, used this distribution for the development of the Polaris Missile Project developed by the US Navy. The general procedure of PERT calculations may be utilized for any assumed distribution provided the validity of the *Central Limit Theorem* is assumed.

This theorem states that if a reasonably large (in practice 4 or more) random variables are added, the sum will be approximately a normal distribution with mean equal to the sum of means and variance = the sum of variances of the random variables. Obviously, the error from the true mean and variance of the sum of the random variables if the critical path (the longest path in the network) contains more and more activities will be smaller. However, if the project is a single activity with some other distribution, the project completion time will obviously not be normal but will follow the distribution of that individual activity.

Apart from a beta distribution, any legitimate distribution to represent the activity times may be chosen. Some of the commonly used distributions are shown in Fig. 6.11.

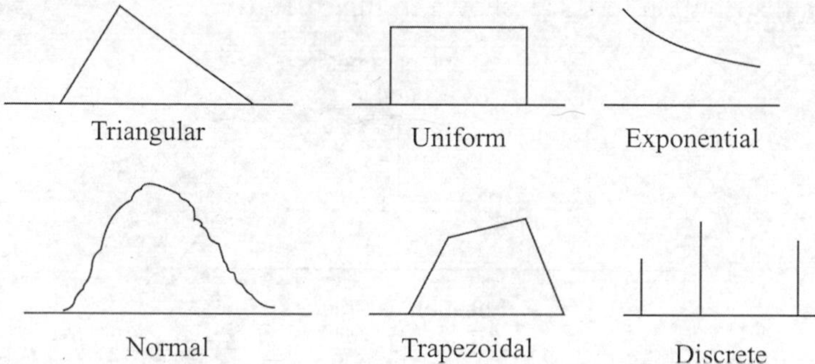

Fig. 6.11 Some common activity time distributions.

PERT calculations with any one of these distributions involve the following steps:

(a) Compute the mean (μ) and variance (σ^2) for each activity.
(b) Conduct a forward pass starting from source to finish node as outlined in the event oriented algorithm using mean activity times, as in a deterministic case.
(c) Similarly, conduct a backward pass and identify the critical path (longest path).
(d) Determine the mean and variance of the identified critical path by adding the activity means (say M) and the variances (say V).
(e) By the Central Limit Theorem, the project duration is approximately normally distributed with mean M and variance V.

The major gain we now have is the complete distribution of the project completion time, which by the above assumptions is normal. Armed with this complete distribution we can now easily compute

(a) Mean project duration = M
(b) Variance of project duration = V
(c) Probability of completing the project by any target date T can simply be computed by the area under the standard normal curve from $-\infty$ to $(T - M)/\sqrt{V}$. This can vary from 0 to 0.5 ($T \leq M$) and from 0.5 to 1 ($T \geq M$).

(d) The probability of completing the project in any interval from T_1 to T_2 can also be easily computed by taking the difference under the cumulative areas between T_2 and T_1 from the standard normal tables. This can establish the confidence limits for the project to be completed in any interval.

The following example illustrates the procedure of standard PERT outlined above:

EXAMPLE 6.1

Job	*Predecessors*	*Time estimates*			*Mean*	*Variance*
		a	*m*	*b*		
A	—	2	4	8	4.33	1
B	—	4	6	10	6.33	1
C	*A*	6	6	6	6.00	0
D	*A*	2	8	14	8.00	4
E	*A*	6	8	12	8.33	1
F	*B, C*	3	6	9	6.00	1
G	*D, F*	8	16	20	15.33	4
H	*D, F*	4	4	4	4.00	0
I	*E, H*	4	8	10	7.66	1

The A-O-A network for the example is shown in Fig. 6.12, with the mean durations as calculated in the above table shown adjacent to each arc.

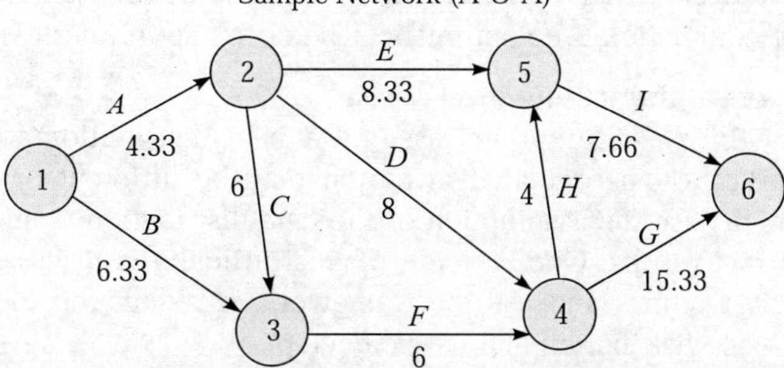

Fig. 6.12 A-O-A network for sample project.

By performing a forward and a backward pass in the usual manner, the results for the event times are shown in Fig. 6.13 and *ACFG* is identified as the critical path with a mean length of 31.66 days.

Distribution of the project duration, by the Central Limit Theorem, is approximately normally distributed with mean = 31.66 days and variance = σ^2 = $(2.45)^2$ as shown in Fig. 6.14.

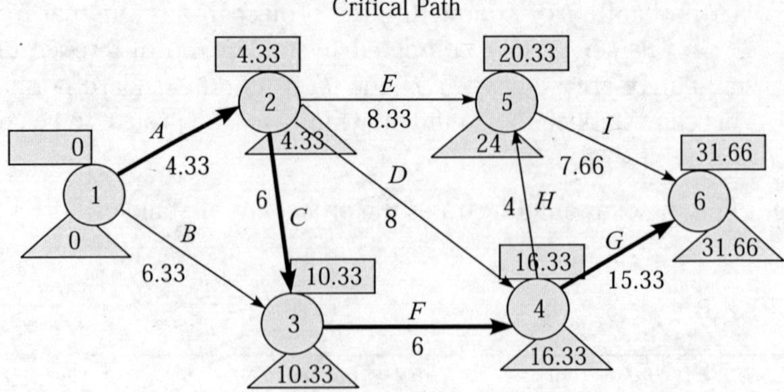

Fig. 6.13 The critical path.

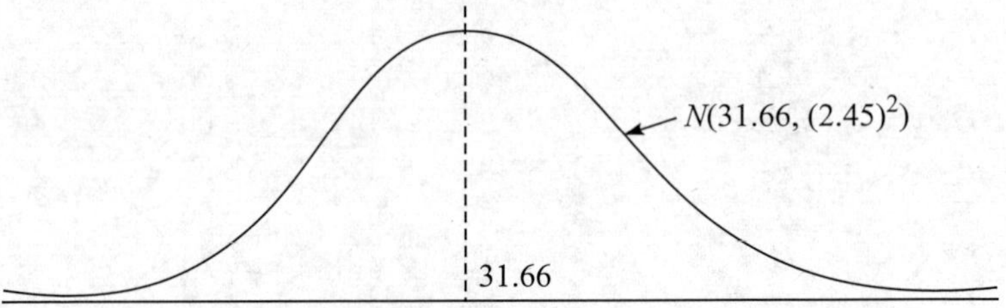

Fig. 6.14 Normal distribution of project duration.

6.8 AN EVALUATION OF PERT

It may be indicated that the standard PERT assumptions tend to make the estimates of completion time optimistic. The errors are primarily due to

- Errors at the activity level
  The PERT assumptions assume a beta distribution for individual activities. The actual distribution may be different or unknown in which case the assumption of the beta distribution would not lead to correct results. One way out of this difficulty is to use sampling for activity times and use the framework of simulation to estimate the project distribution and its parameters.
- Errors of aggregation
  These errors in the estimation of project parameters depend on the network shape, the number of merge events in the network and the number of parallel paths from the source to the sink. Moreover, the correlation between the various paths would also affect the magnitude of errors.

For instance, if a project has a number of independent parallel paths containing a number of activities, then by the Central Limit Theorem each path would be normally distributed with its own mean and variance. If the path with the largest expected length is much greater than the length of other paths, the project duration would be determined primarily by this path, as is assumed in PERT. But if as shown in Fig. 6.15 there are a number of paths which are arranged in the decreasing expected lengths, the probability of achieving the project in some target duration T is p_1* p_2* ... * p_k, which is obviously less than p_1, the probability stipulated under PERT. The following example illustrates this discrepancy between the PERT and the actual probabilities for completing a project with a predefined target date.

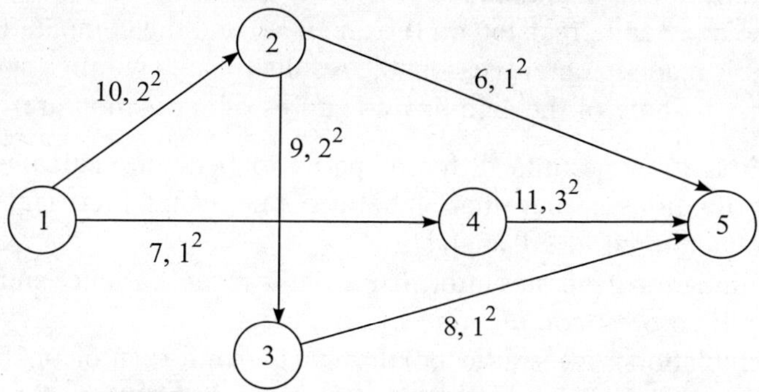

Fig. 6.15 Network with means and variances of jobs.

EXAMPLE 6.2 The error arises in PERT aggregation due to the fact that in PERT the max (expected value of all paths) is computed for the critical path, whereas when the durations are random variables, the expected (max length of all paths) ought to be taken. The latter is generally greater than the former and this is the reason that the PERT estimates are optimistic. For instance in Fig. 6.16, the PERT expected length is 27, whereas the actual expected length would be smaller.

Simulation offers an alternative to compute the actual probability and network parameters. This is explored in the next section.

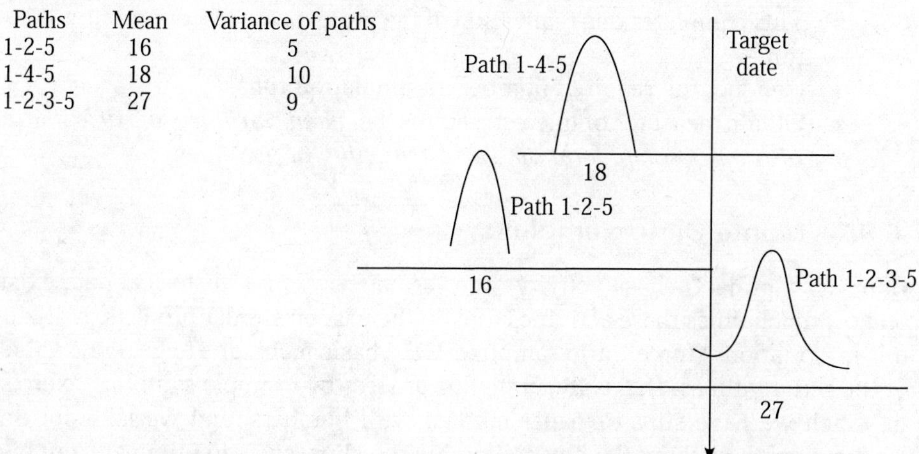

Fig. 6.16 Errors due to ignoring multiple paths in a project.

6.9 PROJECT SIMULATION

Since no simplifying assumptions are made as in PERT, simulation is a more accurate means of estimating the project parameters under general conditions. The project is simulated a number of times (each such simulation being called a network realization) and a summary of the performance characteristics is compiled at the end. Thus, obviously the accuracy and reliability of results depend on the number of simulation runs. As is generally the case, a compromise between accuracy and precision on the one hand and the computational burden on the other is made to obtain reasonable results (results within a specified level of confidence). Some of the significant features of simulation are

- Simulation permits different paths to become critical on different realizations rather than labelling one official critical path as in conventional PERT analysis.
- Simulation generates information of the mean, variance and distribution of the project completion times.
- Simulation is a versatile tool that can give information on the likelihood of any job becoming critical, probability distribution of node slacks or activity floats.

6.9.1 Basic Simulation Approach

The basic simulation approach consists of the following six steps:

- Collect data about the probability distribution of each activity in the project.
- Use Monte Carlo sampling technique to generate the duration of each activity.
- When all activity times are known, basic scheduling consisting of a forward and backward pass is conducted on the network.
- This completes one realization of the project network or one simulation run.
- Conduct the required number of simulation runs.
- Obtain measures of interest, such as the *mean, variance and distribution of project completion time and criticality of activities.*

6.9.2 Monte Carlo Sampling

Consider a project whose activity times are uncertain but historical data exists on how much times these activities took in the past on similar projects. Utilizing this information, Monte Carlo sampling is the basic technique to generate values of the activity times. Let us illustrate this process by a simple sampling exercise in which we have slips of paper marked with numbers, and we take out one randomly after shaking the box containing the slips, so as to eliminate any bias in the selection process. What is important in this process is how the slips have been numbered, and that the numbering scheme conforms to the actual history of the occurrence of these numbers. Suppose there are three activities a, b and c and each has a discrete probability distribution as given below.

Activity a can have a duration of 4, 5 or 6 days with respective probabilities of 0.3, 0.5 and 0.2. Similarly, **activity b** can take 7 or 9 days with probabilities 0.7 and 0.3, respectively. And **activity c** can take 2, 4 or 6 days with probabilities of 0.2, 0.6 and 0.2, respectively. To capture this information, we construct three decision rules, one for each activity, which specify how we shall generate 100 two-digit random number slips (numbered from 00 to 99) which may be utilized for the sampling process to generate the activity times in each of these cases.

DECISION RULE for Activity (a)
100 slips of paper marked 00 – 99

		Activity a	
Slips marked	00 – 29	30 – 79	80 – 99
Duration	4	5	6

DECISION RULE for Activity (b)
100 slips of paper marked 00 – 99

	Activity b	
Slips marked	00 – 69	70 – 99
Duration	7	9

DECISION RULE for Activity (c)
100 slips of paper marked 00 – 99

		Activity c	
Slips marked	00 – 19	20 – 79	80 – 99
Duration	2	4	6

If we now have a box containing these 100 random slips marked 00–99 and we randomly shake the box and pick up one slip, the number on the slip could be utilized to give the duration of the activity as per its decision rule. For instance, if the chosen slip is 69, its interpretation by the above decision rules would represent a duration of 5 for activity a, 7 for activity b and 4 for activity c.

This procedure for utilizing a uniformly distributed random number to generate any discrete distribution is called Monte Carlo sampling and forms the basis of generating the activity times for any distribution. Alternatively if we plot the Cumulative Density Function of the distribution [which is a monotonically non-decreasing function in steps for a discrete distribution, as shown in Fig. 6.17(a), or a continuous function for an arbitrary continuous distribution as shown in Fig. 6.17(b)], any random number r corresponds to a sampled value of the distribution.

6.9.3 Random Numbers

There are various methods of generating uniformly distributed random numbers, which serve as the basic input to generate any probability distribution as indicated

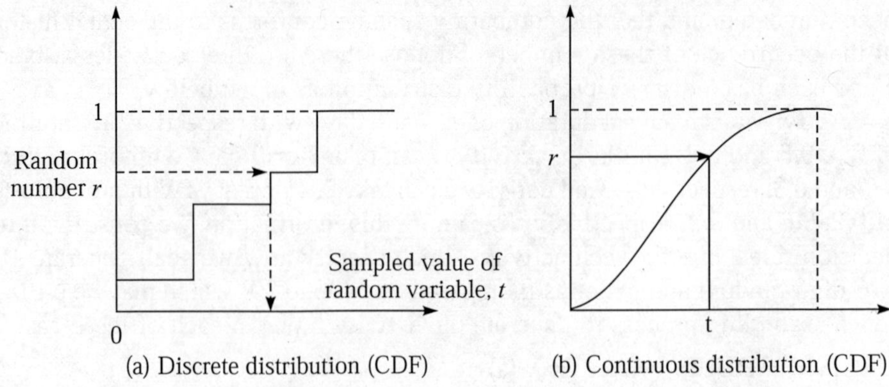

Fig. 6.17 Monte Carlo sampling for any arbitrary distribution.

above. The following are some of the commonly used means of generating random digits (any one or two or three or more digit random numbers may be generated depending on the accuracy required):

- A suitably marked roulette wheel which spins and stops at a given position where the appearing number is read off.
- Slips of paper bearing numbers (00–99) in a box which are shaken randomly before a slip is taken out. The number is noted and the slip is replaced in the box.
- Random number tables which are conveniently available in any statistics text.
- Pseudo random numbers generated on a computer.

Generally, the methods utilizing the roulette wheel or generating numbered slips of paper are cumbersome in practice and either of the other two methods is preferred.

6.9.4 Sample Project

Consider a sample project of installing a new machine at a given site, which consists of five jobs *A*, *B*, *C*, *D* and *E* with predecessors and estimates of time as per the following discrete probability distribution:

Job	*Description*	*Predecessors*	*Possible time durations (discrete probabilities)*
A	Order m/c	—	4, 5, 6 (0.3, 0.5, 0.2)
B	Prepare site	—	4
C	Receive m/c	*A*	2, 4, 6 (0.2, 0.6, 0.2)
D	Electrical connections	*B, C*	2
E	Install m/c	*D*	7, 9 (0.7, 0.3)

The project network for this sample project is shown in Fig. 6.18.

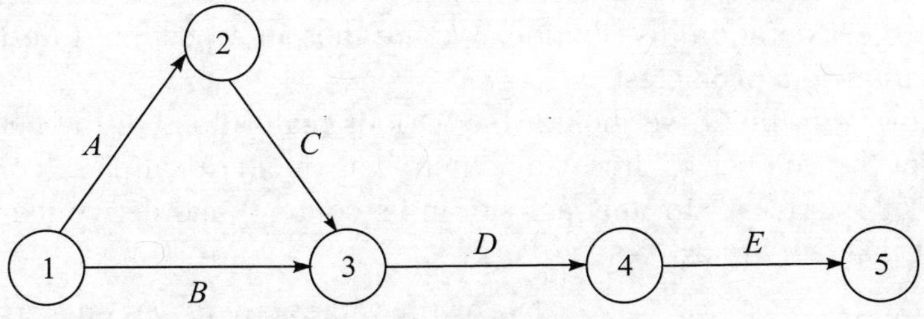

Fig. 6.18 Project network.

Random Number Table

03 68 93 30 90 43 46 59 67 89 56 68 83 …

We will use these random numbers to generate the times for the project activities.

(1st Realization)

Activity	*A*	*B*	*C*	*D*	*E*
Random No.	03	68	93	30	90
Duration	4	4	6	2	9

(Using the probability distribution data)

Project Network

Continuing in this manner the durations of activities can be computed for subsequent realizations.

(2nd Realization)

Activity	*A*	*B*	*C*	*D*	*E*
Random No.	43	46	59	67	89
Duration	5	4	4	2	9

This process would have to be repeated a number of times to obtain correct estimates of the project distribution, the mean, the variance and the criticality indices of various activities. The number of simulation runs required to estimate various project parameters with predefined levels of precision and confidence is explored in Section 6.10.

Compiling Simulation Results

S. No.	*A*	*B*	*C*	*D*	*E*	Critical path	
1	4*	4	6*	2*	9*	21	(* denotes the critical activity)
2	5*	4	4*	2*	9*	20	
…							

Suppose the table as computed above has *N* realizations. Then the *N* values of the critical path generated in the right most column are the sampled values of the project duration and can give a complete idea about the distribution of the project completion time, T. The mean of this column $\overline{T}$ is an estimate of the project mean and the variance of these values is an estimate of the variance of the project duration distribution. We are thus in a position to estimate the major parameters of interest.

Apart from this if we look at the various realizations of the network, we can count the number of times an activity was on a critical path (counting the number of astericks * for that activity in its column) and derive the criticality index of that activity as

$$\text{Criticality index of an activity} = \frac{\text{No. of times the activity was on a critical path}}{\text{No. of simulation runs}}$$

This is a concept that was totally absent in conventional PERT because there only one path was declared as critical and thus an activity was either critical or not. But using the results of simulation, we can get the estimates of the probability that an activity will be on a critical path. This is because simulation permits different paths to become critical on different realizations and captures greater realism in the estimation of various parameters.

Simulation vs PERT

Owing to the assumptions made in standard PERT analysis, both on account of the individual activity distributions (beta) and the manner of aggregation using the Central Limit Theorem and ignoring the non-critical paths, the estimates of mean project duration tend to be optimistic in PERT. The extent of error depends on the network structure and the data. Simulation can be used to compare the PERT results and give an estimate of how much error is introduced by the PERT assumptions. Analytical estimation of the project duration distribution given the activity duration distributions can be attempted, as shown by Elmaghraby in his book on *Activity Networks.* The procedure, however, tends to become complicated for real life networks. Simulation is a more practical tool which can be utilized under varying conditions and assumptions, though a trade-off between computational effort and accuracy has to be maintained.

6.10 ISSUES IN PROJECT SIMULATION

The overall process of simulating a project network is shown in Fig. 6.19.

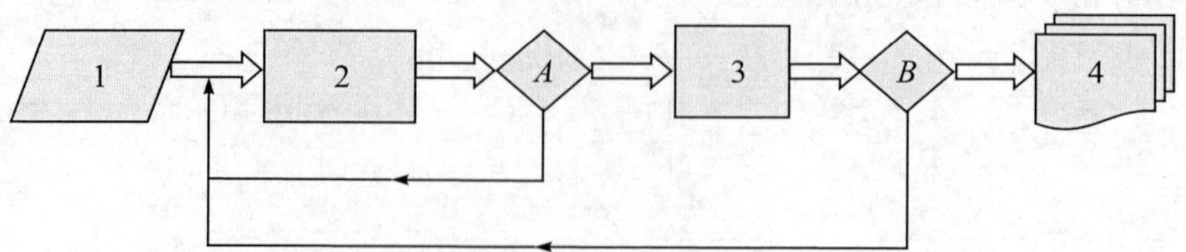

Fig. 6.19 Flow chart for project simulation.

The major sub-modules including the various decision points in the process involve

1. Input network data
2. Monte Carlo sampling for each activity

A Check whether all activities in the network have been considered

3. Basic scheduling for each network realization

B Check whether the requisite number of network realizations has been completed

4. Generation of final reports

The inputs include

- Project network
- Activity distributions
- What is to be estimated?
  - Project mean duration
  - Variance of project duration
  - PDF of project duration
  - Criticality of activities
  - PDF of activity floats
- With what confidence and precision?

Monte Carlo Sampler

Random number generator includes any of the following:

- Paper slips
- Roulette wheel
- Random no. table
- Pseudo random nos. (generated on a computer)

Activity sampled duration for each activity is obtained by utilizing its distribution as shown in Fig. 6.17.

Basic Scheduler

This performs the following computations:

- Forward pass
- Backward pass
- Critical path duration
- Activity floats
- Event slacks

Generating Final Reports

Project duration distribution
Sampled values of project mean T and variance s^2
Population values of project mean μ and variance σ^2

6.10.1 Number of Simulation Runs

This is determined by the

- Precision
- Confidence
- Statistic of interest
  (mean, variance, criticality)

6.10.2 Estimation of Project Variance

Our objective is to estimate the sampled variance s^2 to within 2 per cent of the population variance σ^2 in probability terms this can be written as

Pr $(0.98\ \sigma^2 \le s^2 \le 1.02\ \sigma^2) \ge 0.99$

Precision ± 2%

Confidence 99%

The statistic Ks^2/σ^2 has a Chi-squared Distribution with $(K - 1)$ degrees of freedom.

For large K, this Chi-squared distribution may be approximated as a normal distribution with mean $(K - 1)$ and variance $2(K - 1)$, that is $\approx N(K - 1), 2(K - 1)$.

or

$$\frac{\dfrac{Ks^2}{\sigma^2} - (K-1)}{\sqrt{2(K-1)}} = \text{has an } N(0, 1) \quad \text{(Fig. 6.20)}$$

$$\Pr(0.98\sigma^2 \le s^2 \le 1.02\ \sigma^2) \ge 0.99$$

$$\Pr\left(0.98K \le \frac{Ks^2}{\sigma^2} \le 1.02K\right) \ge 0.99$$

$$\Pr\left[\frac{1 - 0.02K}{\sqrt{2(K-1)}} \le \frac{\dfrac{Ks^2}{\sigma^2} - (K-1)}{\sqrt{2(K-1)}} \le \frac{1 + 0.02K}{\sqrt{2(K-1)}}\right] \ge 0.99$$

$$1 - 2\Phi\left(\frac{1 - 0.02}{\sqrt{2(K-1)}}\right) \ge 0.99$$

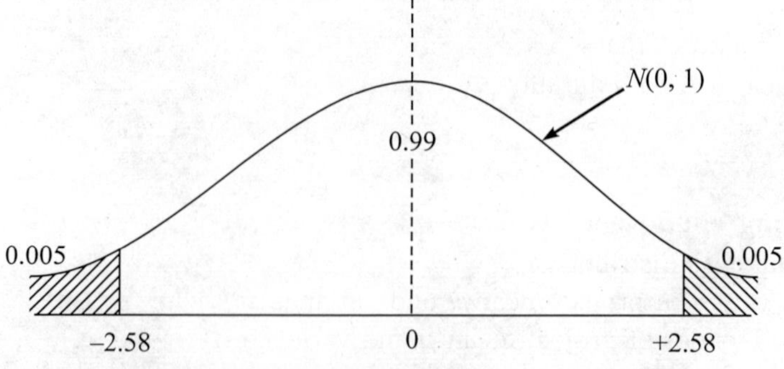

Fig. 6.20 The standard normal distribution.

$$\Phi\left(\frac{1-0.02K}{\sqrt{2(K-1)}}\right) \geq 0.005$$

$$\frac{1-0.02K}{\sqrt{2(K-1)}} \leq -2.58$$

$$K \geq 33{,}295$$

In general for precision P and confidence C the number of simulation runs K can be estimated by the following relation (Fig. 6.21):

$$\Phi\left(\frac{1-PK}{\sqrt{2(K-1)}}\right) \leq \frac{1-C}{2}$$

$$\frac{1-PK}{\sqrt{2(K-1)}} \leq -N_{\frac{1-C}{2}}$$

6.10.3 Estimation of Project Mean Duration

- The project distribution is assumed normally distributed.
- The observed sample mean (of K realizations) follows a t-distribution with $(K-1)$ degrees of freedom.
- For large K, this t-distribution converges to the normal.

It is desired to estimate μ to within 0.01 σ of its true value.

$$\Pr[(\mu - 0.01\sigma) \leq \bar{T} \leq (\mu + 0.01\sigma)] \geq 0.99$$

(Precision: $\mu - 0.01\sigma$ to $\mu + 0.01\sigma$; Confidence: 0.99)

$$\Pr\left[\frac{-0.01\sigma}{\sigma/\sqrt{K}} \leq \frac{\bar{T}-\mu}{\sigma/\sqrt{K}} \leq \frac{0.01\sigma}{\sigma/\sqrt{K}}\right] \geq 0.99$$

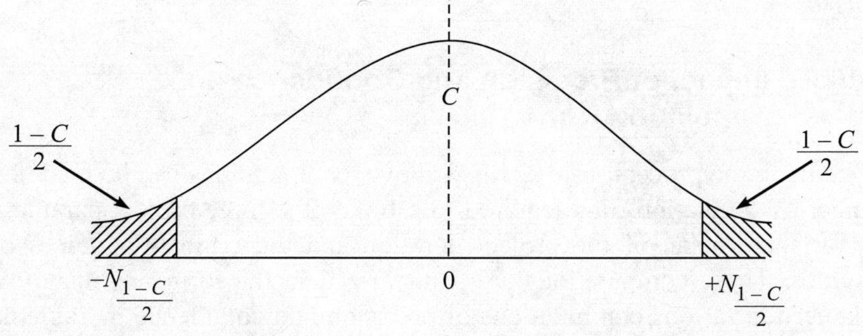

Fig. 6.21 A symmetric normal distribution with bounded area C.

$$\Phi(-0.01\sqrt{K}) \le 0.005$$
$$0.01\sqrt{K} \ge 2.58$$
$$K \ge 66{,}564 \text{ samples}$$

In general for precision P and confidence C the number of simulation runs K can be estimated by the following relation (Fig. 6.21):

$$\Phi(-P\sqrt{K}) \le \frac{1-C}{2}$$

$$P\sqrt{K} \ge N_{\frac{1-C}{2}}$$

$$K \ge \left(\frac{N_{\frac{1-C}{2}}}{P}\right)^2$$

6.10.4 Evaluation of Criticality Indices

In N replications of the project network in a simulation exercise, an activity may be either critical or not critical in each simulation run. If p is the probability of an activity being on a critical path, then the probability that in N realizations it is critical r times is given by a binomial distribution as ${}^{N}C_r\, p^r\, (1 - p)^{N-r}$, $r = 0, 1, 2, \ldots, N$.

For large N which is typically true in this case, this binomial distribution may be approximated by a normal distribution with mean $Np(1 - p)$ and variance $p(1 - p)/N$. If p is estimated from a sample of size N by r, then we know that

$$\Pr\{r - 0.01 \le p \le r = 0.01\} = 1 - 2\Phi[-0.01/\sqrt{p(1-p)/N}\,]$$

Here p is unknown and r is substituted in the right-hand side of the above equation in place of p, or we can be conservative and substitute the worst possible value $p = 0.5$. The same relationship can be used in the reverse direction to determine the required sample size N to guarantee with a specified probability 0.99, say, that a particular interval about the sample values r contains the true value p.

6.10.5 Impact of Precision and Confidence on Simulation Runs

By utilizing the procedures described above, computations can be made for the number of simulation runs required to estimate the three project parameters—the variance, mean of the project duration and the criticality indices of the activities. These computations are summarized in the form of a handy ready reckoner for various combinations of precision and confidence in Table 6.5.

Table 6.5 Number of simulation runs for varying levels of precision and confidence

↓*Precision/ Confidence*→	75%	90%	95%	99%	*Project parameter to be estimated*
10%	284	576	788	1351	Variance
	132	271	384	666	Mean
	33	68	96	166	Criticality index
5%	1097	2209	3114	5364	Variance
	529	1082	1537	2663	Mean
	132	271	384	666	Criticality index
2%	6709	13689	19293	33228	Variance
	3306	6765	9604	16641	Mean
	827	1691	2401	4160	Criticality index
1%	26639	54301	76978	133298	Variance
	13225	27060	38416	66564	Mean
	3306	6765	9604	16641	Criticality index

It is noticed from this table that increasing precision and confidence requirements both increase the computational effort demanded in terms of the number of simulation runs. However, it may be noticed that increase of precision tends to increase the number of simulation runs needed much more drastically as compared to increases in the levels of confidence. In practice, there is often a need to adopt procedures which tend to reduce the computational effort for a given level of precision and confidence. Some of these procedures are hinted at in the next section.

6.10.6 Means to Reduce Computational Effort

There are a number of variance reduction techniques which may be employed in practice to reduce the computational burden in the simulation. Details of these techniques are available elsewhere and the interested reader may refer to Elmaghraby (1977) for details. Some of the generally adopted procedures are listed below:

- Antithetic variates
- Control variates
- Conditional sampling
- Stratified sampling
- Other approaches

6.11 SUMMARY AND CONCLUSIONS

In this chapter, the basic scheduling of both A-O-A and A-O-N project networks has been investigated. All scheduling assumes that activities have a deterministic completion time. Starting with tree enumeration to discover all the paths in a project, event and activity oriented algorithms have been presented to discover the critical path and the total float in the network. The notion of all the four kinds of float, namely total, safety, free and independent, have been discussed with their physical interpretation.

A procedure for direct calculation of floats without drawing the A-O-A network for a given A-O-N network has also been given after the forward and backward pass has been conducted and the *ES*, *EF*, *LS* and *LF* for all the jobs are available.

Project scheduling with uncertain activity times, under a PERT framework, has been discussed with sample computations. The errors in PERT calculations and the alternative of project simulation with notions of the criticality indices of activities have been proposed.

- Project simulation emerges as a powerful tool to handle uncertain activity durations without restrictive assumptions.
- Basic methodology of simulation involving replicating the behaviour of the network by sampling activity times using Monte Carlo simulation has been discussed.
- Monte Carlo simulation approach to generate arbitrary discrete and continuous distributions has been explained and illustrated.
- A small machine installation project has been taken up to illustrate the basic approach of project simulation.
- Compilations at the end of simulation are used to obtain parameters like
  - Project expected duration
  - Variance of project duration
  - Criticality indices of activities
- Simulation results can be used to estimate the errors in the PERT analysis. It is generally seen that PERT gives optimistic results.
- A large number of simulation runs are needed to obtain reasonably reliable estimates. This number has been estimated based on the precision and confidence in the results being estimated.
- Statistical inference is used to determine the number of simulation runs to estimate the project parameters with a pre-specified precision and confidence.
- A ready reckoner for the number of simulation runs for estimating project variance, mean and criticality indices for varying degrees of precision and confidence has been presented.

PROBLEMS

1. For the data in Table 1 below,
   (a) Develop the A-O-A network with a single source and single sink.

(b) What is the number of nodes and arcs in your network? What is the maximum possible number of arcs for the given number of nodes in a legitimate project network?
(c) Enumerate all paths from source to sink by using tree enumeration.
(d) What is the number of paths from source to sink in the network with 1 link, 2 links, ..., *k* links?
(e) What are the upper bounds on the number of paths in (c) and (d) above?
(f) Using a forward pass on the network determine the critical path.
(g) If the critical path can be determined with a forward pass, why do we conduct a backward pass?
(h) If we were interested in the three ordered critical paths, devise a modified forward pass to determine these without path enumeration.
(i) Determine node slacks and all four activity floats.
(j) Determine the longest path through each non-critical node.
(k) Draw a Gantt chart showing the early and late start and finish times of all activities.

2. Repeat all the computations for Question 1 by drawing an A-O-N network, and comment on the differences.

Table 1 Data for problems 1 and 2

Job	*Predecessor*	*Duration*
A	—	6
B	—	4
C	*A*	3
D	*A, B*	5
E	*D*	2
F	*D, E*	8
G	*D, E, F*	5
H	*F, G*	4
I	*E, F*	2
J	*H, I*	6
K	*I, J*	3
L	*J, K*	9

3. Draw both the A-O-A and A-O-A networks for a project with the following job list and precedence relations:

Table 2

Activity	*Must follow*	*Duration (days)*	*Activity*	*Must follow*	*Duration (days)*
A	—	2	*H*	*J, B, C*	2
B	*M. F*	5	*I*	*A, C, E*	5
C	*K*	6	*J*	*M*	4
D	*I, L, G*	9	*K*	—	1
E	—	1	*L*	*M, E*	2
F	*A, C, E*	3	*M*	*K*	3
G	*A*	10			

4. Using the A-O-A network and event oriented calculations determine the *ES, EF, LS, LF* and all the four activity floats and node slacks for the network of Question 1. Which is the critical path(s)?
5. Using the A-O-N network for Question 3 determine the *ES, EF, LS, LF* and floats for all activities, without referring to the A-O-A formulation.
6. A beta distribution is assumed for activity times in PERT. For this distribution,
   (a) Estimate the value of the constant *K* in terms of the shape and location parameters.
   (b) Derive the mean and variance of this distribution.
   (c) For what values of the shape parameters do you get the formulas for the mean and variance that are typically assumed in PERT?
7. For the following probability distributions calculate the mean and variance:
   (a) Uniform distribution with minimum and maximum times of a and b.
   (b) Triangular distribution with minimum, modal and maximum values of a, m and b.
   (c) An exponential distribution with mean m.
   (d) A discrete distribution with times $t_1, t_2, \ldots, t_n$ and corresponding probabilities $p_1, p_2, \ldots, p_n$.
8. Consider the project with data given in Table 3. Assume that the activity times are random variables with the given durations as the mean durations. Assume additionally that the standard deviation of the durations of the activities are 1 for all activities except G and I for which the standard deviations are 2 each.
   (a) Develop the A-O-A network.
   (b) Under standard PERT assumptions determine the critical path.
   (c) Compute probabilities that the project is completed within 50%, 75%, 90%, 110%, 125% and 150% of the critical path duration.
   (d) For the non-critical node in the project, determine the probability of a positive slack.

Table 3

Job	*Predecessors*	*Duration*
A	—	4
B	—	6
C	*A*	6
D	*A*	8
E	*A*	8
F	*B, C*	6
G	*D, F*	15
H	*D, F*	4
I	*E, H*	7

9. Perform the computations of Question 3 under the following situations:
   (a) Each activity has a beta distribution with *a, m, b* values of 4, 8, 12.
   (b) Each activity has a uniform distribution with *a, b* values of 4, 12.
   (c) Each activity has a triangular distribution with *a, m, b* values of 4, 8, 12.
   (d) Each activity has an exponential distribution with mean of 8.
   (e) Each activity has a normal distribution with mean 8 and variance 1.44.
   (f) Each activity has a discrete distribution 6, 7, 8, 9, 10 with equal probabilities.
10. The jobs of the following network have the indicated time estimates

Table 4

Job	*Optimistic*	*Most likely*	*Pessimistic*
(1, 2)	3	6	15
(1, 6)	2	5	14
(2, 3)	6	12	30
(2, 4)	2	5	8
(3, 5)	5	11	17
(4, 5)	3	6	15
(6, 7)	3	9	27
(5, 8)	1	4	7
(7, 8)	4	19	28

   (a) Draw the project network.
   (b) Calculate the length and variance of the critical path.
   (c) What is the probability that the jobs on the critical path will be completed by the due date of 41 days?
   (d) What is the probability that the jobs on the next critical path will be completed by the due date?
   (e) What is your estimate that the entire project will be completed by the due date?

(f) Under standard PERT assumptions, what is the probability of completing the project
- before 30 days?
- between 15 and 35 days?
- after 38 days?

11. Find the number of simulation runs for precision levels of 1%, 2%, 5%, 10% and 20% with confidence levels of 50%, 75%, 90%, 95% and 99% to estimate the project
* – variance
O – mean
□ – criticality indices of activities. Present your results in the form of Table 5.

Table 5

Increasing confidence

	50%	75%	90%	95%	99%
20%					
10%					
5%					
2%					
1%					

12. Simulate the following project. Assume the following distribution data for activities:

Table 6

(1 – 2)	4, 5, 6 discrete with equal probability
(1 – 3)	2, 8, 10 triangular distribution
(1 – 4)	4, 8 uniform distribution
(2 – 3)	Exponential distribution with mean 8
(2 – 6)	Uniform distribution between 10 and 20
(3 – 5)	4, 6, 10 with probabilities 0.3, 0.4, 0.3
(4 – 5)	Normal distribution with mean 20 and variance 4
(4 – 6)	4, 8, 12 triangular distribution
(5 – 6)	Uniform distribution between 12 and 20

Simulate the project for 10 simulation runs and compute
- mean, variance of project duration
- criticality indices for all activities
- mean slack of all events

(use two-digit random numbers)

13. Develop a computer package for simulation of a network with arbitrary distributions for the activities to estimate the distribution of the project duration, mean and variance of the duration, the criticality indices of the activities, the mean floats of the activities and the average event slacks.

CHAPTER

7

Resource Considerations in Project Management

7.1 INTRODUCTION

For the accomplishment of various activities in a project, resources such as men, machines, materials, money, information and energy in its various forms are needed. Explicit planning for requirements of these resources, their procurement and effective usage at the time and site of use is extremely important for the project to be executed properly to required specifications, without unnecessary delays and cost overruns. For purposes of planning, resources can be classified into two broad categories:

(i) Consumable or non-renewable resources
(ii) Renewable resources

Consumable resources are the ones like money, fuel, energy, etc. that once consumed are not available for future consumption and have to be replenished externally. Renewable resources, on the other hand, are the ones that can be used again and again on a daily continuing basis without much degradation in performance. Manpower, equipment, power and energy flow may be treated as renewable under this classification. The total usage of resources (both renewable and non-renewable) varies over the project duration because different activities are being carried out at different stages in the project and each activity being unique has its own requirements of resources and time. Thus, depending on the set of activities in progress from time to time, the aggregate resource usage keeps on fluctuating.

The first fundamental problem for a manager is to determine how much resource of each kind is being consumed or needed at different stages of the project. This is *resource aggregation* which gives the *resource usage profile* (Fig. 7.1). The basic information needed for generating the resource usage

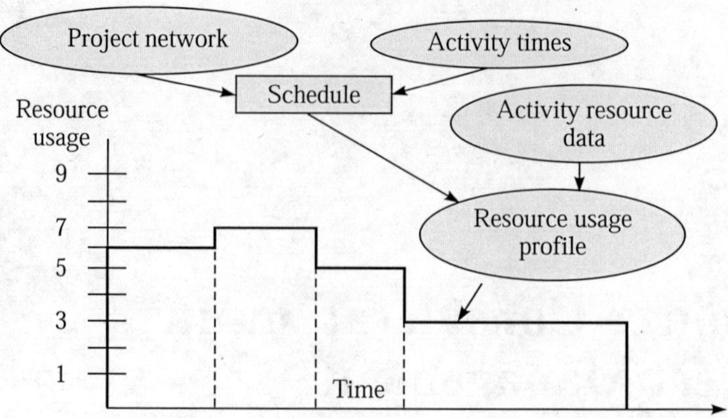

Fig. 7.1 Aggregate resource usage.

profile is the schedule of individual activities and their resource requirements. In treatment of *consumable or non-renewable resources*, like money, one is generally concerned with the resource consumption up to a certain point in time. Mathematically, this may be likened to $\int R(t)\,dt$ of the resource usage profile (Fig. 7.2). This may be useful for establishing targets of consumption as the project proceeds through its various milestones and as a benchmark for project monitoring and control during the stage of project execution (see Chapter 8 for details of these techniques).

In planning of renewable resources like manpower, apart from the resource usage profile indicating the requirements of each resource over time, the concern is with the resource usage at any point in time. For instance, we may want to minimize the peak resource usage or level the resource usage profile or ensure that the peak does not exceed the available resources at any point in time.

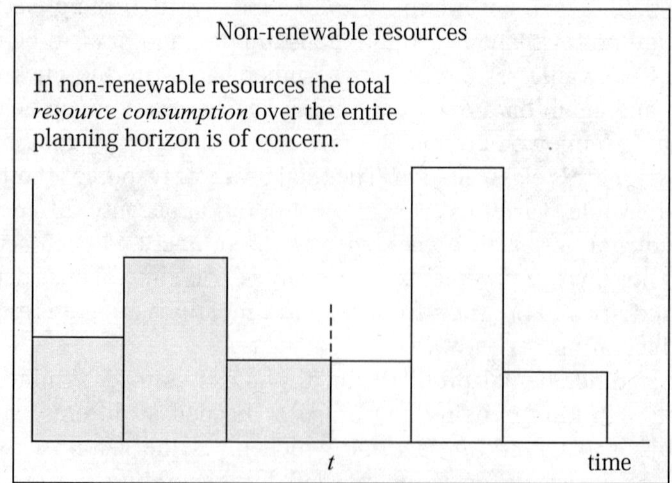

Fig. 7.2 Cumulative resource usage.

Thus, *resource levelling* (Fig. 7.3) and *limited resource allocation* (Fig. 7.4) are the two major problems of interest in planning for renewable resources. This chapter is devoted to the treatment of

(i) Resource aggregation for both consumable and non-consumable resources
(ii) Time–cost trade-offs for consumable resources
(iii) Resource levelling for both renewable and non-renewable resources
(iv) Limited resource allocation for renewable resources

Both heuristic and optimal procedures are discussed with their advantages and disadvantages.

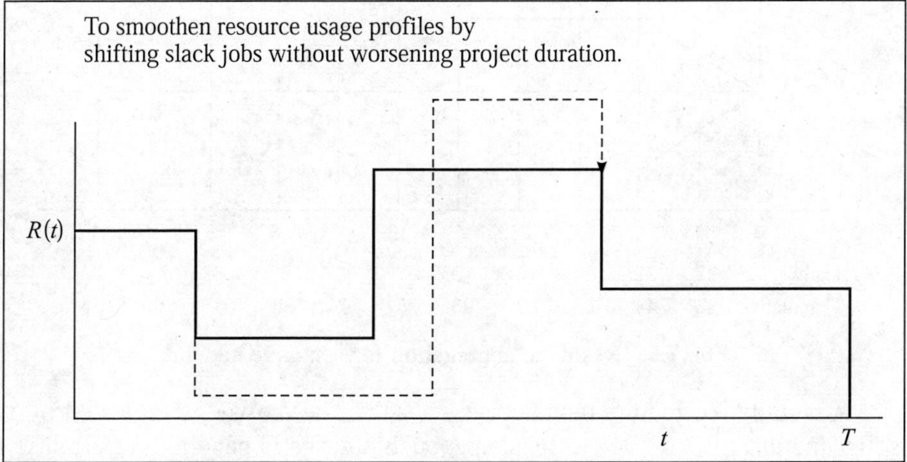

Fig. 7.3 Objectives in resource leveling.

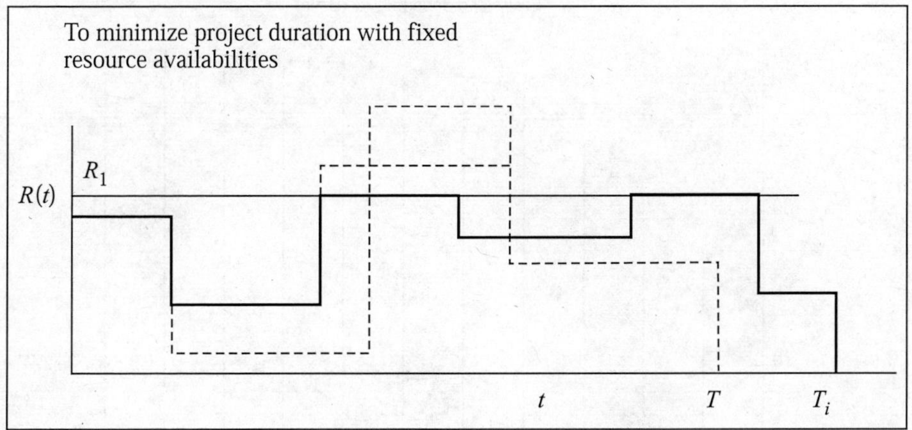

Fig. 7.4 Limited resource allocation.

7.2 RESOURCE AGGREGATION (DEVELOPMENT OF DAILY OR CUMULATIVE RESOURCE USAGE)

Once a project schedule in the form of a Gantt chart is available for the project activities by the basic scheduling algorithms discussed in the previous chapter, it is simple to superimpose the resource requirements of each activity on a time scaled network and derive the resource usage profile by aggregation as shown in Fig. 7.5 for a sample project. Thus, one can obtain the period by period resource requirement of money or manpower or any other resource in this manner.

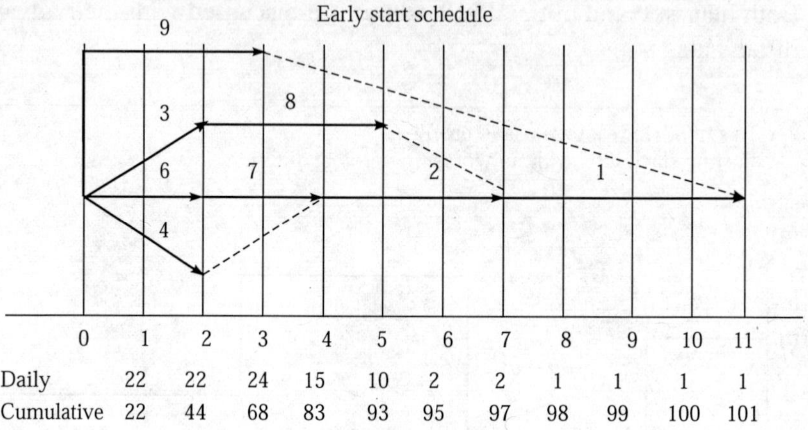

Fig. 7.5 Resource aggregation for a sample network.

A cumulative requirements curve may then be drawn, as indicated by the solid line in Fig. 7.6. Due to its shape, such a curve is generally referred to as an **S curve** and is taken as a basis for budgeting and monitoring expenses and overruns in schedule and cost.

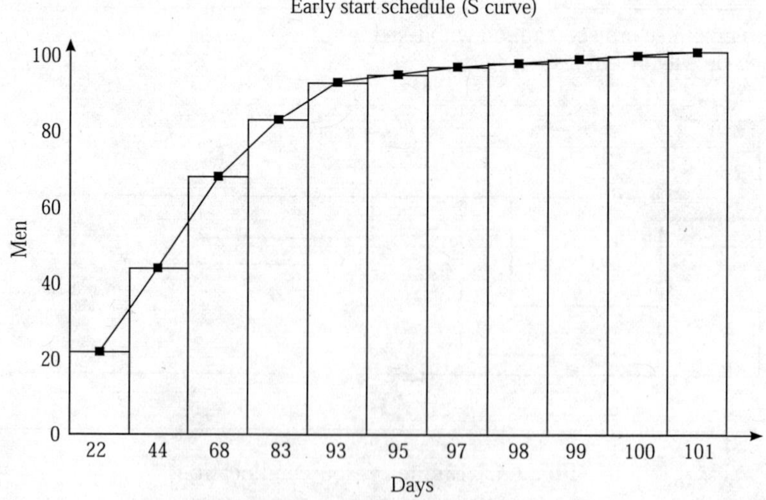

Fig. 7.6 S curve or Cumulative resource curve.

EXAMPLE 7.1 Suppose a project consists of the network shown in Fig. 7.7 with the following data on costs and daily manpower requirements:

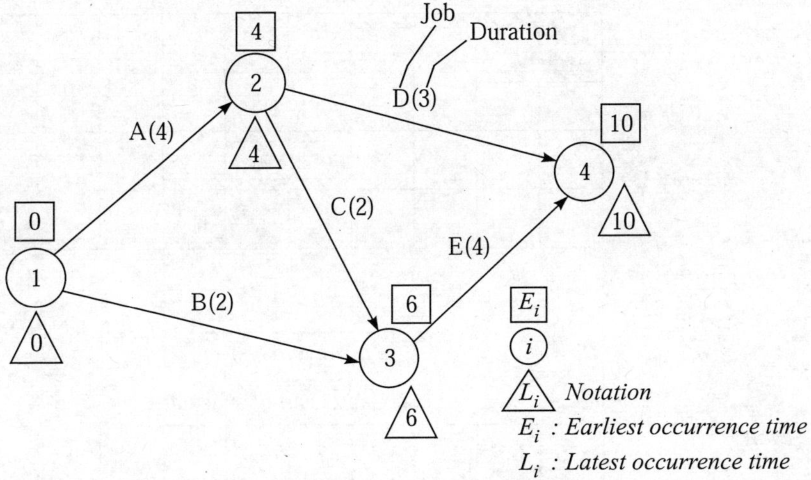

Fig. 7.7 Sample network.

Activity	*From to*	*Total cost* (Rs.)	*Duration* (days)	*Daily cost* (Rs./day)	*Daily manpower needed*
A	1–2	6000	4	1500	2
B	1–3	10,000	2	5000	3
C	2–3	8000	2	4000	1
D	2–4	12,000	3	4000	4
E	3–4	4000	4	1000	4

The project schedule as a Gantt chart is shown in Fig. 7.8(a) wherein the critical path is ACE and the project duration is 10 days. By summing up the daily costs we obtain the expenditure profile shown in Fig. 7.8(b). Similarly, by summing the daily manpower requirements we obtain the manpower profile shown in Fig. 7.8(c). This demonstrates how the resource usage profiles can be obtained for any project, once the schedule is obtained. It is clear that by changing the schedule, the profiles would also consequently change. In project monitoring and control we utilize the cumulative expenditure profile also shown in Fig. 7.8(b) to establish benchmarks for expenditure during the various stages of the project and also to measure the time and cost overruns at any stage. A detailed discussion of these techniques is included in the next chapter on project implementation.

For renewable resources, like manpower, the resource usage profile (Fig. 7.1) is the starting basis for either resource levelling or limited resource allocation. Unevenness in the manpower profile indicates the fluctuations in the requirements of manpower, which may be met by hiring and firing of personnel. This incurs various types of costs and penalties for hiring, training, layoff,

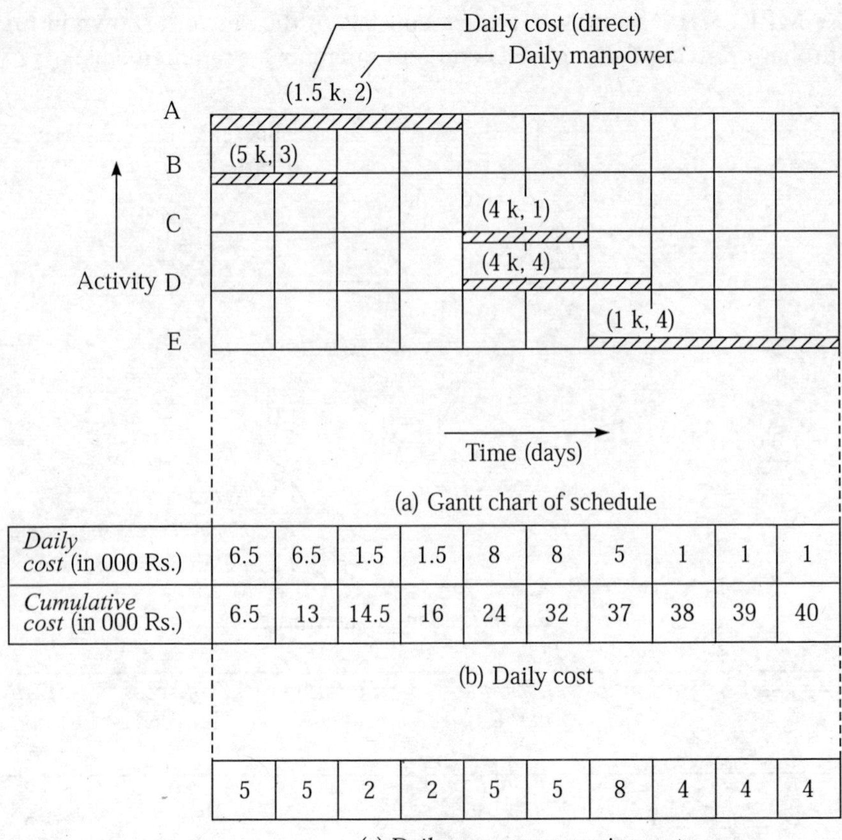

Daily cost (in 000 Rs.)	6.5	6.5	1.5	1.5	8	8	5	1	1	1
Cumulative cost (in 000 Rs.)	6.5	13	14.5	16	24	32	37	38	39	40

(b) Daily cost

5	5	2	2	5	5	8	4	4	4

(c) Daily manpower requirements

Fig. 7.8 Resource aggregation for project network of Fig. 7.7.

goodwill loss, and the loss of time and effort in procurement and disposing of excess manpower. Often, the resources may be specialized and not available readily. In case this free availability of resources is not there and the resources are limited in quantity, resort to limited resource allocation may have to be made where the objective is to ensure that the maximum resource peak at any stage does not exceed the availability. Obviously the critical path is the lower bound on the project duration and it is quite likely that the scarcity of resources may warrant postponement of some critical activities to reduce the resource peak(s) to within available limits. The primary objective in such a problem is to minimize the project duration by staying within resource limits. It may be noted that both resource levelling and limited resource allocation are optimization problems that have received considerable attention in the research literature (see, for instance, References for a state-of-the-art survey). Mathematically, these are difficult problems owing to the absence of a polynomially bounded (NP hard or complete problems) algorithm for these problems. There are, however, a number of heuristic solution procedures that may be employed and some of them are detailed in the discussion below.

In Section 7.3, time–cost trade-offs for utilizing the flexibility in activity durations with consumable resources are discussed. Section 7.4 examines the problem of resource levelling for renewable resources whilst Section 7.5 is devoted to a study of the limited resource allocation problem with renewable resources in projects.

7.3 TIME–COST TRADE-OFFS FOR CONSUMABLE RESOURCES

Consumable resources are best handled by minimizing the total project costs, avoiding wastages and utilizing activity flexibilities by resource application through *time–cost trade-offs.* Since money is generally a surrogate measure of the various consumable resources and expenses incurred in a project, the costs are divided into *direct activity costs* and *project indirect costs.* The direct activity cost is that which is actually incurred on the performance of individual activities, including materials, labour and other activity- specific expenditure that governs its duration. The project indirect costs include the cost of overheads, managerial expenses and infrastructure which is not accountable directly to individual jobs, but is necessary during the duration of the project as a whole. The site rental, the salaries of managers and fixed charges irrespective of the work on the individual jobs would typically account for this. The project indirect costs would typically be increasing with project duration as shown in Fig. 7.9. The behaviour of the direct costs is dependent on the individual activities and their durations and captures the flexibility that exists in individual activity durations with the variations in resource application (Fig. 7.10). In this regard, it is typical to talk of a normal duration, the generally achievable duration with the minimum direct cost. However, with increased effort and expenditure of additional resources, the duration of the activity may be reduced to a level, referred generally as the crash duration of the activity. It may be indicated here that any duration above the normal duration is wasteful in time, since by spending more than necessary resources no reduction in the duration of the activity is obtained. Similarly, the spending of more money than the crash does not lead to any further benefits in terms of a reduced duration, because the technical limits or the technological

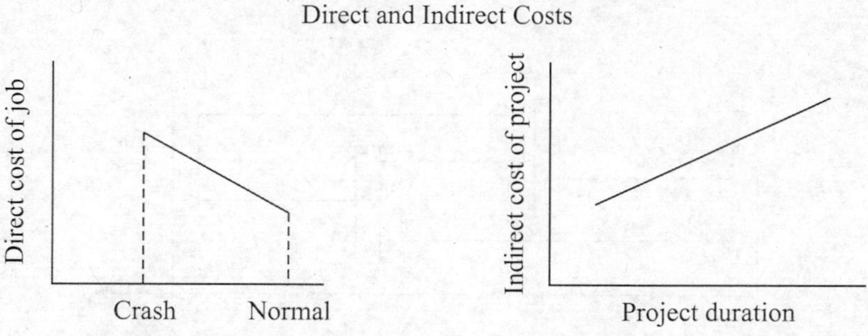

Fig. 7.9 Project indirect costs.

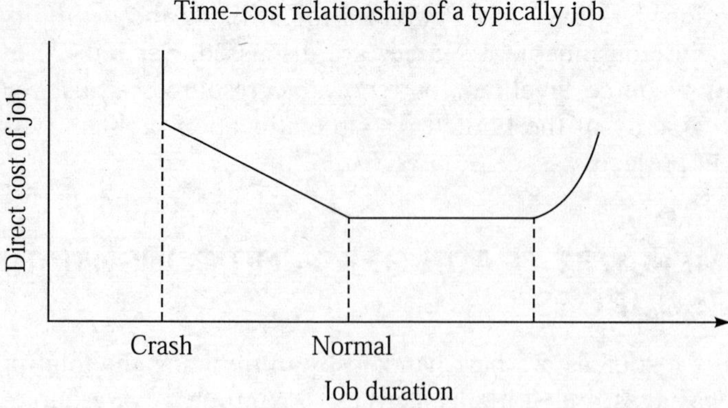

Fig. 7.10 Activity direct costs.

constraints become binding. Thus, the operational range of activity durations lies between the normal (maximum duration and minimum possible cost) and the crash (minimum duration and maximum useful expenditure) limits. This compression in activity durations by the mode of extra resource allocation is termed as *crashing the activity*. The activity thus behaves like a spring with a free length equal to its normal duration that can be compressed to its minimum, the crash duration by an application of a force. This spring analogy was in fact developed by Prager in 1967 to illustrate the notion of project crashing by treating the project as a collection of interconnected springs (Fig. 7.11), where each activity is likened to a spring with a sleeve, where the free length of the spring extends beyond the sleeve to its normal duration and the spring may be compressed to the limit of the sleeve, the crash duration. The system may be solved mechanically by establishing an analogy between the project direct cost and the potential energy of the system with each time–cost relation between

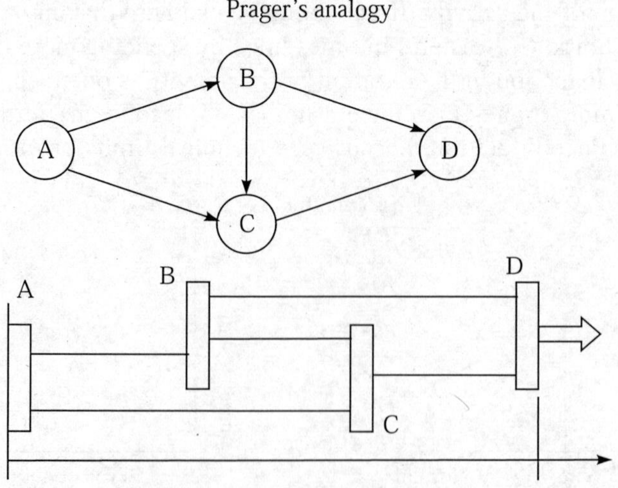

Fig. 7.11 Spring analogy.

activities being modelled as the force-displacement characteristic of the spring. Non-linearities in Activity Costs and Piecewise Linearization

In general, the activity time–cost relationships are assumed to be linear, which implies that the cost of crashing the activity per unit time (the cost slope) is a constant and it is equally costly or difficult as the activity is crashed from the normal to the crash duration [Fig. 7.12(a)]. This assumption may not hold in all cases and it may then be appropriate to model the activity time–cost relationship as one of the following:

(i) Convex
(ii) Concave
(iii) Arbitrary (neither concave nor convex)
(iv) Discontinuous

A convex trade-off [Fig. 7.12(b)] implies that initial crashing near the normal limit is easier and as the activity is crashed it becomes increasingly difficult or costly to further crash the activity. This may be true in situations where technological or human accommodation beyond a point becomes more difficult. A concave relationship [Fig. 7.12(c)], on the other hand, implies initial reluctance or difficulty (to a new idea or concept) and a progressive adoption and enthusiasm to encourage the change, once it is initiated. Whenever the reduction in duration involves distinct technologies or alternative modes of travel (e.g. by land on train or car, by sea or by air) the time–cost relation may be discontinuous segments [Fig. 7.12(d)]or distinct points [Fig. 7.12(e)].

General Crashing Problem for a project network in A-O-A made can be written by assuming that each arc (i, j) has a duration x_{ij} with t_i and t_j being the node occurrence times of nodes i and j respectively. A is the set of all arcs and C the total direct cost.

Minimize $$C = \Sigma c_{ij}\ (x_{ij}) \quad (1)$$

subject to the linear constraints

$$t_j - t_i - x_{ij} \geq 0,\ (ij) \in A \quad (2)$$
$$x_{ij} \geq l_{ij},\ (ij) \in A \quad (3)$$

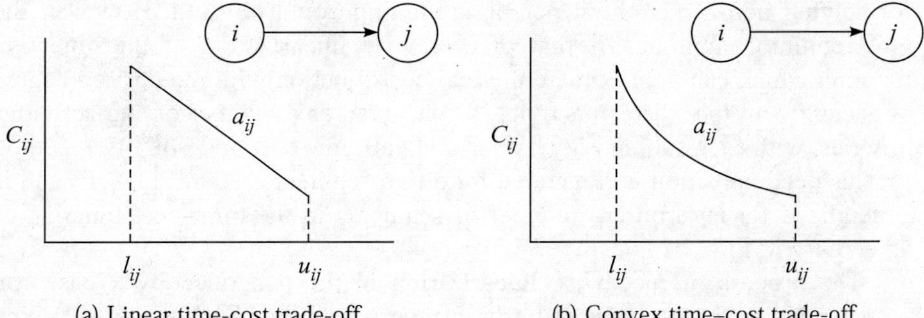

(a) Linear time-cost trade-off. (b) Convex time–cost trade-off.

Fig. 7.12 (*Contd.*)

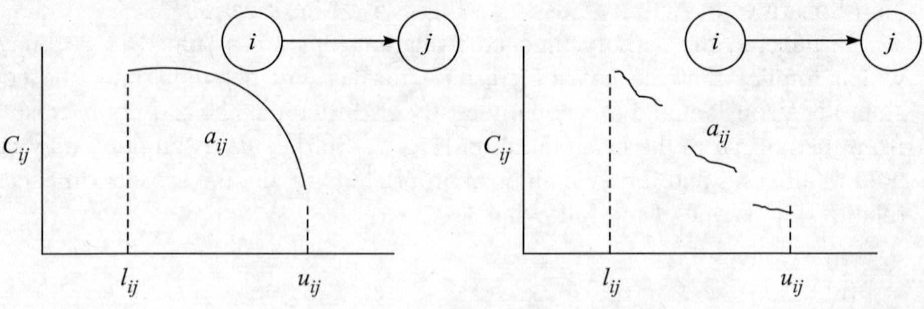

(c) Concave time–cost trade-off. (d) Discontinuous time–cost trade-off.

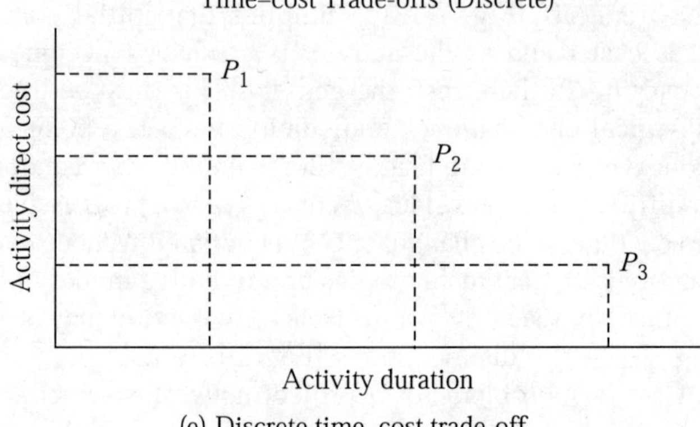

(e) Discrete time–cost trade-off.

Fig. 7.12 Different activity time-cost trade-offs.

$$x_{ij} \leq u_{ij},\ (ij) \in A \tag{4}$$

$$t_n - t_1 = T \tag{5}$$

In this formulation, all the constraints (2), (3) and (4) are linear and if the objective function is linear [as in Fig. 7.12(a)], LP-based methodologies may be employed for solution purposes. In case, however, the objective function is non-linear and belongs to the categories of Figs. 7.12(b), (c) or (d), procedures for solving non-linear or integer programming could be used. However, the most common approach is that of piecewise linearization of the objective function which can approximate the real cost function with the desired degree of accuracy. In this case an activity is conceived as a number of sub-activities in series, with each sub-activity having a linear time–cost trade-off. The method for this decomposition is illustrated for a two-segment case in Fig. 7.13 and is generalized for an arbitrary number of segments in the time–cost function of an activity in Fig. 7.14.

The process of piecewise linearization in the general convex case can be extended to the concave and arbitrary cost functions but for the following

Two-segment Case (Convex Costs)

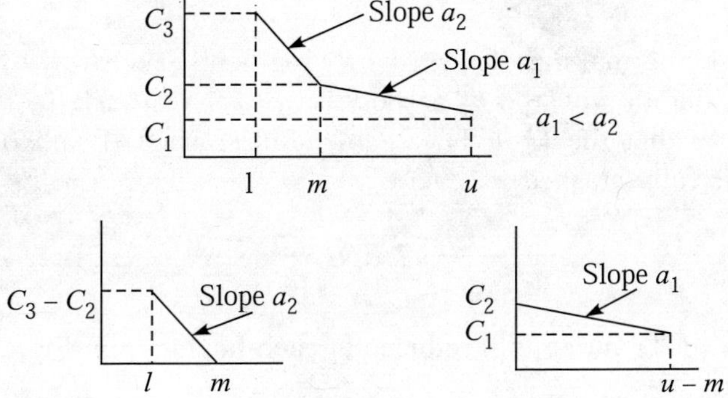

Fig. 7.13 Piecewise linearization: two-segment case.

Multi-segment Case (Convex Costs)

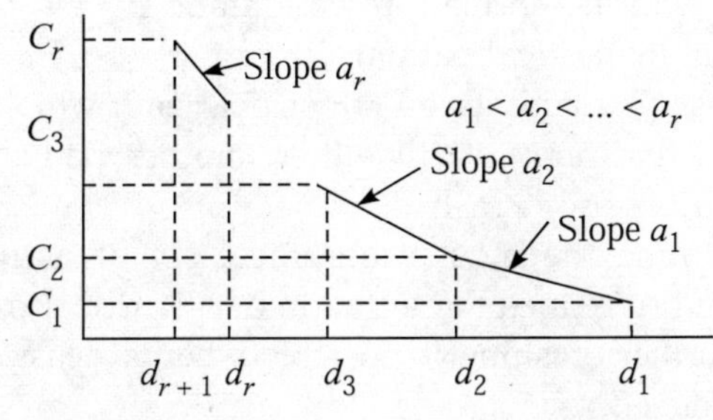

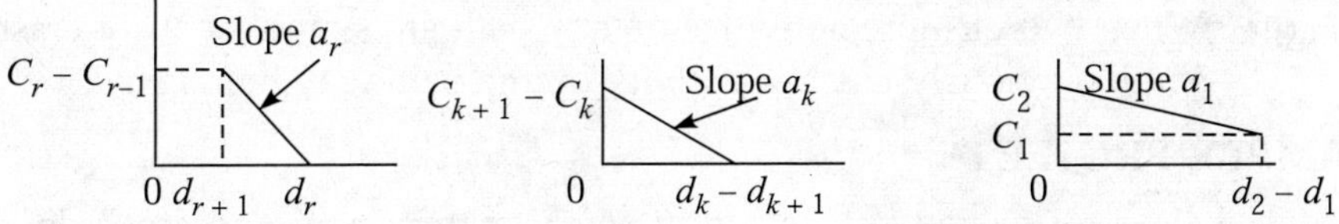

Fig. 7.14 Piecewise linearization—multi-segment case.

complication. Any solution procedure that picks up the segments for crashing in *the order of their cost slopes* would result in an *unnatural sequence* of crashing for concave and arbitrary costs. Thus, restrictions have to be imposed in the formulation through the appropriate use of integer variables so that the segments are crashed in their natural order from higher duration to lower duration.

Arbitrary costs

An activity with *r* segments may be treated as *r* activities in series (Fig. 7.15).

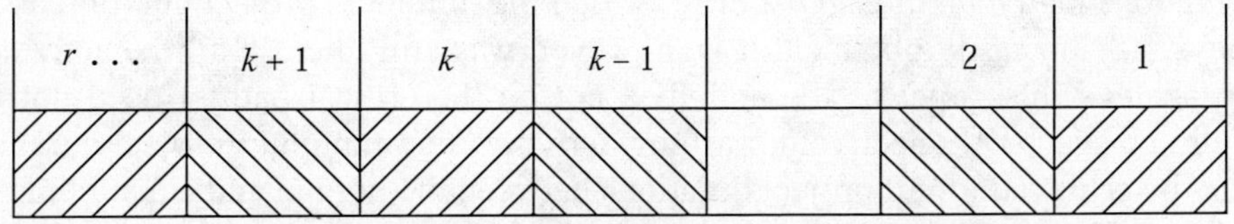

Fig. 7.15 Activity segments with arbitrary costs.

The total duration of activity $(i, j) = \sum_{k=1}^{r} d_k$

where d_k is the normal duration of the kth segment.

And the duration of the kth activity is x_k $(0 \le x_k \le dk)$.

To ensure that the $(k + 1)^{th}$ segment is crashed if and only if the kth requirment is fully crashed

$$\frac{x_k}{d_k - d_{k+1}} \le \delta_k \le \frac{x_{k+1}}{d_{k+1} - d_{k+2}}$$

when δ_k is a (0–1) variable introduced at each boundary in Fig. 7.15.

7.3.1 A Heuristic Solution Procedure for Linear Time–Cost Trade-offs

(a) Start with the normal project duration.
(b) Obtain the critical path(s).
(c) Choose that activity on the critical path which is cheapest to crash.
(d) Crash that activity till either another path becomes critical or the activity is fully crashed.
(e) Determine the most economical set of activities to be crashed or relaxed to reduce the duration of all critical paths.
(f) No further crashing is possible when at least one critical path cannot be reduced.
(g) When two or more activities on any path are simultaneously crashed, some previously crashed activity on the path may be relaxed.

SAMPLE PROJECT

Consider the project network in Fig. 7.16(a), with normal and crash data for activities summarized in the table below. For linear time–cost relationships, the cost slope for any activity = (Crash cost – Normal cost)/(Normal duration – Crash duration). These values are computed for each activity as given in the last column of Fig. 7.16(b).

We enumerate all the paths in the network and tabulate this information in Table 7.1. Assuming all activities to be at their normal durations, the total direct activity cost is the sum of the normal costs of the activities which is Rs. 1320. The project duration is determined by the longest path which is ADG, of length 16 indicated with an asterisk (*). By conducting a forward pass with all crash durations (at a total direct cost of Rs. 2370) the minimum project duration of 11 days may be easily obtained. It is, however, wasteful to crash all the activities to achieve this target as the activities not on the critical path(s) need not be fully crashed. By selectively crashing activities the minimum project duration can be achieved for all project durations between the normal and crash limits of 16 and 11 days, respectively. A plot of the minimum project direct cost for all

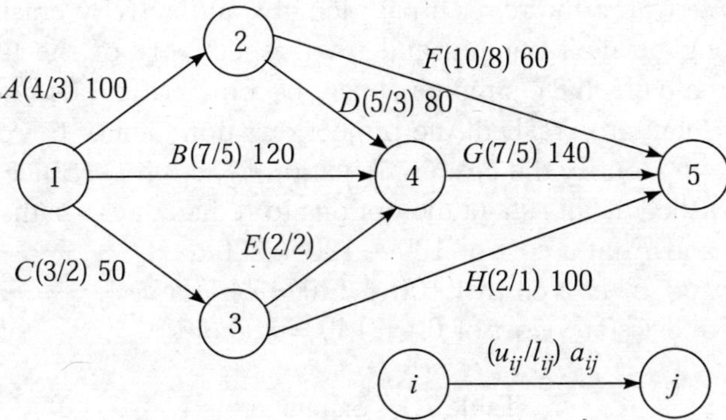

Fig. 7.16(a) A sample network

Activity	*Normal Days*	*(Rs.)*	*Crash Days*	*(Rs.)*	*Cost slope* (Rs./day)
A	4	100	3	200	100
B	7	280	5	520	120
C	3	50	2	100	50
D	5	200	3	360	80
E	2	160	2	160	infinity
F	10	230	8	350	60
G	7	200	5	480	140
H	2	100	1	200	100
Total		1320		2370	

Fig. 7.16(b) Tabular representation for project crashing

feasible durations (between 16 and 11 days, in this case) is called the project cost duration efficient frontier or the Pareto Optimal frontier. For the LP formulation of the project crashing problem, this is the solution to the parametric LP with project duration, T as a parameter varying between the normal project duration T_n to the crash project duration T_c. This project cost efficient frontier is obtained by heuristic reasoning below and subsequently an efficient network flow-based algorithm due to Fulkerson is presented for solving the problem.

The starting point for the project cost duration curve is the all normal project duration with a value of 16 days and a direct cost of Rs. 1320 as the datum. At this stage, *ADG* is the critical path and all the other paths are of lesser durations as seen from the table below. The cheapest way to crash the project is to examine the critical path (*ADG*) and pick up an activity which is least costly to crash. In this case this is the activity *D* with a cost slope of Rs. 80/day, which can be crashed by a maximum of 2 days (referring to the row of activity crash potential in the bottom row of the table). Thus, the critical path of *ADG* can be crashed by 2 days at a cost of Rs. 80/day by crashing activity *D* by 2 days. This would in fact amount to moving in the project cost duration efficient frontier from point

P_1 to point P_2, where the revised path lengths and activity crashing potentials are updated in the next column and row respectively of the table below. At this stage three paths have simultaneously become critical (*ADG*, *AF*, *BG*) and unless all of them are crashed, the project duration cannot be reduced further. We thus have to identify the best combination of activities. Since activity *D* has been fully crashed at this stage the options to reduce these paths are:

Crash *A* and *B* (at a cost of 100 + 120 = 220/day)
Crash *A* and *G* (at a cost of 100 + 140 = 240/day)
Crash *F* and *G* (at a cost of 60 + 140 = 200/day)

Table 7.1 Sample project

Paths				*Activities*				
	A	*B*	*C*	*D*	*E*	*F*	*G*	*H*
ADG	100			80			140	
AF	100					60		
BG		120					140	
CEG			50		X		140	
CH			50					100

Iteration				*Activity slacks*				
1	1	2	1	2	0	2	2	1
2	1	2	1	0	0	2	2	1
3	0	2	1	1	0	2	1	1
4	0	2	1	1	0	1	0	1
5	0	1	1	0	0	0	0	1

Paths	*Path lengths at subsequent iterations*				
ADG	16*	14*	13*	12*	11*
AF	14	14*	13*	12*	11*
BG	14	14*	13*	12*	11*
CEG	12	12	11	10	10
CH	5	5	5	5	5

It appears that crashing *F* and *G* at Rs. 200/day is the cheapest option which can be exercised for 2 days since the crashing potential for both *F* and *G* is 2 days each. However, a little reflection reveals a still better option by noting that crashing both *A* and *G* by 1 day each reduces the length of path *ADG* by 2 days, and there is the possibility of relaxing the previously crashed activity *D* by 1 day resulting in a total cost of Rs. 240 – 80 = Rs. 160/day. The best option, therefore, at this stage is

Crash *A* and *G*: Relax *D* (at a cost of Rs. 160/day)

This option is restricted to only 1 day (the minimum of the crashing potential of *A* and *G*, and the relaxing potential of *D*).

Exercising this option of crashing *A* and *G* and simultaneously relaxing *D* by 1 day is tantamount to moving from point P_2 to point P_3 on the project cost duration efficient frontier of Fig. 7.17.

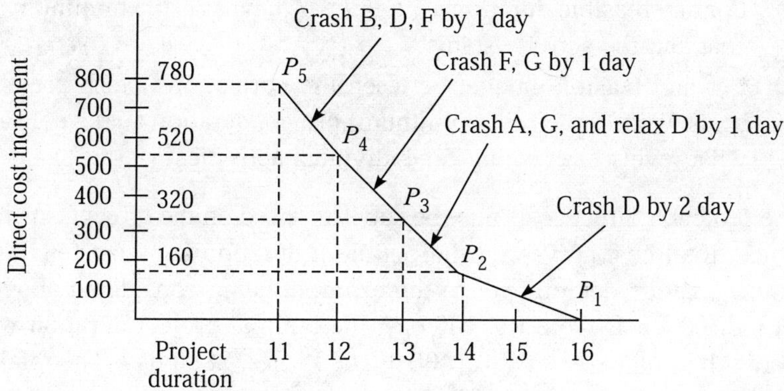

Fig. 7.17 Project cost-duration efficient frontier.

Updating the path lengths and crash potentials in the table of computations reveals that the critical paths are the same three paths (*ADG*, *AF* and *BG*) and now the critical duration has been reduced to 13 days.

Again we are faced with the problem of choosing the minimum cost subset of activities for crashing/relaxing to reduce simultaneously the length of the critical path below 13. Since A has now been fully crashed, the best option at this stage is to crash *F* and *G* (at a cost of Rs. 200/day), an option that can be exercised for at most 1 day at which *G* would be fully crashed. This would reduce the project duration to 12 days corresponding to a movement on the project cost duration efficient frontier from point P_3 to point P_4.

At this stage, the simultaneous reduction of the three critical paths is possible by crashing *B*, *D* and *F* (at a cost of 120 + 80 + 60 = 260/day), an option that can be exercised for only 1 day, limited by the crashing potential of both activities *D* and *F*. With this change, the movement on the project cost duration efficient frontier is from point P_4 to point P_5 and the project duration is 11 days with a total direct cost of Rs. 2100.

Further crashing is not possible whenever any one critical path cannot be crashed further. In this example though *BG* can still be reduced, but the other two critical paths *ADG* and *AF* are fully crashed. Thus, the complete project cost duration efficient frontier is depicted in Fig. 7.17.

It may be noticed that for linear time–cost trade-offs for activities, the project cost duration efficient frontier is piecewise linear, convex with progressively increasing (non-decreasing) cost slopes as we move from right to left. Apart from these characteristics, this efficient frontier also referred to as the Pareto Optimal frontier answers many useful questions for the project manager, such as the following:

(a) What is the minimum and maximum feasible range of durations, T_n and T_c?

(b) What are the corresponding budgets needed to achieve these durations?

(c) For any feasible duration T ($T_c \leq T \leq T_n$), what is the minimum possible cost and the activity status?

(d) For any feasible budget between the normal and crash project direct costs, what is the best (minimum) project duration achievable and with what levels of crashing for individual activities?

The project indirect costs may be superimposed on the direct costs to obtain the project total cost curve and the optimum duration and cost for the project as a whole may be determined. In the example being considered above, if the project indirect costs were Rs. 100/day, the optimal project duration would be 14 days with a total cost of Rs. 1400 + 1480 = Rs. 2880/day. The total project cost curve is shown in Fig. 7.18.

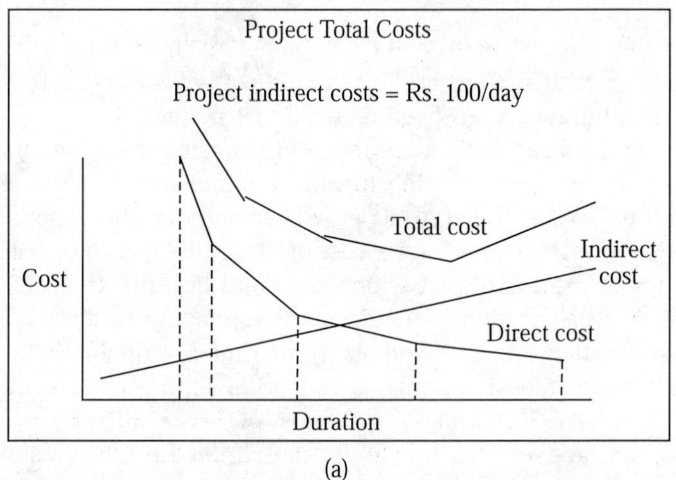

(a)

Project Total Costs

Days	16	15	14	13	12	11
Direct costs	1320	1400	1480	1640	1840	2100
Indirect costs	1600	1500	1400	1300	1200	1100
Total costs	2920	2900	2880	2940	3040	3200

(b)

Fig. 7.18 Project total cost curve.

7.3.2 Mathematical Formulation of the Project Crashing Problem

Activity Direct Costs

For an activity (ij) in the project network

$$C_{ij} = b_{ij} - a_{ij}x_{ij}, \text{ for } l_{ij} \le x_{ij} \le u_{ij}$$

Precedence Constraints

Node occurrence times for nodes should satisfy

$$t_j \ge = t_i + x_{ij}, \text{ for all } (ij) \text{ in } A \text{ in } G\ (N, A)$$
$$j = 2, 3\ , \ldots, n;\ t_1 = 0,\ t_n = \text{Project duration}$$

Problem Statement

The problem is to determine activity durations, x_{ij} and node realization times, t_j to minimize total activity direct cost for all possible project durations between the normal and crash limits.

Parametric LP Formulation

$$\begin{aligned}
\text{Minimize} \quad & Z = C_{ij} = \sum(b_{ij} - a_{ij}x_{ij}) \\
\text{Subject to} \quad & t_i - t_j + x_{ij} \le 0, \text{ for all } (ij) \in A \\
& x_{ij} \le = u_{ij}, \text{ for all } (ij) \in A \\
& x_{ij} \ge = l_{ij}, \text{ for all } (ij) \in A \\
& t_n - t_1 = T,\ T \text{ lying in } (T_c, T_n)
\end{aligned}$$

(T_c and T_n are the crash and normal project durations respectively.)

The basis of the network flow procedure for solving the project crashing problem using the approach of Ford and Fulkerson (1966) is developed below using the primal-dual formulation of the above parametric linear program. We first write the primal *LP* in the canonical form, write its dual and then develop the optimality conditions from complementary slackness which govern the operation of the algorithm.

Primal *LP*

Maximize $Z(T) = a_{ij}\ x_{ij}$

subject to — Dual variables

$$\begin{aligned}
t_i - t_j + x_{ij} &\le = 0, \text{ for } (ij) \text{ in } A && f_{ij} \\
x_{ij} &\le = u_{ij}, \text{ for } (ij) \text{ in } A && g_{ij} \\
-x_{ij} &\le = -l_{ij}, \text{ for } (ij) \text{ in } A && h_{ij} \\
-t_1 + t_n &= T && v
\end{aligned}$$

Dual *LP*

$$\begin{aligned}
\text{Minimize} \quad & Tv + u_{ij}g_{ij} - l_{ij}h_{ij} \\
\text{subject to} \quad & f_{ij} + g_{ij} - h_{ij} = a_{ij}, \text{ for } (ij) \text{ in } A \\
& [f_{ij} - f_{ji}] = v,\ i = 1 \\
& \qquad = 0,\ i \ne 1, n \\
& \qquad = -v,\ i = n
\end{aligned}$$

Flow Interpretation

- f_{ij} = flow in arc (ij)
- a_{ij} = capacity of arc (ij)

- g_{ij} = residual capacity of arc (ij)
- h_{ij} = flow in excess of capacity in arc (ij)

Optimality Condition – I

$g_{ij} > 0$ implies

(i) $h_{ij} = 0$

(ii) $x_{ij} = u_{ij}$

(iii) this is the range of $f_{ij}(1)$

Again by complementary slackness

if $t_i - t_j + u_{ij} < 0$, then $f_{ij}(1) = 0$

if $0 < f_{ij}(1) \leq a_{ij}$, then $t_i - t_j + u_{ij} = 0$

If we define $s_{ij}(1) = t_i - t_j + u_{ij}$, then positive flow, $f_{ij}(1) > 0$ is permissible only if $s_{ij}(1) = 0$.

Optimality Condition – II

$h_{ij} > 0$ implies

(i) $g_{ij} = 0$

(ii) $x_{ij} = l_{ij}$

(iii) this is the range of $f_{ij}(2)$

Again by complementary slackness

if $t_i - t_j + l_{ij} < 0$, then $f_{ij}(2) = 0$

if $f_{ij}(2) > 0$, then $t_i - t_j + l_{ij} = 0$ & $f_{ij}(1) = a_{ij}$

If we define $s_{ij}(2) = t_i - t_j + l_{ij}$, then positive flow, $f_{ij}(2) > 0$ is permissible only if $s_{ij}(2) = 0$ and $f_{ij}(1) = a_{ij}$.

These optimality conditions and the behaviour of the variables f_{ij}, g_{ij} and h_{ij} are shown in Fig. 7.19.

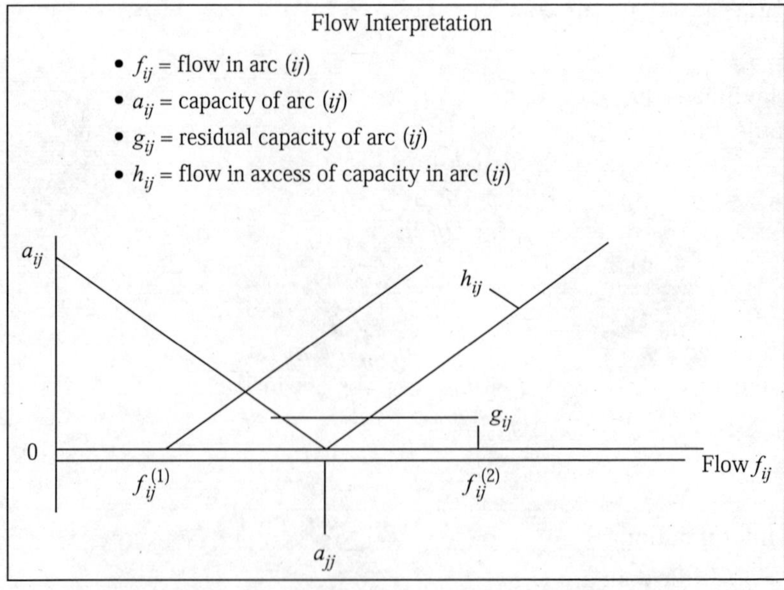

Fig. 7.19 Behaviour of dual variables (arc flows) at optimality.

7.3.3 Fulkerson's Flow Procedure

- A primal-dual algorithm based on the two optimality conditions stated in Section 7.3.2.
- Each project activity or arc is capable of carrying two kinds of flow (imagine two compartments in each arc).
- The algorithm proceeds to augment flows at a breakthrough and alter node times at a non-breakthrough.
- The three key features of the algorithm are
  - Labelling of nodes
  - Breakthrough (finite and infinite)
  - Non-breakthrough
- The algorithm starts from the normal project duration and successively identifies the most economical set of activities for crashing or relaxing till the crash project duration is reached.

A flow chart depicting the major steps in the algorithm is shown in Fig. 7.20.

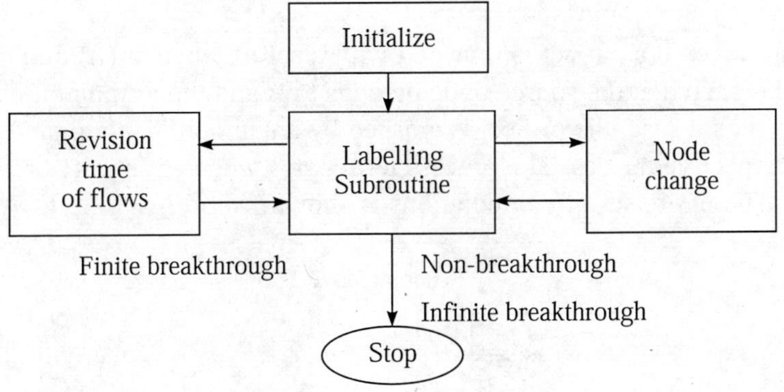

Fig. 7.20 Flow chart of Fulkersons's crashing procedure.

Illustration on a Sample Project

Fulkerson's flow algorithm for project crashing following the above steps is illustrated on the network of Fig. 7.16 which was solved using the heuristic procedure.

Initialization:

We initialize the network with all zero arc flows [$f_{ij}(1) = f_{ij}(2) = 0$, for all arcs (ij) in the network], and set the arc capacities equal to their respective cost slopes. The initial node times are determined by conducting a forward pass with activity times equal to their normal durations (Fig. 7.21). Through successive applications of the routine after a series of breakthroughs and non-breakthroughs as illustrated in subsequent figures, we obtain the final solution. At each breakthrough the value of the flow (v) increases as a consequence of the discovery of a flow augmenting path. When, however, a flow augmenting path

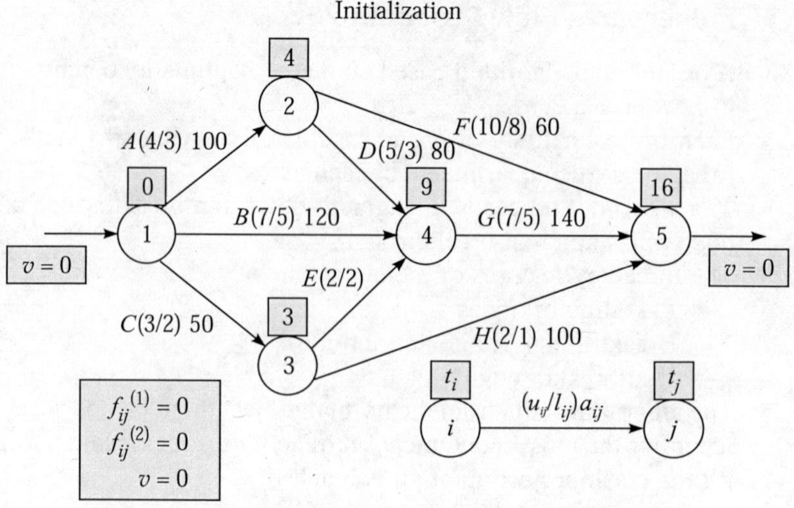

Fig. 7.21 Initialization of sample network.

is not discovered a cut-set is revealed with a set of labelled (X) and unlabelled (Y) nodes such that the source node belongs to X and the terminal node belongs to Y. In such a case, the project is crashed by an amount δ, computed as shown in the respective figures. The process terminates when an infinite breakthrough occurs. The entire set of computations is shown from Figs. 7.22 to 7.45.

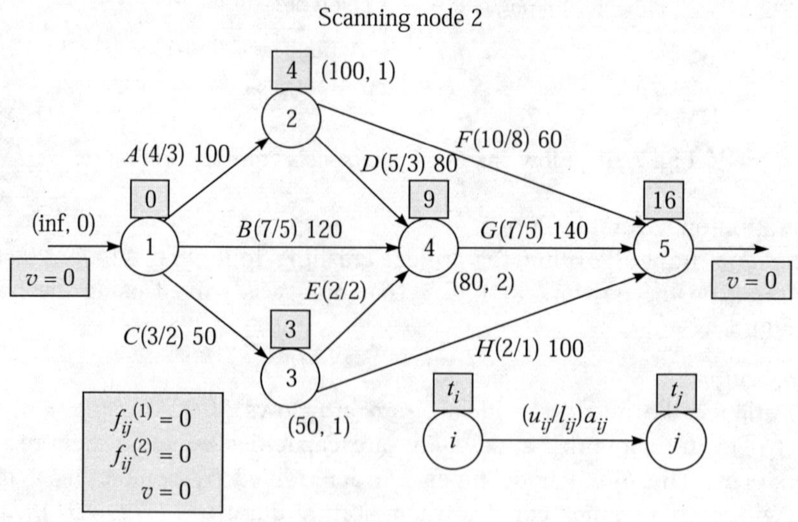

Fig. 7.22 Scanning node 2.

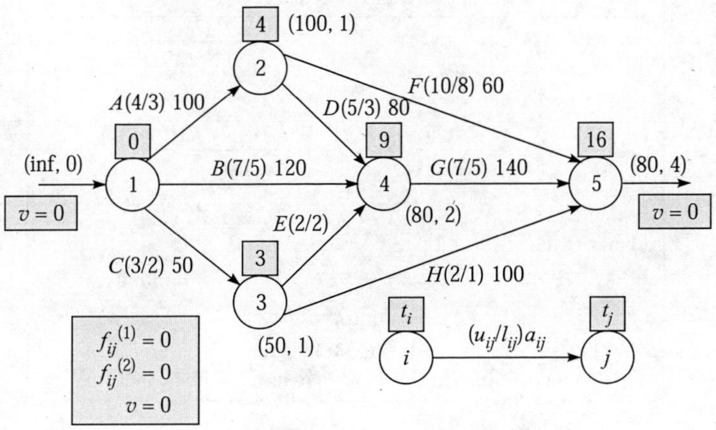

Fig. 7.23 Scanning node 4 leads to breakthrough 1.

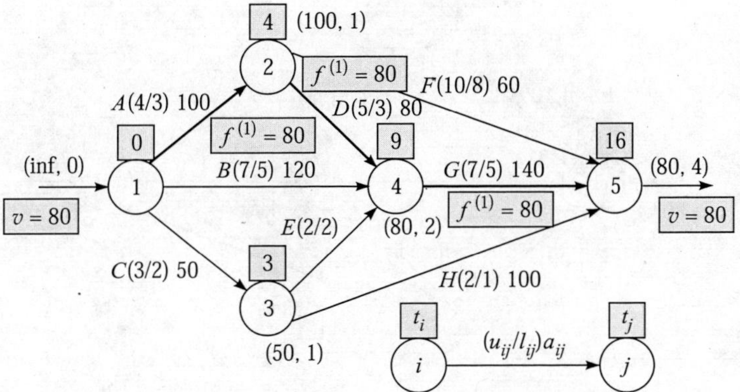

Fig. 7.24 Flow revision after breakthrough 1.

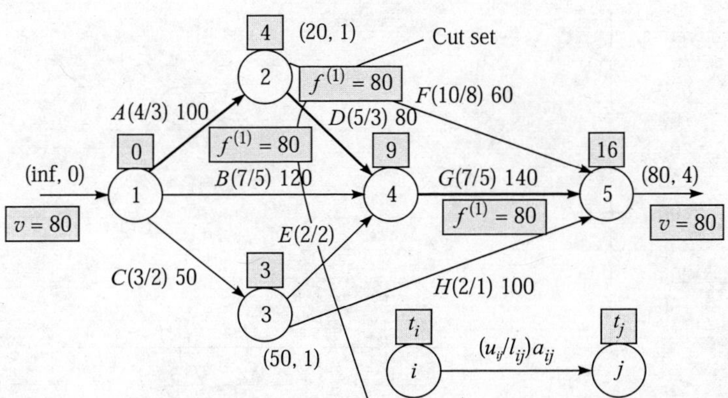

Fig. 7.25(a) Non-breakthrough 1.

Analysis at non-breakthrough 1					
Forward arcs			Reverse arcs		
(i, j)	$s_{ij}^{(1)}$	$s_{ij}^{(2)}$	(i, j)	$s_{ij}^{(1)}$	$s_{ij}^{(2)}$
(1, 4)	– 2	– 4			
(2, 4)	0	– 2		NULL SET	
(2, 5)	– 2	– 4			
(3, 4)	– 4	– 4			
(3, 5)	–11	–12			
	$\delta_t = 2$			δ_2 = Infinity	
$\delta = \min(\delta_1, \delta_2) = 2$					
Crash D (2, 4) by 2 days					
(Other activities in cut set have reduced slack by 2 days)					

Fig. 7.25(b) Analysis at non-breakthrough 1.

Project crashed (16-14 days) after N1

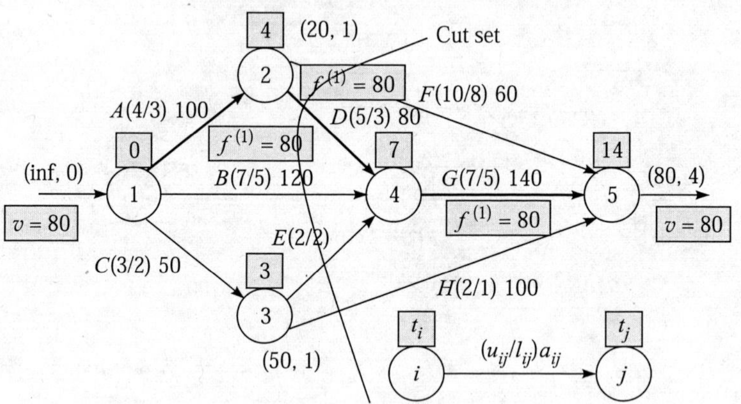

Fig. 7.26 Project crashed at N1 (16–14 days).

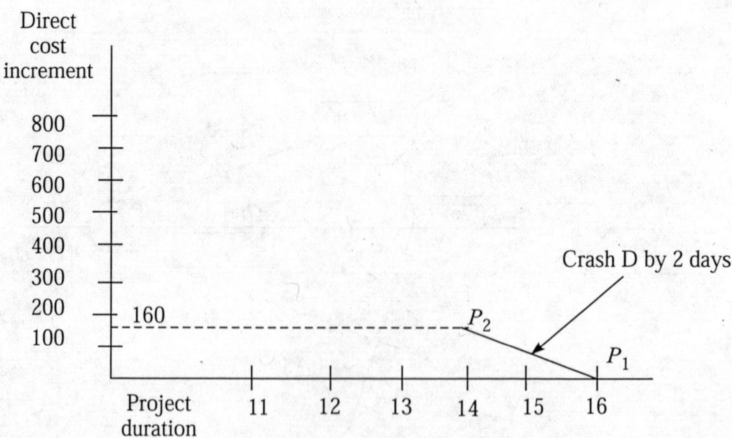

Fig. 7.27 Point P_1 to P_2.

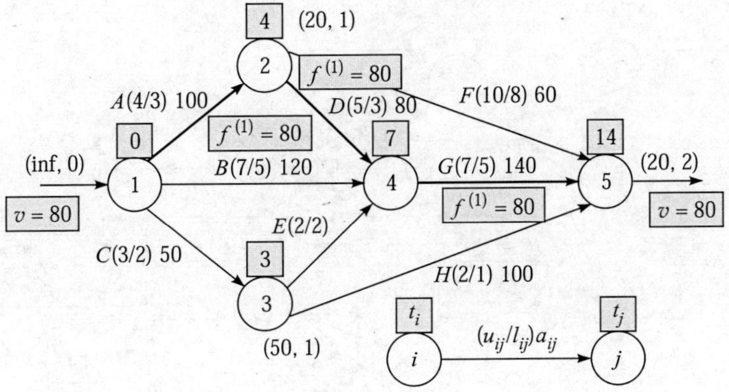

Fig. 7.28 Labelling after N1 reveals breakthrough 2.

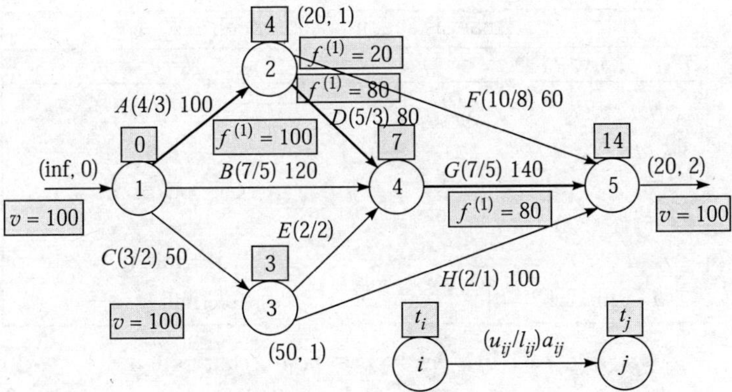

Fig. 7.29 Breakthrough 2.

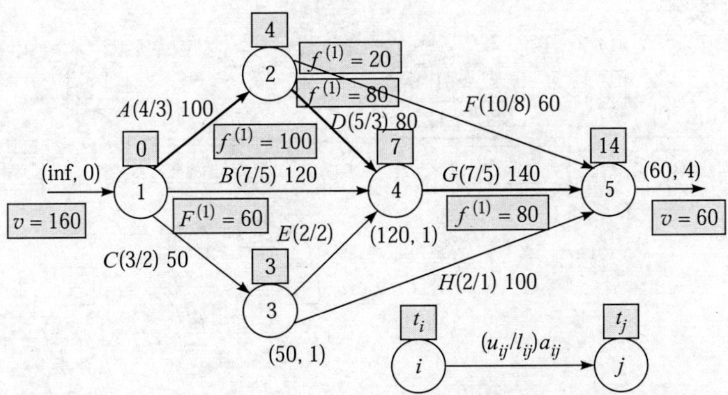

Fig. 7.30 Breakthrough 3.

Non-breakthrough 2

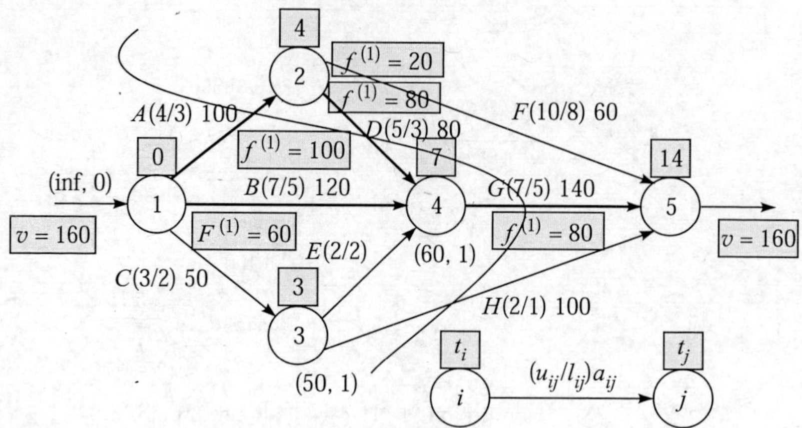

Fig. 7.31(a) Non-breakthrough 2.

Analysis at non-breakthrough 2					
Forward arcs			Reverse arcs		
(i, j)	$s_{ij}^{(1)}$	$s_{ij}^{(2)}$	(i, j)	$s_{ij}^{(1)}$	$s_{ij}^{(2)}$
(1, 2)	0	– 1		2	0
(3, 5)	2	0			
(4, 5)	0	– 2			
			$\delta_2 = \min\,(2) = 2$		
$\delta_t = \min\,(1, 2) = 1$			$\delta = \min\,(1, 2) = 1$		

Fig. 7.31(b) Analysis at non-breakthrough 2.

Node Revision after N2

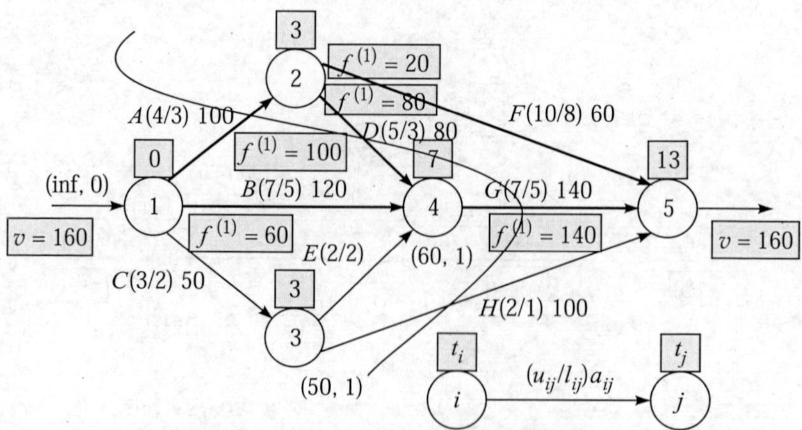

Fig. 7.32 Node revision after N2.

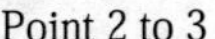

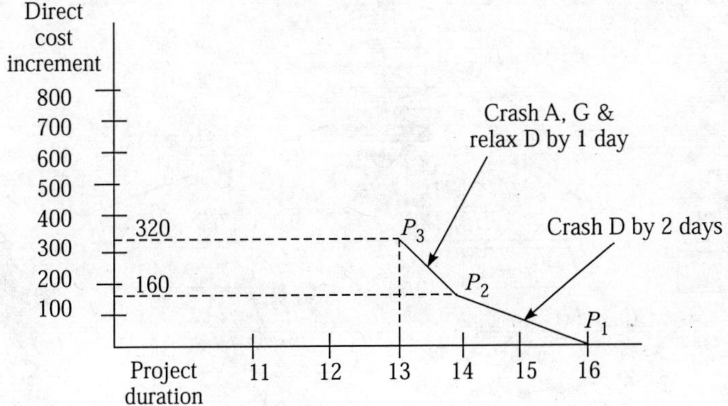

Fig. 7.33 Point P_2 to P_3.

Labelling Reveals Breakthrough 4

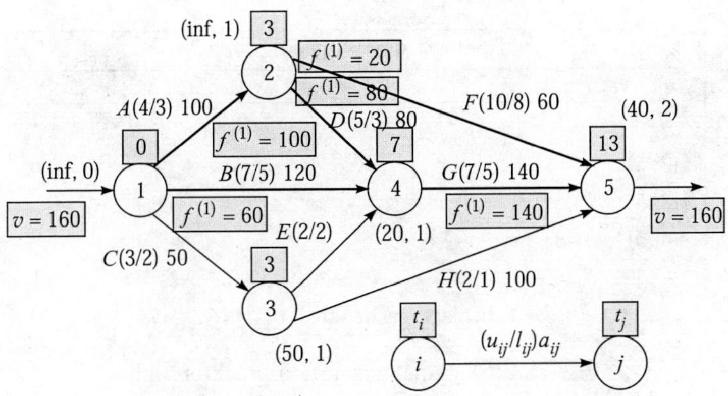

Fig. 7.34 Labelling reveals breakthrough 4.

Flow Revision after
Breakthrough 4 (v = 160 – 200)

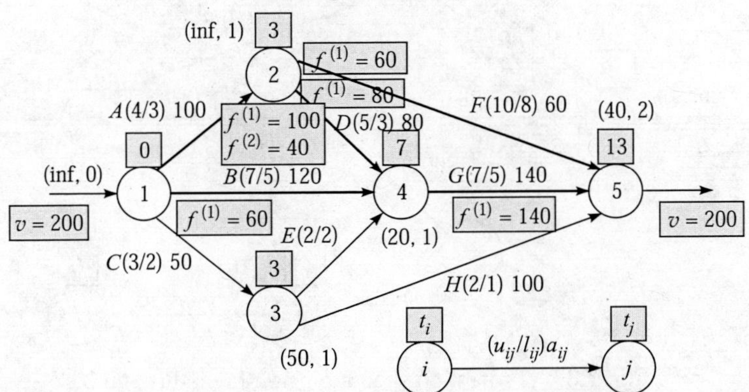

Fig. 7.35 Flow revision after breakthrough 4.

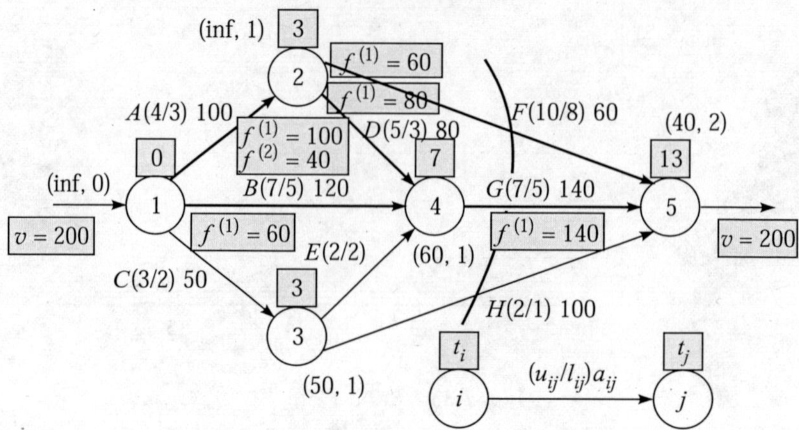

Fig. 7.36(a) Non-breakthrough 3.

Analysis at non-breakthrough 3					
Forward arcs			Reverse arcs		
(i, j)	$s_{ij}^{(1)}$	$s_{ij}^{(2)}$	(i, j)	$s_{ij}^{(1)}$	$s_{ij}^{(2)}$
(2, 5)	0	– 2			
(3, 5)	1	– 1		NULL SET	
(4, 5)	–8	– 9			
	$\delta_1 = 1$			$\delta_2 = \infty$	
$\delta = 1$, Project crashed by 1 day to 12 days					

Fig. 7.36(b) Analysis at non-breakthrough 3.

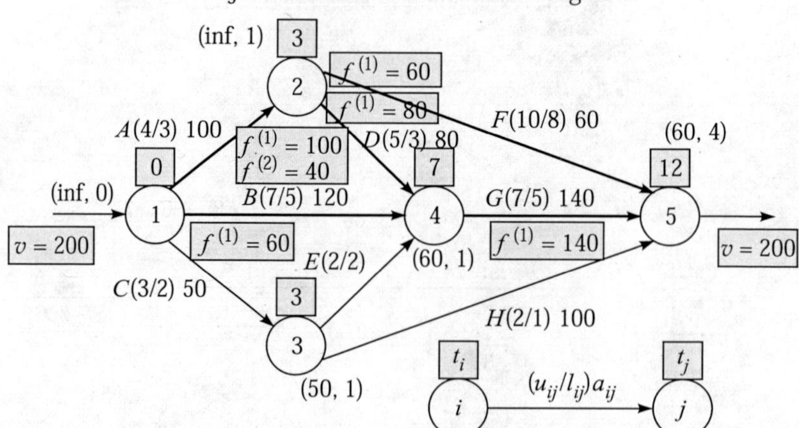

Fig. 7.37 Project crashed after non-breakthrough 3.

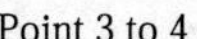

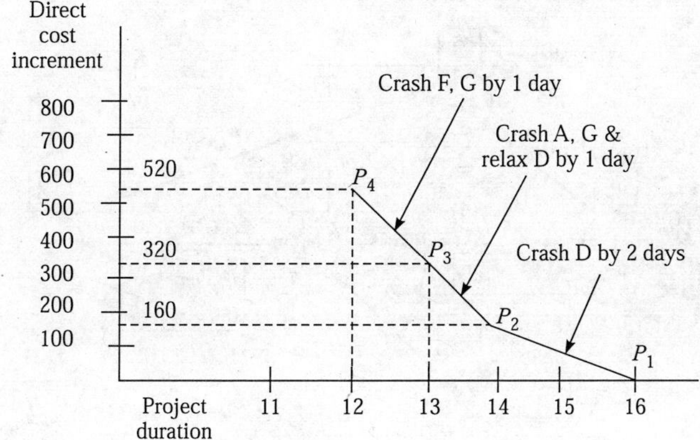

Fig. 7.38 Point P_3 to P_4.

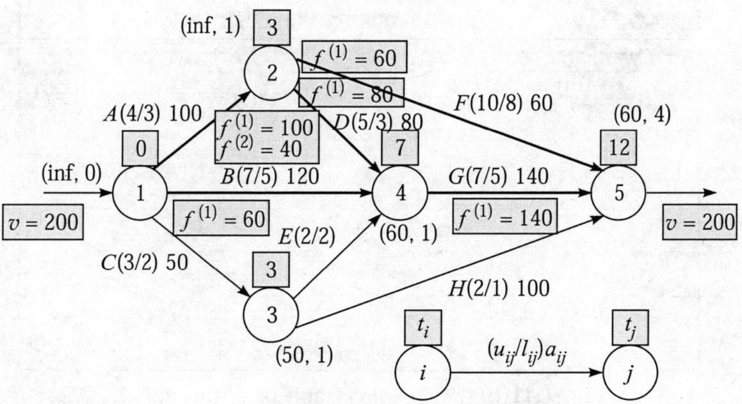

Fig. 7.39 Labelling reveals breakthrough 5.

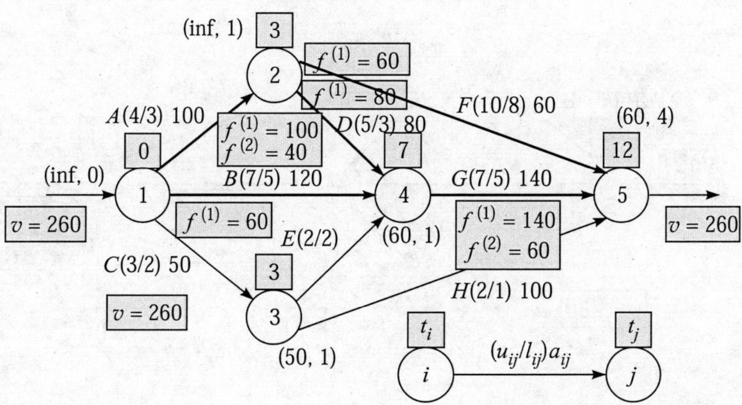

Fig. 7.40 Breakthrough 5.

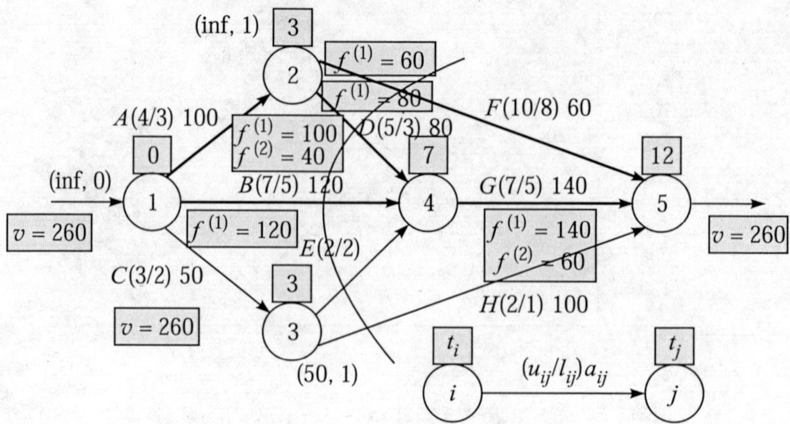

Fig. 7.41(a) Non-breakthrough 4.

Analysis at non-breakthrough 4					
Forward arcs			Reverse arcs		
(i, j)	$s_{ij}^{(1)}$	$s_{ij}^{(2)}$	(i, j)	$s_{ij}^{(1)}$	$s_{ij}^{(2)}$
(2, 5)	1	– 1			
(2, 4)	1	– 1		NULL SET	
(3, 4)	–2	– 2			
(3, 5)	–7	– 8			
$\delta_1 = 1$					
$\delta = \min(1, \infty) = 1$				$\delta_2 = \infty$	
Project crashed by 1 day to 11 days					

Fig. 7.41(b) Analysis at non-breakthrough 4.

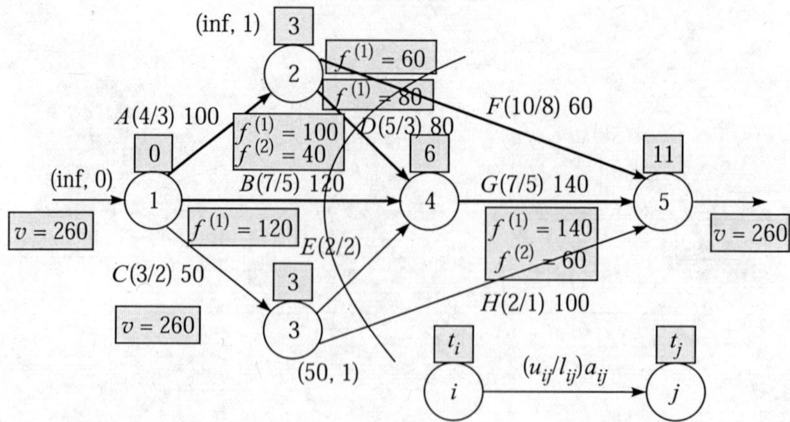

Fig. 7.42 Project crashed from 12-11 days after N4.

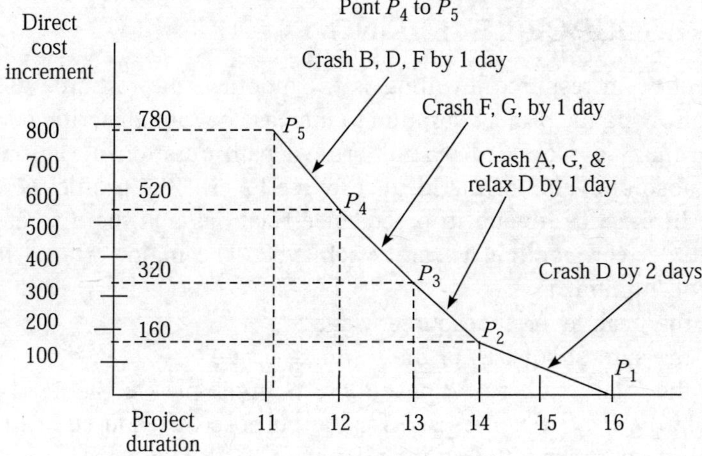

Fig. 7.43 Point P_4 to P_5.

Infinite Breakthrough 6 (v = 260 – ∞)

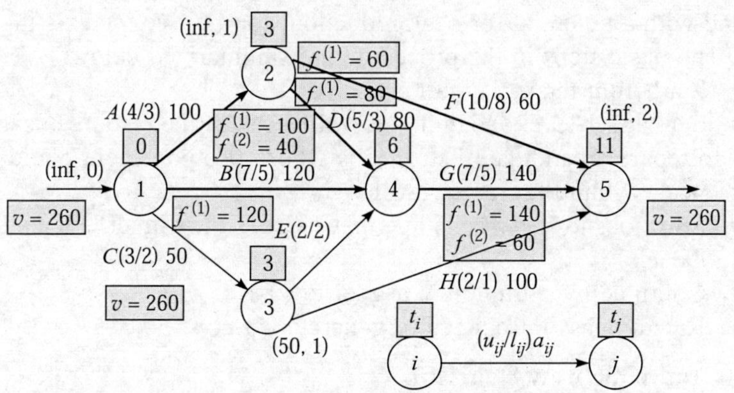

Fig. 7.44 Infinite breakthrough 6.

Summary of Computations

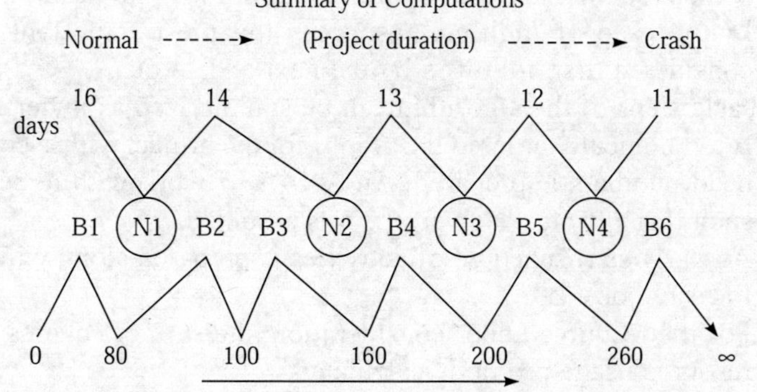

Fig. 7.45 Summary of computations.

7.4 RESOURCE LEVELLING

The objective in resource levelling is to smoothen the resource usage profile without allowing the project duration to increase beyond the critical path length. The total man-days divided by this critical path duration in days would thus give the absolute value of the ideal resource level if the profile were perfectly levelled. In practice, owing to precedence relations and the discrete nature of activities, perfect levelling is rarely achieved. The major criteria in levelling could be to minimize

- the peak level of resource usage.
- the sum of squares of the resource usage.
- the total number of dips and crests in the profile.

Generally, heuristics are used for the purpose of resource levelling which tend to shift activities utilizing their slacks.

Workload Smoothing Heuristic

This heuristic proposed by Levy, Thompson & Wiest (1962) examines the resource peak and attempts to shift the eligible activities (those with adequate slack and with a potential for peak reduction) to improve the existing resource profile. The basic steps in the procedure are summarized below:

- Start from the early start schedule.
- Set trigger level one unit below the peak of the resource usage profile.
- Prepare a candidate list of jobs whose postponement could bring the peak within the trigger level.
- Shift jobs to find a schedule that satisfies the trigger level; stop if none exists.
- Continue by setting new trigger levels.
- Randomness introduced to generate variety.

Burgess and Killebrew Heuristic

- This is a heuristic procedure designed to minimize the total sum of squares of the resource usage.
- It thus looks at the whole profile and not just the peak(s).
- In the case of multiple resources the most important resource is considered first, followed by the next and so on.

The basic steps of the algorithm can be summarized as under:

1. A topologically ordered list of jobs for the project with ascending arrow head numbers is prepared. An A-O-A network with nodes numbered such that $i < j$ for each arc (i, j) is assumed.
2. An early start schedule of activities is prepared along with total floats for each job.
3. For the resource under consideration, the sum of squares of the daily resource usage profile is calculated.
4. Starting at the bottom of the list of jobs, each activity is shifted to the right, one period at a time up to a maximum permitted by its float or

precedence needs of subsequent activities. For each such shift, the sum of squares of resource usage is updated and the activity fixed at the latest slot, yielding the lowest sum of squares. This is to permit the utilization of float of preceding activities to the greatest extent possible.

5. The exercise in step 4 is repeated for all the activities in turn from bottom to top, completing a rescheduling cycle, and a feasible schedule with a given sum of squares of resource usage.
6. Additional rescheduling cycles are carried out till no further reduction in sum of squares of resource usage occurs.
7. Since the topological ordering for the activities may not be unique, the above procedure (steps 2–6) could be repeated with any other topological order of activities (not necessarily increasing arrow head numbers).
8. The best feasible solution generated in steps 1–7 is chosen for implementation.

Example Network

An application of this procedure to the example network of Fig. 7.46 with two resources A (manpower) and B (special equipment) yields:

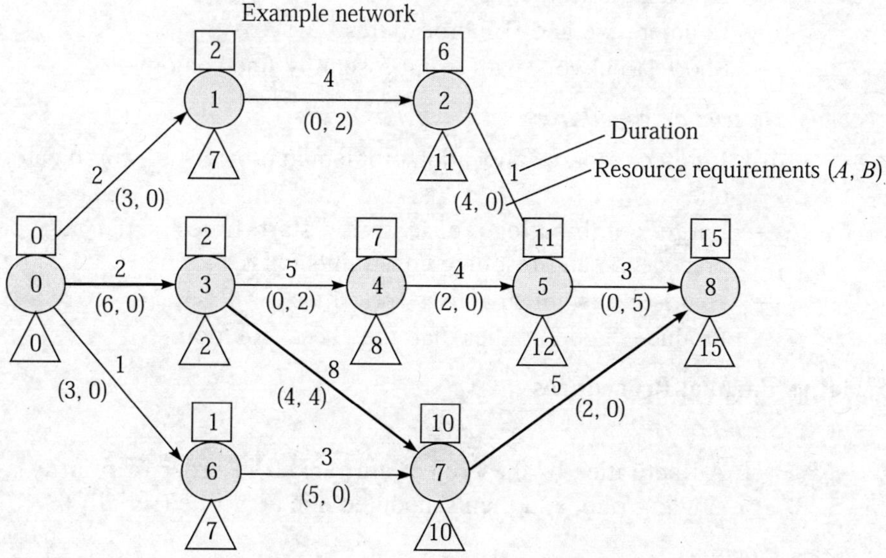

Fig. 7.46 Example network.

	Sum of Squares	
	Initial	***Final***
Resource A	738	626
Resource B	416	375

Both the initial and final solutions are shown in Fig. 7.47.

Before & After Comparison														
12	14	09	09	04	04	08	06	06	06	04	02	02	02	02
(Initial Resource A profile)														
06	**06**	**07**	**07**	**07**	**09**	**09**	**09**	**06**	**06**	**04**	**08**	**02**	**02**	**02**
(Final Resource A profile)														
00	00	08	08	08	08	06	04	04	04	00	05	05	05	00
(Initial Resource B profile)														
00	**00**	**04**	**06**	**06**	**06**	**06**	**08**	**06**	**06**	**02**	**00**	**05**	**05**	**05**
(Final Resource B profile)														

Fig. 7.47 Initial and final results of levelling.

7.5 LIMITED RESOURCE ALLOCATION

Solution Techniques

- ***Optimization procedures***
  - *LP*-based formulations
  - Enumerative and ILP procedures
  - Shortest network path using assembly line analogy
- ***Heuristic procedures***
  - Limited resource allocation problem in projects is a combinatorial one
  - Large combinations of activity start times satisfying both precedence and resource constraints exist
  - Heuristics establish activity priorities
  - Produce "good" rather than the "best" solution

Serial vs Parallel Procedures

- ***Serial***
  - All activities of the project are ranked in order of priority as a single group, and then scheduled one at a time (serially).
- ***Parallel***
  - All activities starting in a given time period are ranked as groups and resources allocated. At each successive time period a new rank ordering of all eligible activities is made and the process continued.
  - Computational experience generally favours parallel heuristics in comparison to serial heuristics.

Heuristic Procedures

Commonly Used Heuristics

- MINSLK: Minimum activity slack
- LFT: Minimum late finish time
- RSM: Resource scheduling method
- GRD: Greatest resource demand
- GRU : Greatest resource utilization*
- SIO: Shortest imminent operation
- MJP: Most jobs possible*
- RAN: Random activity selection

(*Involves ILP)

Comparison of Heuristics

Heuristic	*Percentage of problems for which optimum found*
MINSLK	29%
LFT	20%
RSM	14%
GRD	13%
RAN	5%
GRU	2%
MJP	2%
SIO	1%

Percent Increase above Optimal Duration

MINSLK	5.6%
LFT	6.7%
RSM	6.8%
RAN	11.4%
GRU	13.1%
GRD	13.1%
SIO	15.3%
MJP	16.0%

Wiest's Heuristics for Resource Allocation

- Allocate resources serially in time. That is, start on the first day and schedule all jobs possible, then do the same for the next day, and so on.
- When several jobs compete for the same resources, give preference to the jobs with the least slack.
- Reschedule non-critical jobs, if possible, to free resources for scheduling critical jobs.

An application of this procedure to the sample network of Fig. 7.48 yields the final solution of Fig. 7.49.

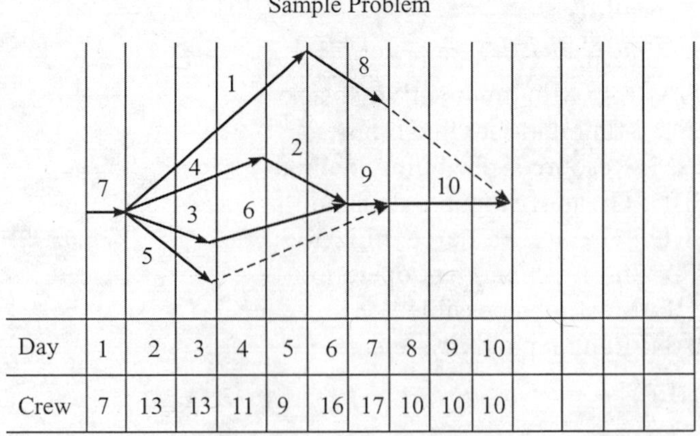

Fig. 7.48 Sample problem for limited resource allocation.

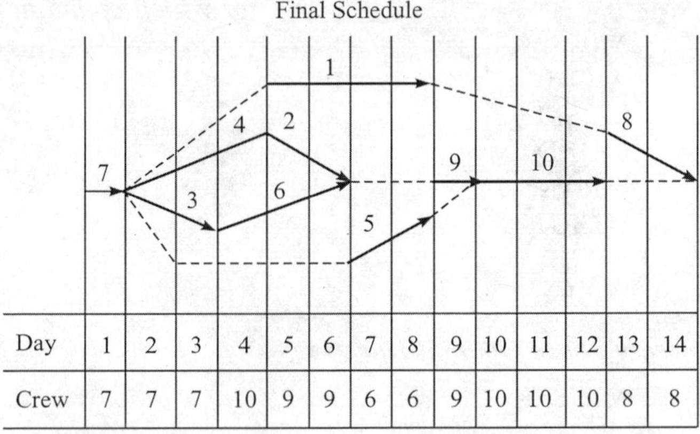

Fig. 7.49 Final schedule after resource allocation.

7.6 MANAGING A LIST OF INDEPENDENT TASKS

7.6.1 Problem Statement

Find the best way to manage a task list, given that each task has an independent time and resource requirement with total resource availability of R.

If there be a lower limit L and an upper limit U on the resource, what should be the values of L and U to manage the tasks in minimum time?

7.6.2 Development of Solution Procedure

Assuming that there are n tasks with times $t_1, t_2, \ldots, t_n$ and resource requirements of $r_1, r_2, \ldots, r_n$, respectively, clearly the total task time can be minimized if the tasks are done concurrently. Denoting this minimum time by $T_{\min}$, we have $T_{\min} = \text{Max}[t_1, t_2, \ldots, t_n]$ and the maximum resource requirement is U, where

$$U = (r_1 + r_2 + \ldots + r_n)$$

Thus, the total job may be considered a pseudo job with resource requirement R (= U in this case) and time T_{min} represented by the rectangle in Fig. 7.50.

Arranging jobs in a sequence such that $t_1 \geq t_2 \ldots \geq t_n$ (as shown by the pyramid style in Fig. 7.50), for the indicated project duration, the resource limit can be reduced only by filling in the gaps in the above pyramidal structure. There can obviously be various combinations that are possible, but we would like to minimize the manpower for accomplishing all the jobs without sacrificing time (*the resource levelling problem*).

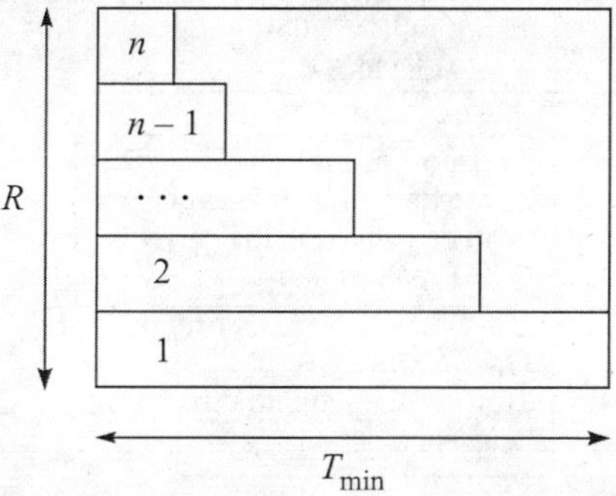

Fig. 7.50 Jobs done concurrently (arranged in pyramid style).

7.6.3 Algorithm 1 for Resource Levelling

The following heuristic algorithm based on the properties of the shortest/longest processing time in the n job – 1 machine sequencing problem is suggested for bunching of jobs in a given list of tasks for processing. The flow chart of the proposed procedure is given in Fig. 7.51.

7.6.4 Algorithm 2 for Limited Resource Allocation Problem

Once the resources are levelled as given above, we would like to reduce the resource level from R to L. After the levelling is complete via algorithm 1, the resource peak can be reduced only by shifting some jobs beyond the critical path duration.

1. Check all the k levels $L = L$ to L_{max} for the maximum gap ($t_{max} - \sum$times of S_L). Let this be at r^{th} level denoted by $G_r = t_{max} - \sum$times of S_L.
2. Slide the current job with the minimum duration into this gap and find the revised project duration T, corresponding to the new critical chain.
3. Take this new critical chain. Put it at the base of pyramid.
4. Recall algorithm 1 with the reduced subset of jobs arranged according to SPT rule.
5. Compute the revised resource peak R. (This corresponds to a movement from one non-dominated point to a neighbouring non-dominated point, i.e. P_x to P_{x+1}).

6. Is the maximum possible duration reached or/and the resource peak $= \max(r_1 \dots r_n)$?. If so then stop, if not, go to step 1.

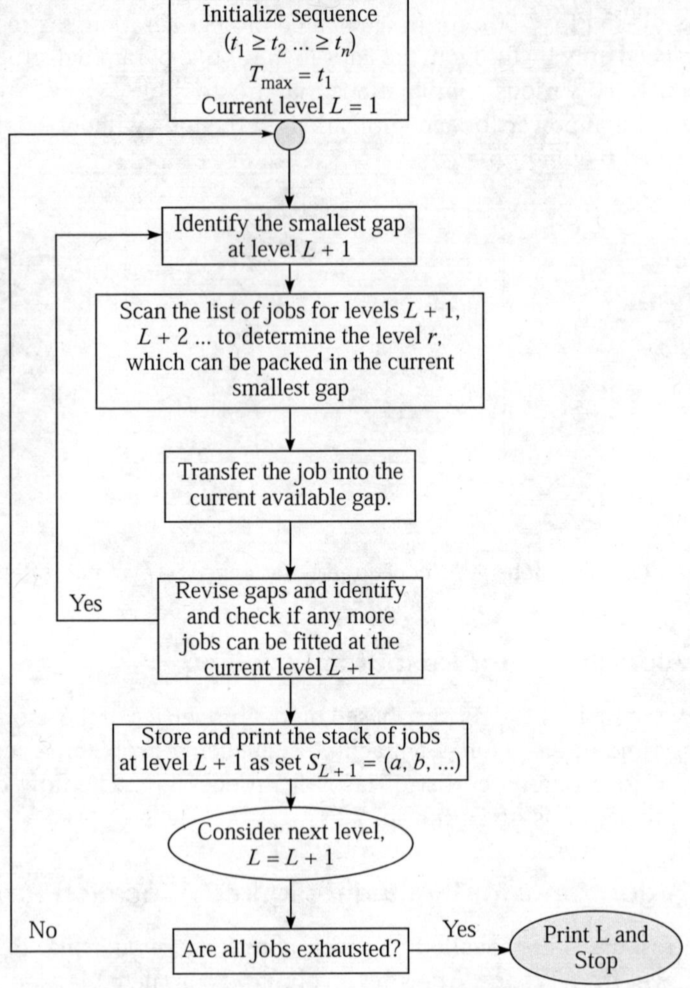

Fig. 7.51 Flow chart for the proposed algorithm 1.

7.6.5 Sample Problem

Let there be six tasks with the times 8, 2, 4, 6, 1 and 14.

Step 1 Arrange the tasks according to task times in decreasing order (Fig. 7.52).

$t_1 - 14$
$t_2 - 8$
$t_3 - 6$
$t_4 - 4$
$t_5 - 2$
$t_6 - 1$

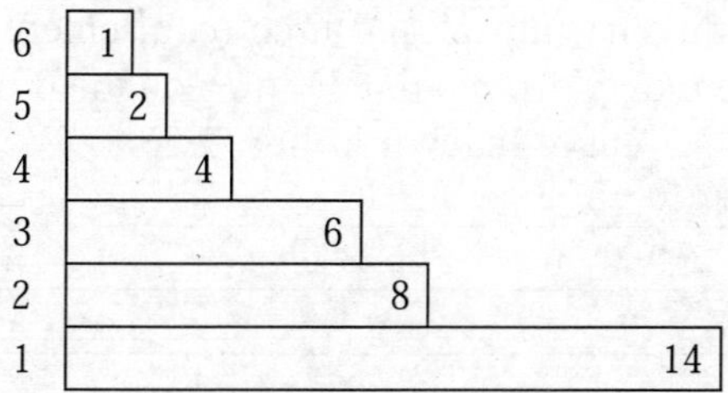

Fig. 7.52 Task list as per SPT/LPT.

Step 2 Arrange the tasks according to algorithm 1.

(a) At level 2, the gap (14 – 8) can be filled by job 3 (scanning upwards) leaving zero gap at level 2 (Fig. 7.53).

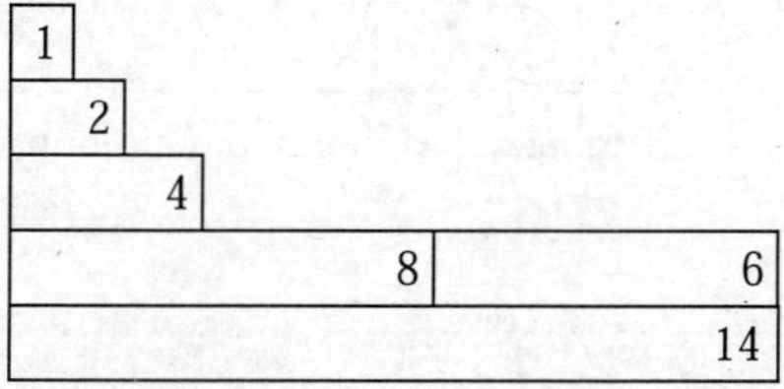

Fig. 7.53 Two levels completed (job at level 3 of duration 6 accommodated at level 2).

(b) Incrementing the current level from 2 to 3, we find that the remaining 3 jobs can all be accommodated at level 3. And thus the final solution is as given below (Fig. 7.54).

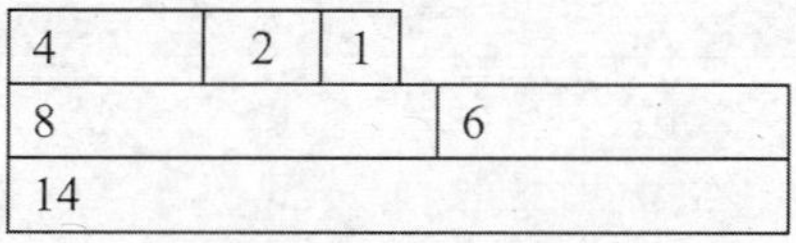

Fig. 7.54 Optimal solution to the resource levelling problem.

The peak resource requirement is 3. The final solution may be represented as the set of jobs at each level as follows:

$$S_1 = \{1\},\ T_1 = 14$$
$$S_2 = \{2, 3\},\ T_2 = 14$$
$$S_3 = \{4, 5, 6\},\ T_3 = 7$$

This makes the available gap at the third level maximum with value 7. The candidate jobs other than those in the level which can be accommodated in the maximum gap are jobs = {3}. Notice that the shifting of this job into the available slot of 7 yields a float of 1 and does not reduce the peak, but is an illustration of one of the many possible schedules with a peak of 3.

If we want to reduce the peak of 3 to 2, we apply algorithm 2, which essentially shifts job 4 of duration 4 to the critical chain (now of length 18 instead of 14) and rearranges the remaining jobs to yield the schedule shown in Fig. 7.55. This schedule has a peak resource requirement of 2 and the duration of 18. Thus, we have moved from point P_1 to P_2 on the project resource duration efficient frontier ($Z-T$ curve) shown in Fig. 7.56.

8	6	2	1
14		4	

Fig. 7.55 Limited resource allocation problem (with peak 2).

The resource requirement is 2. The duration of the tasks is now 18 days.

A movement on this curve from P_2 to P_3 is possible only if all jobs are done in series which implies a duration of $(t_1 + t_2 \ldots t_6)$. Obviously any increase in duration beyond 35 days is wasteful. Thus, the entire resource duration efficient frontier consists of the points P_1, P_2 and P_3 for this example (Fig. 7.56).

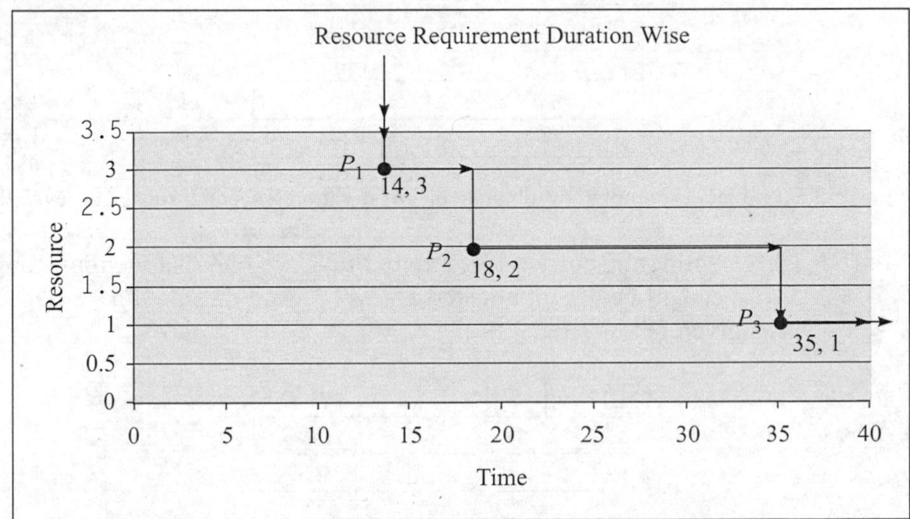

Fig. 7.56 Project resource-duration efficient frontier.

Considering that the man days for an activity i are $r_i t_i$, the total requirement of man days = the work content of the jobs, $W = \sum r_i t_i$. The manpower employed may be given by the rectangle of minimum area enclosing the schedule (which, if there is no wastage, would be of area W, but in actual would be $W' \geq W$ owing to schedule non-pre-emption of an activity and the integral number of levels, etc. W/W' may be treated as a packing ratio which could be a measure of the efficiency of the schedule. For the example under consideration, Table 7.2 summarizes the results.

Table 7.2 Summary of results for non-dominated solutions

Resource level	1	2	3
Minimum possible duration (days)	35	17.5	11.66
Actual optimal duration (days)	35	18	14
Packing ratio (%) or efficiency of the schedule	1.000	0.972	0.833

In this section, a systematic procedure to generate the resource-constrained project scheduling efficient frontier has been proposed as a series of vertical (resource levelling) and horizontal (limited resource allocation) movements for a job list without precedence restrictions. This results in very valuable planning information for a project manager who can utilize this information to allocate resources to projects depending on availability and convenience. The two algorithms proposed are illustrated with a sample problem. More computational work needs to be done to assess the efficiency of these algorithms under various job environments. Clearly, there is no guarantee of optimality in these heuristic algorithms, though preliminary experience shows that they produce "good" working solutions. In the next section, we investigate how integer programming models can be developed and used for solving the general project scheduling problems of levelling and resource allocation with precedence restrictions.

7.7 MATHEMATICAL PROGRAMMING FORMULATIONS

7.7.1 Task Splitting Not Allowed

Suppose there are five jobs with durations 5, 7, 4, 3, 2 and resource requirements 2, 3, 1, 2, 4, respectively. If all the jobs are done in parallel at their earliest start time (0), the resource peak is 12 (Fig. 7.57). Without increasing the duration of 7 days of the jobs, we would like to minimize the peak.

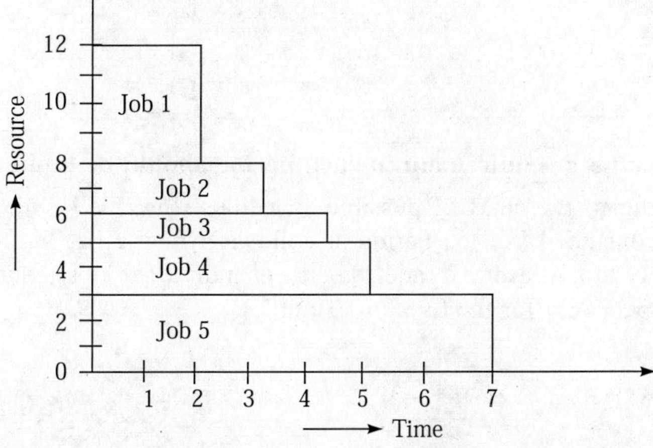

Fig. 7.57 Jobs done in parallel.

Definition of integer variables

Job 1 of duration 2 can start in period 1, 2, ..., or 6 (to be completed by day 7) and we can define $x_{11}, x_{12}, \ldots, x_{16}$ as (0,1) variables indicating start times of job 1. Similarly,

job 2 may start in period 1, 2, 3, 4 or 5 resulting in variables $x_{21}, x_{22}, \ldots,$ and x_{25}

job 3 may start in period 1, 2, 3 or 4 (corresponding variables x_{31}, x_{32}, x_{33} and x_{34})

job 4 may start in period 1, 2 or 3 (corresponding variable x_{41}, x_{42} and x_{43})

job 5 may start only in period 1 (x_{51} being the only choice)

Thus, if a job i is to be started earliest in time s_i and finished latest by f_i, then it can be started in $(f_i - s_i + t_i)$ discrete slots starting at $s_i, s_{i+1}, \ldots, (f_i - t_i)$. The possible start times of the five activities are shown in Fig. 7.58, and the corresponding schedules are depicted in Fig. 7.59.

		Time period							
Job	Resource	1	2	3	4	5	6	7	Duration
1	4	x_{11}	x_{12}	x_{13}	x_{14}	x_{15}	x_{16}		2
2	2	x_{21}	x_{22}	x_{23}	x_{24}	x_{25}			3
3	1	x_{31}	x_{32}	x_{33}	x_{34}				4
4	2	x_{41}	x_{42}	x_{43}					5
5	3	x_{51}							7

Fig. 7.58 Possible start times of the five activities.

Constraints

I. Each activity must be done from one amongst its possible start times

$$x_{11} + x_{12} + x_{13} + x_{14} + x_{15} + x_{16} = 1$$
$$x_{21} + x_{22} + x_{23} + x_{24} + x_{25} = 1$$
$$x_{31} + x_{32} + x_{33} + x_{34} = 1$$
$$x_{41} + x_{42} + x_{43} = 1$$
$$x_{51} = 1$$

II. The resource requirement in each period should be limited to *R*

By referring to the chart of possible schedules (Fig. 7.59), we can write the resource consumed in each period as follows, where r_1, r_2, r_3, r_4 and r_5 refer respectively to the resource requirements of individual jobs (equal to 2, 3, 1, 2 and 4, respectively for the five job example):

For period 1

$r_1x_{11} + r_2x_{21} + r_3x_{31} + r_4x_{41} + r_5x_{51} \leq R$

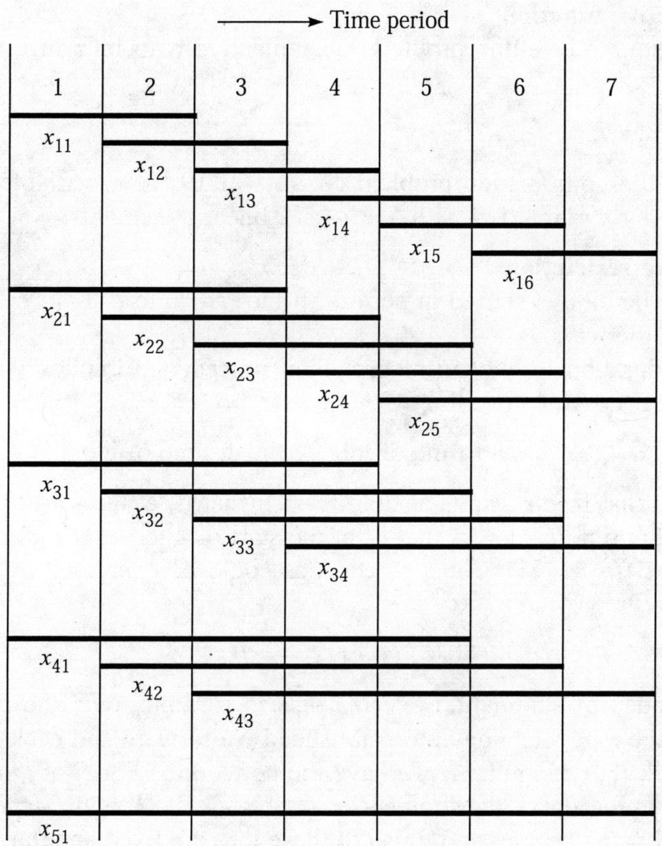

Fig. 7.59 Corresponding schedules.

For period 2

$r_1(x_{11} + x_{12}) + r_2(x_{21} + x_{22}) + r_3(x_{31} + x_{32}) + r_4\ (x_{41} + x_{42}) + r_5x_{51} \leq R$

For period 3

$r_1(x_{12} + x_{13}) + r_2(x_{22} + x_{23}) + r_3(x_{31} + x_{32} + x_{33}) + r_4(x_{41} + x_{42} + x_{43}) + r_5x_{51} \leq R$

For period 4

$r_1(x_{13} + x_{14}) + r_2(x_{22} + x_{23} + x_{24}) + r_3(x_{31} + x_{32} + x_{33} + x_{34}) + r_4\ (x_{41} + x_{42} + x_{43})$
$+ r_5x_{51} \leq R$

For period 5

$r_1(x_{14} + x_{15}) + r_2(x_{23} + x_{24} + x_{25}) + r_3(x_{32} + x_{33} + x_{34}) + r_4\ (x_{41} + x_{42} + x_{43})$
$+ r_5x_{51} \leq R$

For period 6

$r_1(x_{15} + x_{16}) + r_2(x_{24} + x_{25}) + r_3(x_{33} + x_{34}) + r_4\ (x_{42} + x_{43}) + r_5x_{21} \leq R$

For period 7

$r_1x_{16} + r_2x_{25} + r_3x_{34} + r_4x_{43} + r_5x_{51} \leq R$

III. Objective function

For the resource levelling problem, our objective is to minimize the resource peak *R*.

Minimize *R*.

Thus, the optimization problem consists of 19 (0, 1) variables of type x_{ij} plus 1 integer variable (*R*) with 5 + 7 = 12 linear constraints.

Precedence restrictions

If $x_{it} = 1$ when job is started in period t [time $(t - 1)$ to t]
$= 0$, otherwise
and d_i = duration of job i (integer) then precedence implies that for every immediate successor j of job i

start time of job $j \geq$ finish time of job i

Notice that if job i starts at time $(t - 1)$ (that is, at the start of period t), it would end at time $t - 1 + d$, that is, at the start of interval $(t + d)$ or the end of the interval $(t + d - 1)$. Thus, precedence could be expressed by a constraint of the type

$$\sum(t - 1)x_{jt} - \sum t x_{it} \geq d_i$$

The index of summation over t needs to run only over the possible start values of the job which may be established by a forward and backward pass on the network. For example, if we have the network of Fig. 7.60, then there are four binary precedence constraints $A < C$, $A < D$, $B < E$, and $C < E$. *ACE* being the critical path, the start and finish of these jobs are fixed and the project has a duration of 6 days, in which *D* can start in the 3rd, 4th or 5th period (variables xD_3, xD_4, xD_5) while B can start in 1st, 2nd or 3rd period (variables xB_1, xB_2, xB_3) (Fig. 7.61).

Here, the precedence restrictions would be taken care of by including the following two constraints $B < E$ and $A < D$:

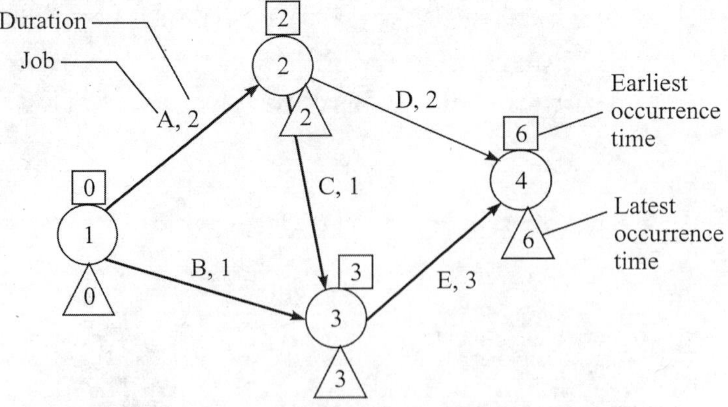

Fig. 7.60 A sample network.

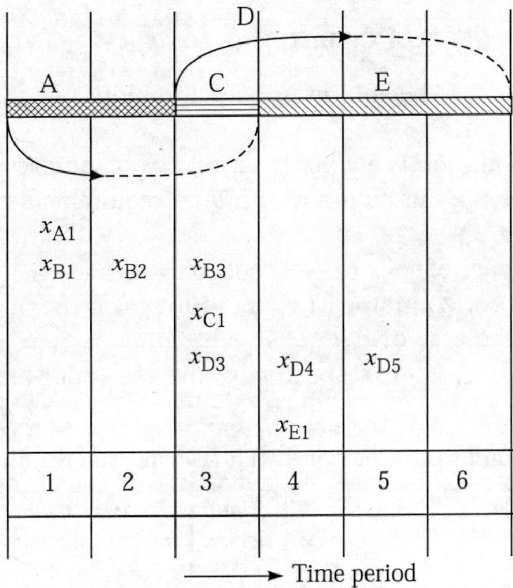

Fig. 7.61 Schedule showing critical and non-critical activities.

The constraint $B < E$ implies
Finish time of $B \leq$ start time of E

$0 \times x_{B_1} + 1 \times x_{B_2} + 2 \times x_{B_3} + 1$ (duration of activity B) ≤ 3 (start time of successor E)

Similarly the constraint $A < D$ implies
Start time of $D \geq$ finish time of A

$2 \times x_{D_3} + 3 \times x_{D_4} + 4 \times x_{D_5} \geq 2$ (finish time of A)

The limited resource allocation problem

Here again we define integer variables $x_{it} = 1, 0$, depending on whether a job is started in period t. The objective now is to minimize project duration T, subject to resource availability, precedence and job completion constraints which have been developed above. Now, however, R is specified and the objective is to minimize project duration T in the above formulation.

If we take some planning horizon H (which guarantees the feasibility of the problem) $\sum txlt + dl \leq T$ (for l belonging to the set of last jobs)

With the inclusion of these constraints the objective function may be stated as

Min $Z = T$
Subject to
Activity completion
Resource consumption and
Precedence restrictions

7.7.2 Task Splitting Permitted

If we allow the tasks to be split in unit duration jobs, we may define a variable x_{it} as follows:

x_{it} = 1, if the *i*th, job is active in period *t*, 0 otherwise

Let (d_i, r_i) be the duration and resource requirements respectively of the *i*th job.

N = total number of jobs to be scheduled

T = planning horizon [at least equal to max $(d_1, d_2, \ldots, d_n)$]

Considering the case of five jobs with durations 5, 7, 4, 3, 2 and resource requirements 2, 3, 1, 2, 4, respectively, the relevant variables and data are depicted in Table 7.3.

Table 7.3 Variables with task splitting permitted

Job	*Time period 1*	*Time period 2*	*Time period 3*	*Time period 4*	*Time period 5*	*Time period 6*	*Time period 7*	*Duration*	*Resource*
1	x_{11}	x_{12}	x_{13}	x_{14}	x_{15}	x_{16}	x_{17}	5	2
2	x_{21}	x_{22}	x_{23}	x_{24}	x_{25}	x_{26}	x_{27}	7	3
3	x_{31}	x_{32}	x_{33}	x_{34}	x_{35}	x_{36}	x_{37}	4	1
4	x_{41}	x_{42}	x_{43}	x_{44}	x_{45}	x_{46}	x_{47}	3	2
5	x_{51}	x_{52}	x_{53}	x_{54}	x_{55}	x_{56}	x_{57}	2	4

Constraints may be formulated as given below:

I. Job completion constraints (row sums = duration of the respective job)

$$\Sigma(j = 1,7)\ x_{1j} = 5$$
$$\Sigma(j = 1,7)\ x_{2j} = 7$$
$$\Sigma(j = 1,7)\ x_{3j} = 4$$
$$\Sigma(j = 1,7)\ x_{4j} = 3$$
$$\Sigma(j = 1,7)\ x_{5j} = 2$$

II. Resource consumption constraints

$$\Sigma(\text{i} = 1,5)\ r_i x_{ij} \le R,\ j = 1,\ldots, 7$$

III. Objective function for resource levelling

Minimize R.

Thus, the total number of (0, 1) variables in this formulation is $nT + 1$ (integer variable R) = 35 + 1 = 36 in this case, and the number of constraints is $(n + T)$, that is, 12 in this example.

It is, however, not very convenient to express the minimum project completion time constraint in this formulation. Thus, this formulation is more suited to the resource levelling framework but not directly to the limited resource allocation problem.

7.8 SUMMARY AND CONCLUSIONS

In this chapter, the importance of renewable and non-renewable resources in projects has been emphasized. Consumable or non-renewable resources are handled through resource aggregation and crashing procedures, whilst renewable resources need to be handled by resource levelling or limited resource allocation.

Project crashing by heuristic reasoning has been explained with an example project. A variety of time–cost trade-off functions including linear, convex, concave and discontinuous have been proposed for different situations in practice. A mathematical formulation for the general project crashing problem is proposed with the option of piecewise linearization to handle non-linearity in the cost function.

Fulkerson's network flow procedure based on primal-dual concepts of linear programming for generating the project cost curve is explained with an example.

Limited resource allocation has been contrasted with resource aggregation and resource levelling. Trigger level setting and sum of squares procedures for resource levelling have been discussed. Optimization and heuristic procedures for the solution of the limited resource allocation problem in projects have been compared. Popularity of heuristics in practical applications is owing to their simplicity and intuitive appeal. The comparative performance of eight commonly used heuristics is presented. Wiest's procedure based on three simple heuristics has been discussed and illustrated on a sample problem.

Heuristic algorithms have been proposed to manage and schedule a list of independent tasks. An illustration of the Pareto-Optimal frontier for handling resources and multiple tasks has been included.

Mathematical programming formulations have been proposed for the resource levelling and the resource allocation problem with and without job splitting.

PROBLEMS

1. Distinguish between renewable and non-renewable resources in project management indicating the kinds of procedures used to handle each category.
2. For a small project, the predecessors and the normal and crash times and costs are given in the table below.

Time and cost data

	Job	*Predecessors*	*Normal*		*Crash*	
			Duration (hours)	*Cost* (Rs.)	*Duration* (hours)	*Cost* (Rs.)
A	Remove and disassemble motor	—	8	80	6	94
B	Clear and paint frame	*A*	7	40	4	70
C	Rewind armature	*A*	12	100	4	196
D	Replace bearings	*A*	9	70	5	102
E	Assemble and install motor	*B, C, D*	6	50	6	50

If the time–cost trade-off function is linear, determine the total cost duration efficient frontier using heuristic reasoning. Assume an indirect project cost of Rs. 20/hour.

3. Use Fulkerson's network flow procedure to generate the project cost curve for the project given in Question 2.
4. As the project overhead cost increases, the minimum total cost of the project would tend to shift from normal to crash. Plot this optimum (duration and total cost) for varying values of the project overhead cost for the feasible range of project durations for the project in Question 2.
5. In the project of Question 2 assume that the jobs can be done at either normal or crash, but not at any pace in between. Plot the relationship between project completion time and minimum total project cost. (Solve by path enumeration and heuristic reasoning.)
6. In the project of Question 2 assume that a linear cost–time relationship exists between job duration and cost and that a job may be scheduled not only at the normal and crash duration but at any integer duration in between. With overhead costs of Rs. 25/hour, plot the cost–time relationship.
7. For the project network with the following data, develop the complete project-time cost efficient frontier

Arc (I, j)	L_{ij}	U_{ij}	a_{ij}
(1, 2)	4	6	8
(1, 3)	4	8	9
(1, 4)	3	5	3
(2, 4)	3	3	∞
(2, 5)	3	5	4
(3, 6)	8	12	20
(4, 6)	5	8	5
(5, 6)	6	6	∞

Use Fulkerson's crashing algorithm.

8. For the A-O-N project network shown below in the figure, answer the following questions:

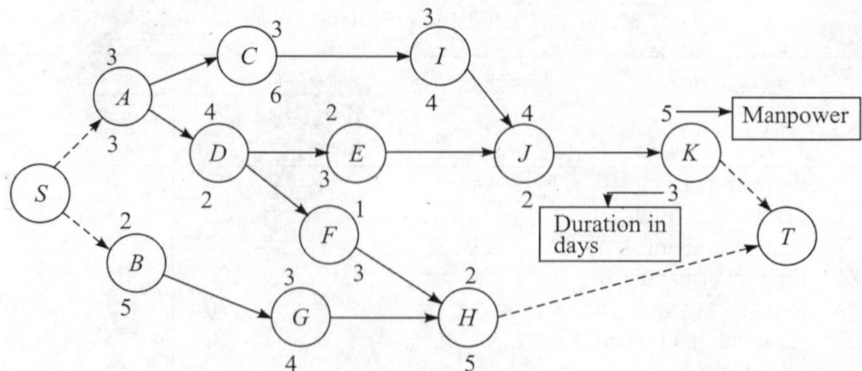

(a) Using a forward pass on the network determine the critical path.
(b) Determine node slacks and all the four activity floats.
(c) Draw a Gantt chart showing the early and late start and finish times of all activities.
(d) For both the early and late start schedules, develop the resource profiles.
(e) Determine a schedule for a resource availability of 7 men daily and the corresponding bound on the project duration. How do these values change if the resource availability is only 6 men daily?

9. For the project with the following data obtain the best levelled resource profile using the procedure of Burgess and Killebrew. Compare the initial and final sum of squares of manpower levels.

Activity	*Predecessor*	*Duration* (days)	*Daily manpower requirements*
A_1	—	4	6
A_2	—	2	4
A_3	A_1	1	3
A_4	A_1	6	2
A_5	A_2, A_3	3	5
A_6	A_4, A_5	4	3
A_7	A_4, A_5	2	8
A_8	A_6	1	5

10. The project below has to be scheduled for execution. What is the minimum time in which it can be completed assuming unlimited supply of manpower? If only 10 men were available what is the minimum bound on the duration? Using Wiest's heuristics for resource allocation determine the minimum duration schedule for the project.

Job	*Predecessors*	*Duration* (days)	*Manpower needed*
A	—	4	8
B	*A*	6	6
C	*A*	2	8
D	*B*	5	4
E	*C*	3	7
F	*D, E*	6	4
G	*C*	5	9

11. Formulate the resource levelling problem for the project of Question 10 as an integer linear program assuming (a) no job splitting and

(b) job splitting permissible. Solve by using any standard integer programming code.

12. A set of 7 independent jobs has the following durations and manpower requirements: Job 1 2 3 4 5 6 7
Time (days) 10 4 6 2 12 20 15
Manpower 4 6 2 8 3 9 12
Find the minimum possible project duration to complete all the tasks and level the resource profile. What is the minimum resource peak and the corresponding schedule of doing the jobs?
13. For the set of jobs in Question 12, determine the minimum cost schedule if only 12 men were available.

CHAPTER

8

Project Monitoring and Control

8.1 INTRODUCTION

Once the project plan is finalized and the schedule is developed, the important stage of project execution begins, where work is done as per the intended plan. This involves the proper utilization of resources of men, equipment and materials to execute the job plan so as to **maintain time schedules, minimize wastages and cost overruns and maintain the requisite quality specifications**. It is in this regard that project monitoring and control is crucial during the implementation phase of the project. The task of the project manager is to be able to balance and maintain a reasonable check on these three major project attributes. The earned value technique often referred to as PERT/Cost has been and still is one of the most popular methods of project monitoring and control.

More recently, the critical chain method of project monitoring based on Goldratt's theory of constraints has also come into prominent use with its emphasis on aggressive project estimates and redistributing project and resource buffers. Both these approaches are discussed in this chapter.

8.2 PROJECT MONITORING AND CONTROL USING PERT/COST

Some of the salient features of the PERT/Cost system, developed by the Department of Defence and NASA, USA in 1962, are as follows:

- It is primarily a network cost accounting system.
- The key concept used is that costs are to be measured and controlled primarily on a project basis rather than according to the functional organization of a firm.
- Activities/groups of activities are micro-cost centres and this system advocates that all measurements of progress be based on this philosophy.
- The responsibility for expenditure should coincide with the responsibility for managing the activities that give rise to the expenditure.

- It seems strange that one who sanctions the expenditure has nothing to do with activity implementation and actual cost control. This kind of attitude and organization leads to unnecessary bureaucracy and delays.

The notion of work packages is central to PERT/Cost.

- A project may be divided into work packages in various ways.
- A division into too many small activities
  - may facilitate detailed planning and scheduling.
  - is not convenient for cost control purposes.
- A division into very large chunks
  - deprives the project of necessary detail.
  - is not conducive to effective monitoring and control.

In keeping with the above guidelines the recommended work package should be

- Manageable in size—neither too small nor too big*.
- One whose responsibility can be clearly identified.
- Still small enough and manageable for planning and control purposes.

The assumption is generally made in PERT/Cost that the expenditure on a work package is uniform throughout its duration. This may be reasonable as a number of activities are included in the work package.

If, however, this is not reasonable in a certain situation, the work package could be redefined. For instance, it may be logical to assume that a large portion of the expenditure occurs in the beginning of a contract when advance payments are to be made, followed by a lean period where a maintenance allowance is adequate followed by a peak in expenditure towards the close of the contract when all the final bills are to be settled. The actual expenditure profile which might be non-uniform may be approximated by a series of uniformly distributed work packages in series with almost uniform expenditure as indicated in Fig. 8.1.

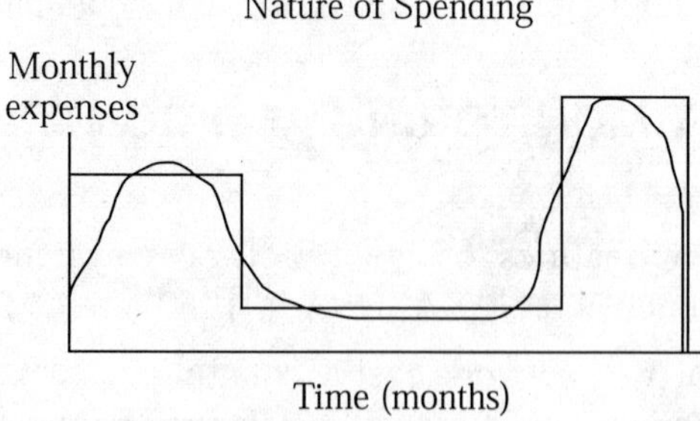

Fig. 8.1 Actual and approximated expenditure profiles.

* The DOD/NASA guide considered $100,000 worth and 3 months duration as appropriate, but these figures depend on the context. The project total scope, cost and duration should be appropriately considered in defining the work packages. A major activity or a sub-network of the overall project may be considered as a work package.

8.2.1 The Early Start vis-à-vis the Late Start Schedule

Consider a project shown in Fig. 8.2, in which the cost and duration data is summarized in Table 8.1. With the assumption of a uniform rate of spending, the cost per period for the project is obtained by dividing the cost of each work

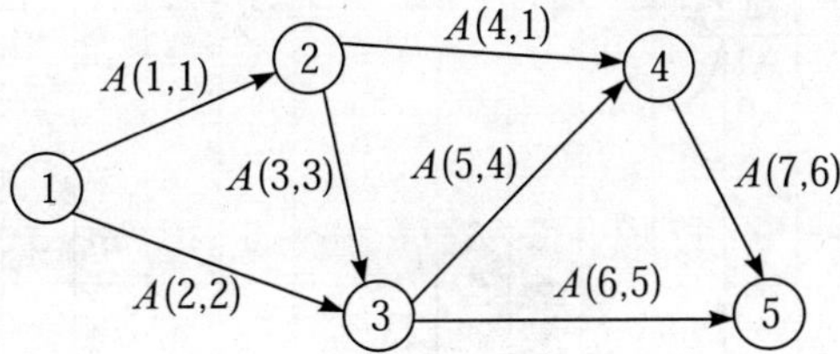

Fig. 8.2 Sample project.

Table 8.1 Time and cost data

Activity	*Time in months*	*Cost* (Rs.)	*Cost/month* (Rs. in thousand)
A_1	1	5,000	5
A_2	2	8,000	4
A_3	3	9,000	3
A_4	1	10,000	10
A_5	4	8,000	2
A_6	5	20,000	4
A_7	6	36,000	6

package by its duration. Then by a simple application of a forward and backward pass both the early and late start schedules could be computed. These are shown as time-scaled networks in Figs. 8.3 and 8.4, respectively. Also shown at the bottom of each of these figures are the period and cumulative expenditures obtained by aggregating the costs of different activities in progress in each period. It is easy to observe that both the early start and late start schedules incur the same total cost in the long run, but the timing of the expenditure varies. Considering the time value of money, the late start schedule would require a lower NPV and hence a lesser loan from a financial institution as compared to the early start schedule. This difference, however, is compensated by the fact that there are floats for delays of non-critical activities which can be utilized as buffers in case of inordinate delays in activities in the early start schedule, whereas in the late start schedule all activities are critical in the sense that a delay in any one would lead to a delay in the project. Thus, the choice of a schedule between an early start and the late start should be done with caution. In situations where risks are high an early start schedule offers maximum security. However, in situations where vendor and environmental reliability is high, as happens in a just-in-time environment, the late start schedule would offer economic benefits.

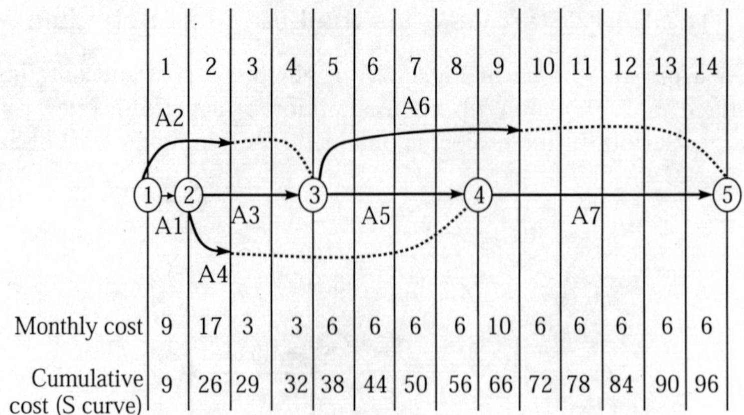

Fig. 8.3 Early start time-scaled network.

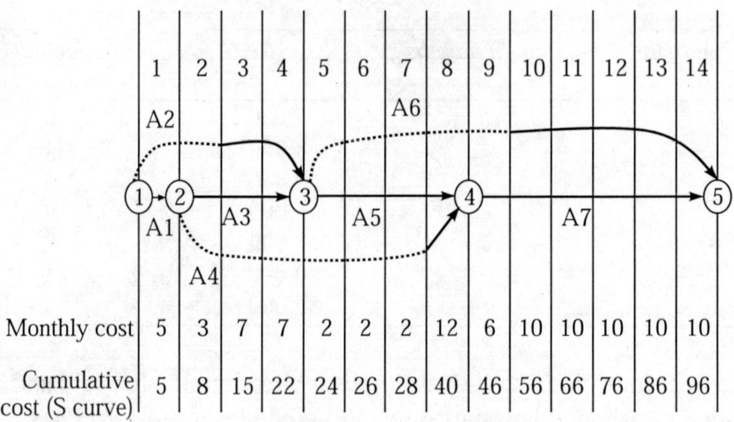

Fig. 8.4 Late start time-scaled network.

The patterns of cumulative expenditure planned for the project for both an early start and a late start schedule are shown in Figs. 8.3 and 8.4, respectively. Any schedule in between these limits may be chosen as the planned schedule for implementation. Because of their similarity to the letter S, cumulative cost curves are commonly referred to as S curves. It may be mentioned that there is a very large number of schedules that may be chosen as the budgeted plan, within the following framework:

Start time of an activity = Early start + α(total float), where $0 \leq \alpha \leq 1$ with the additional restriction that precedence relations for all activities be met. This implies that when activities on a sub-critical path are in series, utilizing the float of succeeding activities would deprive the preceding activities from that share of the total float.

Thus, $\alpha = 1$ represents a late start schedule for the activity suitable when perfect reliability exists. Similarly, $\alpha = 0$ represents an early start schedule that provides maximum buffer against risky situations. The decision maker may choose a suitable value of α for all activities based on his judgment and may finalize the initial budgeted schedule and cost curve.

8.2.2 The Earned Value Approach to Project Monitoring

As the project progresses information on the following three attributes is collected at each review period as shown in Fig. 8.5.

(a) The budgeted cost and value curve represented by curve *A*
(b) The actual cost of work performed (ACWP) represented by curve *B*
(c) The budgeted cost of work performed (BCWP) represented by curve *C*

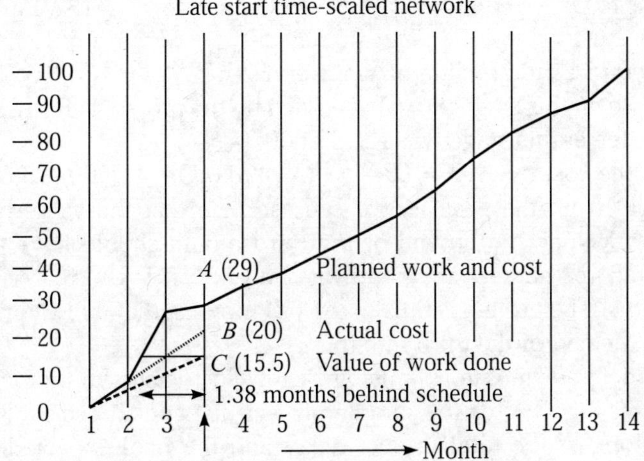

Fig. 8.5 Earned value concept (S curves).

At any point of time *t*, when the project is monitored, the curve *A* gives the value of work that should have been performed by that time. The actual work performed as determined from site conditions is given on curve *C*. Thus, if curve *C* is below curve *A*, we can conclude that we are running behind schedule. A horizontal projection from curve *C* to the point where it intersects curve *A* gives how much the project is lagging from its schedule. Moreover in accomplishing the work *C*, the actual cost incurred is *B*.

Hence the cost overrun = $(B - C)/C \times 100$ as a percentage

Schedule lag (or lead) = Horizontal distance from *C* to *A* (lag if *C* is to the right of *A* and lead if *C* is to the left of *A*)

An illustration of these computations for the network of Fig. 8.2 is given below. Suppose the early start schedule of Fig. 8.3 is chosen as the budgeted cost and value curve (*A*) for purposes of implementation. Consider a status report of the project taken at the end of three months.

According to the plan, the budgeted cost of the planned work from the *S* curve should be Rs. 29,000 at the end of the third month (***point A***). However, the actual figures at site may be different.

Actual money spent to date (***point B***) = Rs. 20,000.

Suppose, the following information on the budgeted cost of actual work performed (BCWP) from a site report is as follows:
C

Activities scheduled to be done	*Actual status*	*Budgeted cost*
(i) A_1 to be completed	Completed	Rs. 5000
(ii) A_2 to be completed	$\frac{1}{2}$ Complete	Rs. 4000
(iii) A_4 to be completed	20% Complete	Rs. 2000
(iv) A_3 to be $\frac{2}{3}$ completed	$\frac{1}{2}$ Complete	Rs. 4500

Thus, ***point C***, total value of work done (BCWP) = Rs. 15,500

Therefore, at this stage the value earned by the project is Rs 15,500, whereas the target value at this stage was Rs. 29,000.

Hence, the cost overrun = $(B - C)/C$ = (20,000 – 15,500)/15,500 = 29.03%

Similarly from the *S* curve we can estimate that the value of Rs. 15,500 worth of work done by the end of the third month should have actually been accomplished in the second month at the end of 1 + (26 – 15.5)/(26 – 9) = 1.62 months. The project is thus (3 – 1.62) months, that is, 1.38 months behind schedule at the end of the third month.

This concept of monitoring using PERT/Cost is shown by the three curves *A*, *B* and *C* in Fig. 8.5 for the sample project just considered.

Projections of the total project delay and the final expected cost may be made from the *S* curves by extrapolating the curves *C* and *B* respectively to the completion of the project. Wherever curve *C* is expected to hit the 100% of the original budgeted cost and value curve would give an estimate of the project completion time. And where the actual cost curve *B* hits, the project completion gives an estimate of the overrun in cost (Fig. 8.6).

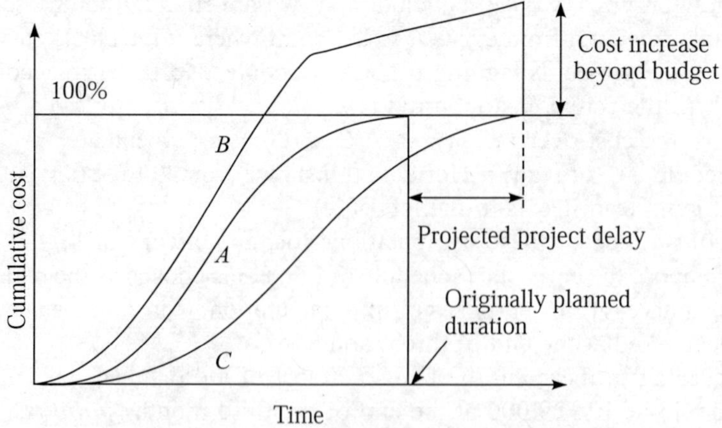

Fig. 8.6 Projection of project delay and cost overrun.

These indices give an overall idea of how the project is performing. In a large project, some activities could be ahead of schedule, others on or behind schedule but the earned value concept gives the project manager an idea of how his entire project on the whole is performing with regard to both time and cost. Since both performances on schedule and cost are important, the cost and schedule performance indices can be computed as

Cost performance index (CPI) = C/B

Schedule performance index (SPI) = C/A

This information could be tracked on a graph (Fig. 8.7) and the performance of the project over time could be seen as a movement in one of the four possible regions of performance on project schedule and cost.

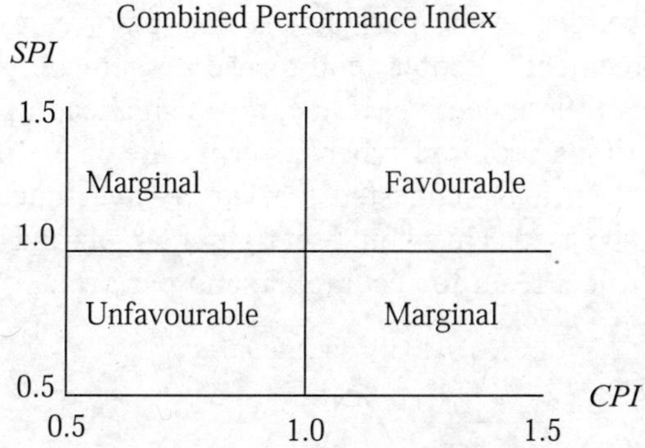

Fig. 8.7 Forecast of project completion cost and time.

Once these indices are computed, they can be used to identify the reasons for the overruns in cost and time and the culprit activities can be spotted to take corrective action. It is important to mention here that no monitoring device can replace the judicious corrective actions of a project manager to keep the project on course. They, however, provide the signals for a manager to intervene and help him take the right corrective measures for the defaulting activities in time so that further delays and overruns can be prevented.

8.3 THE CRITICAL CHAIN FRAMEWORK OF GOLDRATT

This concept of project management based on Goldratt's theory of constraints employs aggressive time estimates for individual activities and abandons the conventional milestone concept in project execution. Instead it focuses on both the time and resource requirements to consider the *critical chain* rather than the critical path (which is based only on the time) and makes use of centrally allocated resource and time buffers to drastically attempt cuts in project lead times.

The problems common to all projects are the high probability of budget overruns, time overruns and *many times* compromising the content.

The typical reasons for project delays can be classified as official and unofficial reasons.

Commonly given official reasons include

- vendor/subcontractor not cooperating
- materials, machines not reaching in time
- rework for quality, etc.

Some of the unofficial reasons for delays may include

- personal lapses
- preoccupation with too many tasks
- inadequate experience, etc.

8.3.1 Aggressive Time Estimates for Activities

Uncertainties embedded in the projects are the major causes of what may be called "mis-management". People tend to use pessimistic (75–80%) estimates for jobs as there is little incentive, if any, to finish ahead of time, but there are plenty of explanations required when projects are late. In the critical chain framework (Fig. 8.8), it is suggested that aggressive time estimates (50% or median estimates) be used. This would set tighter targets and exert psychological pressure on the project team to accomplish and perform.

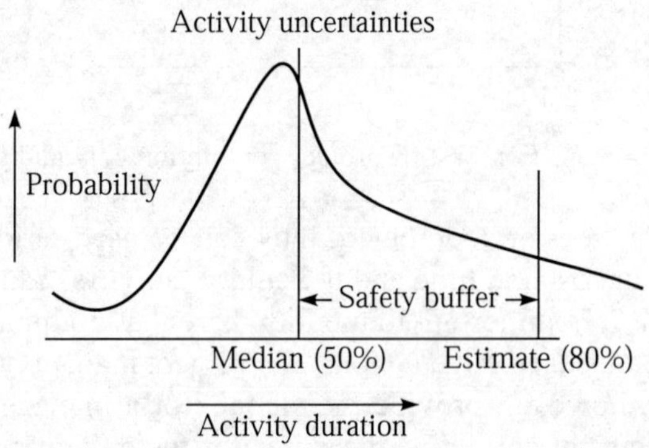

Fig. 8.8 Cost and schedule performance indices.

8.3.2 Inadequacy of Early and Late Start Schedules

The inadequacies of both the early and late start schedules are recognized in the critical chain methodology.

- In early start the project leader has to concentrate on a large number of activities to begin with. Thus he loses focus.
- In late start all activities are critical and focussing is not possible at all.
- We have to find the mechanism that will enable the project leader to *focus.*

Three mechanisms that are typically employed to add safety in conventional project management (or to waste that safety) are:

- ***Student syndrome***: There is no rush, so start at the last minute. There is a tendency to postpone the tasks which are not immediately due, which forces one to adopt a last minute strategy for doing the tasks. This tendency is referred to as the Student syndrome and results in laxity in the execution of the project activities.
- ***Multi-tasking***: Often considered to be a valuable and time-saving strategy has no real benefits as Fig. 8.9 shows. If three tasks *A*, *B* and *C* are done sequentially then these tasks are over at times 10, 20 and 30, respectively as shown assuming that each task has a duration of 10 units. However, if multi-tasking is done by splitting the tasks into two parts each and parts of the tasks are undertaken as shown in the figure, there is no saving in the total time, but the completion of individual tasks is delayed. The first task is completed at time 20, rather than at 10 as was the case without multi-tasking. This kills lead time available to subsequent jobs and is thus wasteful.

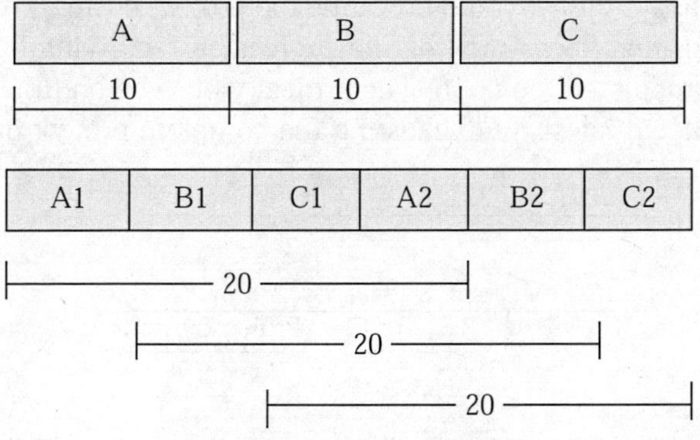

Fig. 8.9 Multi-tasking.

- ***Dependencies between steps***: As Fig. 8.10 shows the milestone concept causes delays to accumulate and advances to be wasted. The early starts are wasted and the largest delay is passed on to the next step.

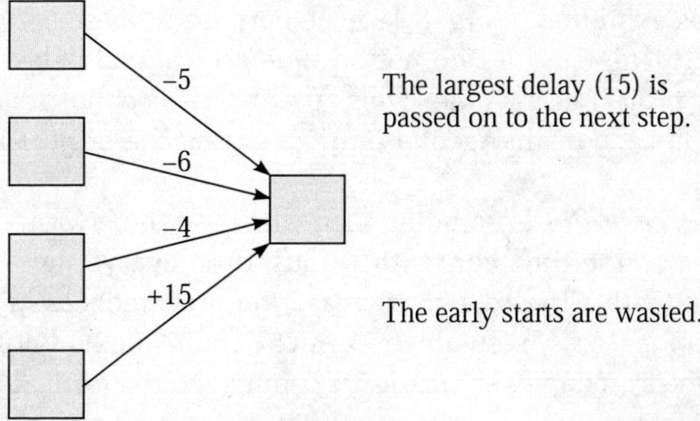

Fig. 8.10 Wastage of early starts.

These discrepancies are handled in the critical chain methodology by using aggressive time estimates (there is a 50–50 chance of accomplishing the activity in these times) so that wastages are minimized. Moreover, a roadrunner concept rather than the milestone concept is used, meaning that whenever the predecessor activities at an event are completed the next activities are undertaken even if the milestone time has not been achieved, and by eliminating the notion of individual buffers for activities by including a centralized project buffer which is placed at the end so that any activity could borrow or add to it depending on whether it is running late or early. This buffer serves as a bank balance which could be shared by all the activities so that early activities on the path contribute their share and their benefits are passed on rather than wasted.

8.3.3 Various Buffers for Project Monitoring

- ***Project buffer*** (for the critical path): The project buffer is placed at the end of the project as shown in Fig. 8.11. The individual delays in critical activities would consume the project buffer. Project monitoring would thus keep track of the project buffer giving a warning if it is being depleted too soon. The project would be on time if the project is completed latest by exhausting the complete project buffer.

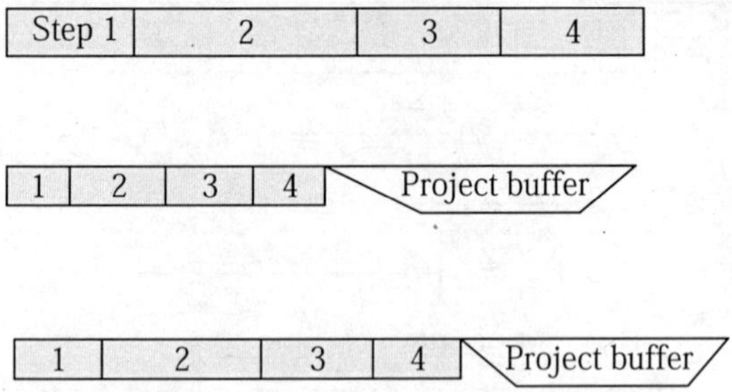

Fig. 8.11 Notion of project buffer.

- ***Feeding buffer*** (for non-critical feeding paths): For paths feeding into the critical path a feeding buffer is placed at the end of each sub-critical path as exhibited in Fig. 8.12. The purpose of these is to ensure that the non-critical activities do not become critical and delay the completion of the project as a whole. Thus, after the project buffer an eye has to be kept on each of the feeding buffers during the project implementation stage.
- ***Resource buffer*** (reminding men who have to perform critical tasks, so that when the time comes they must drop everything and work on the critical path): In order to increase the preparedness of the task force, indications are given in the critical chain methodology to have the resources (manpower) ready to commence the critical activities when they become due. This ensures that the critical path is not delayed for want of resources.

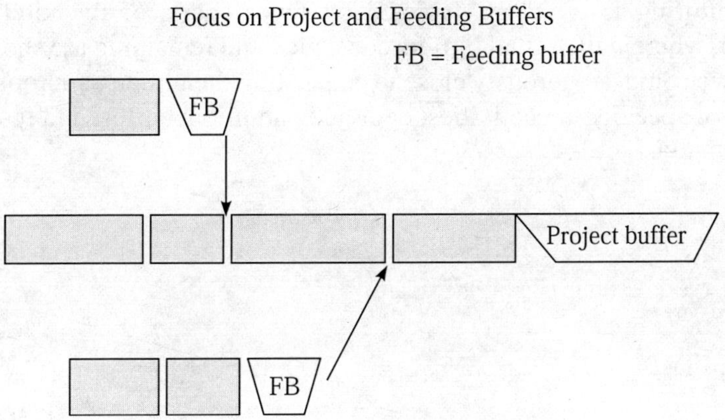

Focus on Project and Feeding Buffers

FB = Feeding buffer

FB

Project buffer

FB

Fig. 8.12 Project and feeding buffers.

It may be indicated that the notion of a critical chain employs the longest path with both time and resource restrictions. The conventional critical path would be a lower bound on the time for the project. Owing to the limited availability of resources the duration could be longer (recall the limited resource allocation problem considered in Chapter 7) as shown in Fig. 8.13. Thus, the critical chain has to be monitored and not the conventional critical path.

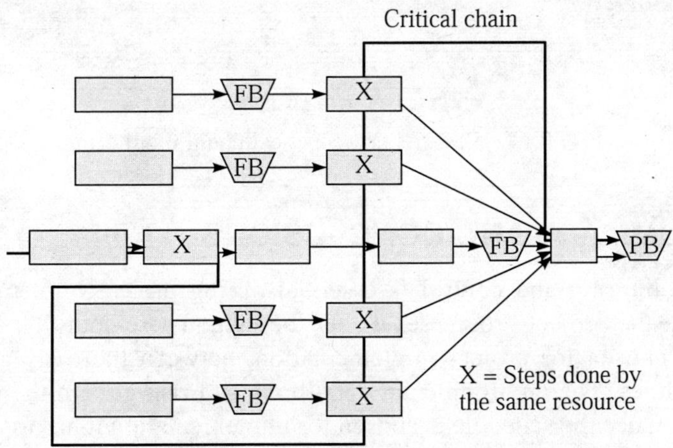

Fig. 8.13 The critical chain.

8.3.4 How to Measure Project Progress?

Unlike the earned value approach, where the value of the entire work done including both critical and non-critical activities is recorded and monitored, in the critical chain methodology monitoring is done *only on the critical chain* by asking at every review date the question:

What percentage of the critical path have we already completed?

This is answered by a focus on project and feeding buffers.

Monitoring is typically depicted by fever charts of the kind shown in Fig. 8.14, wherein the actual buffers consumed and remaining are shown. At any stage if we come dangerously close to exhausting the buffers, appropriate action in terms of speeding up activities, deploying additional effort and resources has to be initiated.

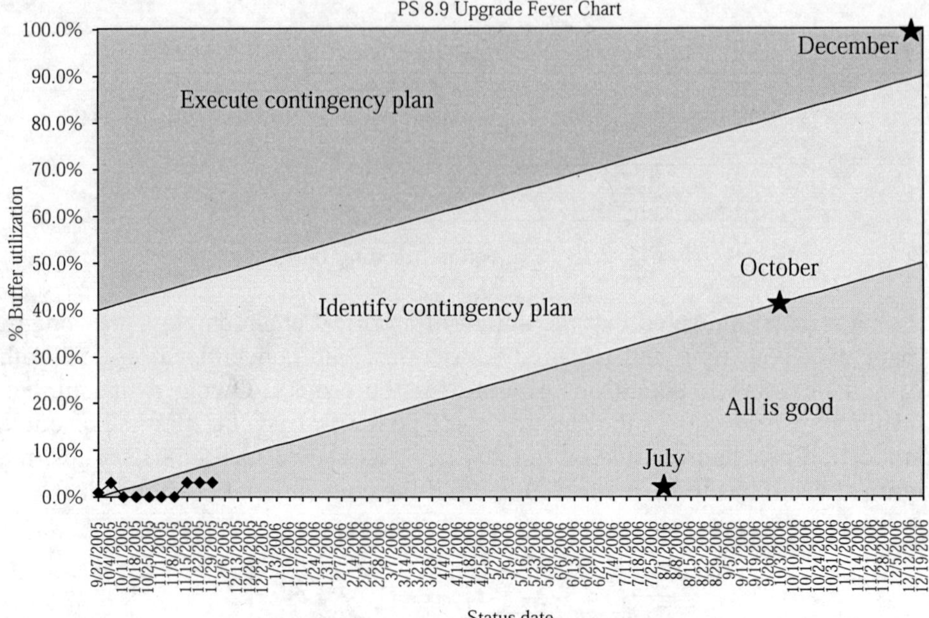

Fig. 8.14 Fever chart in critical chain monitoring.

8.4 SUMMARY AND CONCLUSIONS

Project monitoring and control is essential during project implementation to ensure that the project progresses as per the plan. There could be a variety of schedules chosen for project implementation, between the early and the late start schedules. The environmental conditions and risk govern the schedule to be chosen. Once the schedule is chosen for implementation it has to be followed up by an appropriate monitoring mechanism. In this chapter, two monitoring schemes have been discussed.

PERT/Cost which is based on the notion of cost accounting of work packages uses the earned value approach and utilizes the *S* curve to record and predict time and cost overruns for the project as a whole.

The Critical Chain methodology utilizing The Theory of Constraints proposed by Goldratt has also been outlined. This monitoring scheme in a nutshell is summarized by the following important features:

1. Monitoring by critical path
2. Change of attitude (no false alarms)

3. No milestones any more
4. Trim times to 50% (from 80 to 90%) so people are not sure whether they can finish the step on time
5. Reduction of multi-tasking
6. People more focussed
7. Utilization of resource and feeding buffers in fever charts for project monitoring

PROBLEMS

1. The project with the following data is to be implemented:

Activity	*Duration* (months)	*Cost* (thousand Rs.)
A (1, 2)	4	8
B (1, 3)	3	9
C (2, 3)	2	10
D (2, 4)	4	12
E (3, 4)	5	15
F (3, 5)	6	12
G (4, 5)	1	10

(a) Compare the pattern of expenditure for both an early start and a late start schedule.

(b) If the rate of interest is 12% per annum, compute the NPV for both the early and the late start schedules.

(c) The late start schedule is chosen for implementation and the progress is monitored after 6 months. The following status is observed:

Activity *A*: 50% complete
Activity *B*: completed
Other activities: not yet started
Total spending to date: Rs. 18,000

What is time and cost overrun?

Compute the cost and schedule performance indices and show the performance of the project on a consolidated front.

(d) Assuming that the durations and costs of the project remain unaltered, what is your projection of the revised project completion time and cost from now onwards?

(e) If you feel that the original estimates of time and cost for activities were optimistic and that the remaining durations of all activities would have to be scaled up by 25% as compared to the original estimates, whilst the estimates of cost would go up by 50%, what would be your projection of the project completion time and the phasing of expenditure?

2. The project with the following data has activities which may be considered uniformly distributed between a lower and an upper limit:

Activity	*Immediate predecessors*	*Lower bound on duration* (days)	*Upper bound on duration* (days)
A	—	10	14
B	—	14	20
C	*A*	20	30
D	*B, C*	6	10
E	*A*	12	16
F	*D, E*	15	25

(a) Assuming an 80% estimate for each activity compute the critical path.
(b) If 50% estimates are utilized for each activity, what would be the critical path length?
(c) Assuming that the project target completion date is the one computed in (a), add the project and feeding buffers at the appropriate places using the critical chain framework.
(d) The project is monitored on day 30 and it is found that activities *A* and *C* are completed, while *B* is 50% complete. Comment on the status of the project and the various feeding buffers on a fever chart.

3. A project has the following precedence relations:

Activity	*A*	*B*	*C*	*D*	*E*	*F*	*G*	*H*
Predecessors	—	*E*	*A*	*G*	*C*	*B, D*	—	*F*
Duration (days)	14	10	2	8	6	10	6	12
Cost (Rs.)	140	100	144	96	60	50	72	120

The project is planned for implementation using the late start schedule. After 40 days, activities *A, C* and *G* are completed and E is half complete.

(a) Determine the budgeted cost and value of the work at the end of 40 days.
(b) What is the actual cost incurred at the end of 40 days?
(c) What is the value of work accomplished at the end of 40 days?
(d) Determine the time and cost overruns at the end of 40 days?
(e) Compute the cost and schedule performance indices.

4. In the above project of Question 3, if the durations of the remaining activities were estimated to increase by 25%, what would be the estimate of project completion time and cost after the initial monitoring at 40 days?

5. How is the notion of a work package relevant in PERT/Cost? What are the considerations determining the size and cost of a typical work package in a project?
6. Distinguish between monitoring and control. Is PERT/Cost a monitoring package or a control package for a project? List typical control actions that may be initiated after the receipt of a project monitoring report.
7. Compare the relative merits and demerits of the earned value method with the critical chain methodology for project monitoring.

CHAPTER

9

Computers, e-Markets and Their Role in Project Management

9.1 INTRODUCTION

With changing technologies, free global trade and a perennial competitive race among individuals, societies and nations at large, it is becoming increasingly imperative to use and develop appropriate technologies for the safety, growth and benefit of mankind at large.

The advent of computers and the consequent e-markets available on the World Wide Web have simplified life and provided man with the material comforts he has been dreaming of. Now that this is almost a reality there still exists a gnawing fear in the responsible managers and custodians of today about the sincerity of purpose of potential opponents.

The solution to this state of affairs lies very clearly in the development of a "universal conscience" totally devoid of any sinister or evil intentions to harm any one else. This can clearly be achieved by a purging of the human mind, especially for the people at the helm of affairs, who are entrusted with the task of managing their respective organizations.

This chapter reviews briefly the available computer packages for project management, e.g. Primavera and Microsoft Project (for latest versions consult the World Wide Web). The pros and cons of available software packages in project management are compared and directions for future developments are also explored.

One significant development in the offing seems to be the advent of Quantum Computers, which could revolutionize the project management scenario in the race between hardware and software development. There is a global competition today encouraging faster and miniaturized computer development (refer to Vishal Sahni, *Quantum Computing*, Tata-McGraw Hill, 2007). The changing paradigms may be depicted as shown in Fig. 9.1.

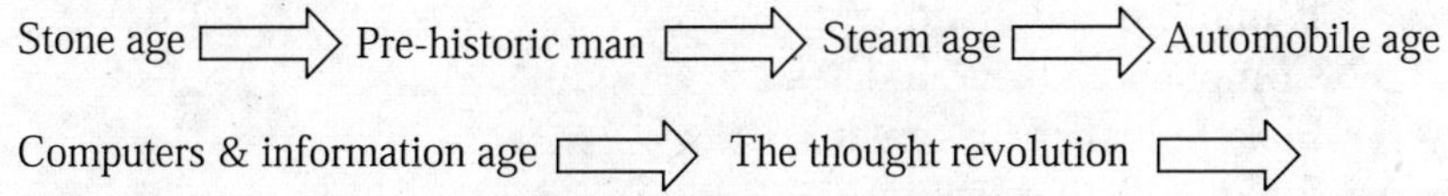

Fig. 9.1 Changing paradigms with the ages.

A quote by one of the famous and richest entrepreneurs of the age, Bill Gates, one of the developers of Microsoft, reads as under:

"If the 1980s were about quality, and the 1990s were about reengineering, then the 2000s will be about velocity. About how quickly the nature of business will change. About how quickly business will be transacted. ... These changes will occur because of a disarmingly simple idea: the flow of digital information." (Bill Gates, *Business @ The Speed of Thought Using a Digital Nervous System, 1999*)

Inspired by such statements, the role of seamless information management in management of any system cannot be overemphasized. And we hope to see a phenomenal growth in the area of applications of both hardware and software in revolutionizing the future computer and the way we live.

9.2 THE GROWING USE OF COMPUTERS IN PROJECT MANAGEMENT

With the increasing usage of computers and Internet, project management is witnessing changes in scope, speed and economy never seen before. Computer usage varies from basic e-mailing to project management software to project management websites (Fig. 9.2).

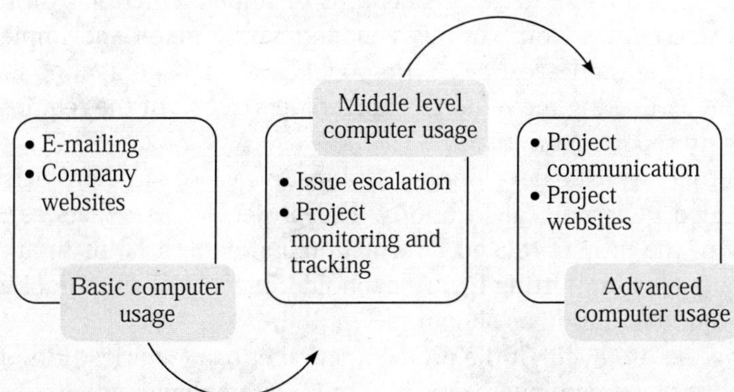

Fig. 9.2 The usage level of computers in project management.

With the availability of computers at every stage of project management, it is not necessary for the project manager to be physically available at the project site. Project managers and stakeholders increasingly work from remote locations and are able to come together for important meetings and consultations. The usage of computers include

- E-mailing and chatting
- Company website updates
- Stakeholder management
- Stakeholders selection
- E-procurement
- E-marketing
- Project communication
- Project management website development
- Issue resolution and escalation
- Project monitoring and tracking
- Project delivery reports
- Monthly MIS
- Outsourcing
- Vendor development

With increasing use of information technology, there is greater liaison between stakeholders, consultants and clients for smooth implementation of the project. Project communication, e.g. website development, regular feedbacks to the clients and other stakeholders, and monthly MIS, is more smooth and timely. Many self-generated reports are being used for project monitoring and tracking. Daily and fortnightly progress monitoring, and website tracking of the project are a common feature of modern project management.

Another aspect of e-project management is regular audit of the system through regular reports and studies. The audit of the quality of implementation (for quality standards) can be done on an ongoing basis and not after the complete installation is done. The best in class implementation can be insured by comparing and using the best standards of implementation available on the Internet. Price quotes from various vendors can be taken and implementation can be ensured at the lowest price. Regional level management of stakeholders can be done by making the regional stakeholders aware of the requirements and taking timely reports from them.

The project website development is done in case of large projects, spanning over extended geographical locations. The project website acts as the central repository of the project-related information and data. It helps in all aspects of project management, starting form stakeholder management to tracking to issue escalation and resolution as shown in Fig. 9.3.

During the life cycle of the project computer usage varies (Fig. 9.4). At the start of the project, computers are used in effective development of the Report for Feasibility of the Project (RFP) and project scope definition. The usage of computer at the conceiving stage of the project is restricted to typing of RFP. More effective usage of computers starts when the decision of stakeholders and vendors is done. The rating of vendors is done using the predefined rating standards. Once the vendors are decided and the implementation of the project starts, computers are used in tracking, project communication, etc.

Project communic- ation
Stakeholder management
Reporting and tracking
Project website

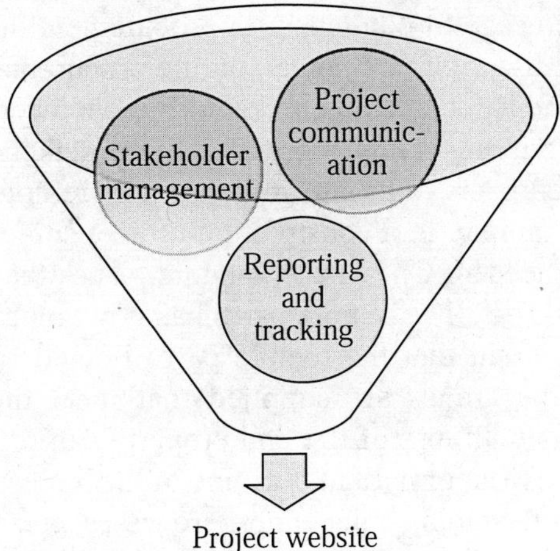

Fig. 9.3 Usage of project website.

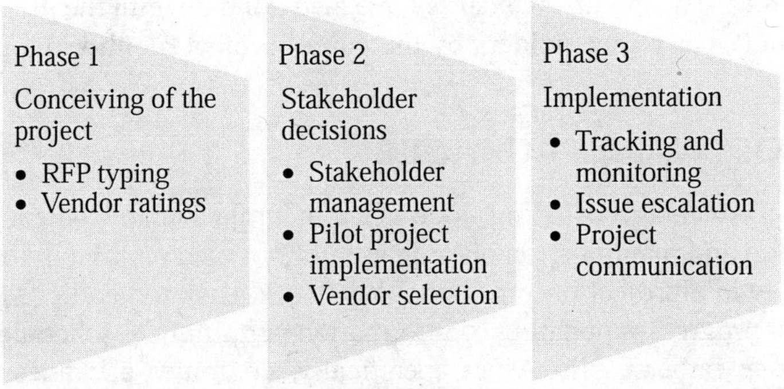

Phase 1
Conceiving of the project
• RFP typing
• Vendor ratings
Phase 2
Stakeholder decisions
• Stakeholder management
• Pilot project implementation
• Vendor selection
Phase 3
Implementation
• Tracking and monitoring
• Issue escalation
• Project communication

Fig. 9.4 Computers in various stages of the project life-cycle.

Project communication plays a significant role in project management and project success. Project communication involves pamphlets, project status reports, etc. Computers play an important role in project communication. Figure 9.5 depicts the usage of computers in various aspects of project communication.

Public awareness
• Implementation status
• Issue escalation and resolution
Peripheral stakeholder awareness
• Pamphlets
• Implementation status
• Issue escalation
Stakeholder awareness
• Status reports
• Monthly MIS
• Issue resolution

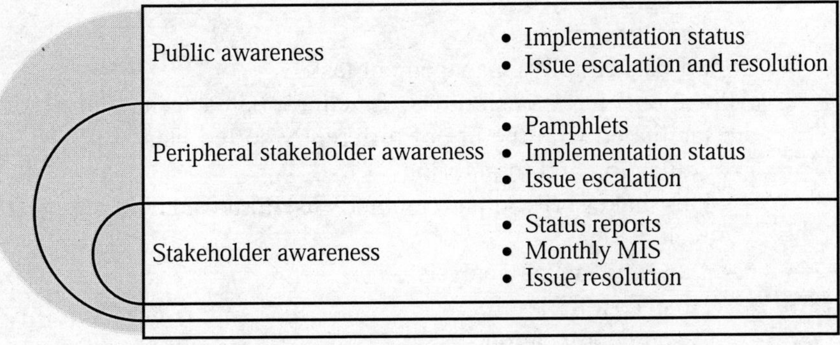

Fig. 9.5 Communication in projects.

e-Market is the usage of computers in procurement of goods and services. With the increasing usage of computers, online procurement is the need of the hour. The procurement includes using remote manpower, remotely available resources and outsourcing. Now more and more stakeholders have become the peripheral stakeholders, who are in some way remotely connected to the project team. For example, in a construction project some specialized forklifts and cranes may be needed. One of the vendors places the order with a remote supplier of such forklifts. The remote party has now got a stake in the project. It is extremely important that the remote party is made aware of the project requirements and the cranes are supplied that meet the quality standards. Otherwise, accidents with loss of life and property can result.

Outsourcing is also an important outcome of the increasing computer usage. Now the manpower, technology, machines, processes, etc. can all be outsourced to a remote party, which is not directly connected to the project. The increasing stress on outsourcing means greater usage of remotely available technologies and resources. The quality standards have also gone up with the greater training of the remote party stakeholders by the parent project monitoring group.

9.3 SOFTWARE PACKAGES

The major advantage of using computers in project management is that the organization and manipulation of large volumes of data pertaining to the variety of activities in a project becomes convenient and easy to handle. Moreover, as the project progresses updating of information pertaining to schedules and costs can be done rather easily. More specifically, computer packages for project management help in

- Easy sorting of activities
  This sorting could be based on criteria depending on the situation at hand. The following are some of the commonly used criteria for preparing such lists:
  - Float
  - Early and late start dates
  - Responsibility codes
  - Activity numbers
- Sorted lists simplify management tasks
  Allocation of responsibilities, function-related tasks and accounting are facilitated with the use of differently sorted lists.
- Easy updation and monitoring
  - This makes critical path methods useful throughout a project's life cycle.
- Facilitates advanced analysis
  - Time–cost trade-offs
  - Resource allocation
  - Cost control

9.3.1 When is a Computer Needed?

Practical projects typically have a large number of activities running from hundreds to thousands. Manual computations with such large networks become cumbersome and time consuming. The usage of a computer is warranted more as the following factors increase:

- Network size
- Computer availability
- Expected frequency of updating
- Desired output listings
- Advanced analysis
- Network format

9.3.2 Comparative Features of Software Packages

Computer packages can have many distinguishing features and capabilities. Some of these are summarized below:

(1) The type of network it can handle: A-O-A/A-O-N/Precedence diagramming.

(2) The event numbering scheme
$i < j$ format
Random numbering (greater flexibility)

(3) Capacity
A few hundred to 500,000 activities

(4) The provision for calendar dates
Base starting date
5/6/7 day week
Provision for holidays

(5) Scheduled dates
The critical path may have positive, zero or negative float.

(6) Multiple initial and terminal events
Help merging of parallel projects

(7) Error detection
Loops
Improper time estimates

(8) Output sorts

(9) Report generator
Flexibility of report

(10) Graphical output
Bar charts
Resource requirement distributions
Network diagrams

(11) Updating
Modified forward pass to incorporate review date information

(12) Network condensation
Condensation of large to small networks
Integration of two or more condensed networks
Expansion of condensed to large detailed networks
(13) Statistical analysis
Three time estimates
Probability computations
(14) Interactive processing
Keyboard entry and checks

9.3.3 Trends in Project Software and Commercial Availability

- Both proliferation and evolution
- Basic structure of earlier packages:
  - Arrow networks (A-O-A)
  - Numbering with ($i < j$)
  - One output tabulation
  - Single starting/ending node
  - No resource allocation
- Newer versions include the following modified features:
  - Network scheme (A-O-N/PDM)
  - Graphic reports
  - Resource allocation
  - Hardware/software advances
  - Vendors and distribution network
- 22 packages with addresses of vendors listed by Moder, Phillips and Davis (1983)

There has been a steady increase in the number of software packages that are available in the market for project management. The ratings of 10 available packages for project management in a recent review is given in Table 9.1.

9.3.4 Features to Check in Project Software

- ***What do you want the software to do?***
  - Bar chart and flow chart capabilities?
  - What types of output reports?
  - Handling resource and budget allocations?
  - Show working schedules on a calender.
  - Is package user friendly?
  - Do the software manufacturer and distributor have a good reputation?
- ***Ensure that the software package can perform at least the following functions:***

  (1) Permits easy development and changes in project bar charts and flow charts and notes the critical path.

Table 9.1 Project management software review product comparisons (2009)

	#1	#2	#3	#4	#5	#6	#7	#8	#9	#10
■■■■ Excellent ■■■□ Very good ■■□□ Good ■□□□ Fair □□□□ Poor	*Microsoft Project*	*Mind View*	*Project Kick Start*	*Rational Plan Multi Project*	*Fast Track Schedule*	*Service Desktop Pro*	*Milestones*	*MinuteMan*	*Fusion Desk Professional*	*VIP Team To Do List*
Overall rating	■■■■	■■■◧	■■■◧	■■□□	■■□□	■■□□	■■□□	■◧□□	■◧□□	■□□□
Ratings										
Collaboration	■■■□	■■◧□	■■□□	■■□□	■◧□□	■■□□	■□□□	■□□□	■□□□	◧□□□
Resource management	■■■■	■■◧□	■■◧□	■■■□	■■■□	■■□□	■□□□	■■□□	◧□□□	◧□□□
Project management	■■■■	■■■◧	■■■□	■■■□	■■■□	■■□□	■■■□	■■□□	■□□□	■□□□
Ease of use	■■■◧	■■■■	■■■■	■◧□□	■□□□	■□□□	■■◧□	■■□□	■■■□	■■■□
Help/Support	■■■◧	■■■□	■■■■	◧□□□	■■□□	■■■□	■■◧□	■□□□	■■□□	■□□□
Lowest price	**$449.99**	**$389.00**	**$199.00**	**$98.00**	**$334.99**	**$99.95**	**$269.00**	**$49.95**	**$89.95**	**$99.95**

Source http://project-management-software-review.toptenreviews.com/

(2) Allows you to see a bar chart or flow chart on the computer screen before printing it. And the charts are easy to follow on the screen.
(3) Permits you to combine resource and budget information into the project file and to retrieve useful reports on this information.
(4) Allows you to tie your project plan to a real calendar, with allowances for weekends and holidays.
(5) Alerts you to over-scheduling of individuals or groups, as well as to errors in the logic of your dependencies.
(6) Allows you to construct "what if?" scenarios so that you can engage in contingency planning and update modifications.
(7) Has a good demonstration file to show you what the program can do; also has user-friendly user's manual.

- ***Experiment with the package on a project you have already completed. Let the package convince you that it could have helped.***
  Remember that the computer software, with its reports and files, is only a tool to help you manage the project. The computer will not manage it for you. That is your job as a project leader.

9.4 NETWORKING IN ORGANIZATIONS

Today the customers, the organization and the suppliers are heavily networked and have an access to the most intricate knowledge of the organizations involved. These linkages are shown in Fig. 9.6. In this increasingly networked world it becomes important to be aware of associated activities and organizations.

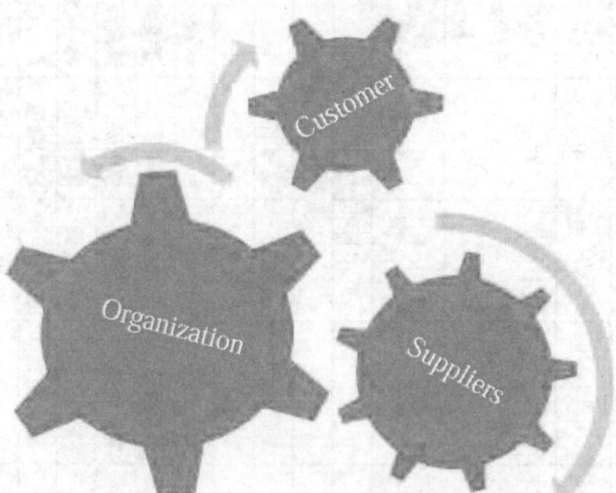

Fig. 9.6 Networked organizations.

In the ever-networked world, LAN and WAN are increasingly becoming common place. They help in easy interaction between the various stakeholders involved in the project. Figure 9.7 shows the implementation of LAN and WAN in the various offices to be connected through a network.

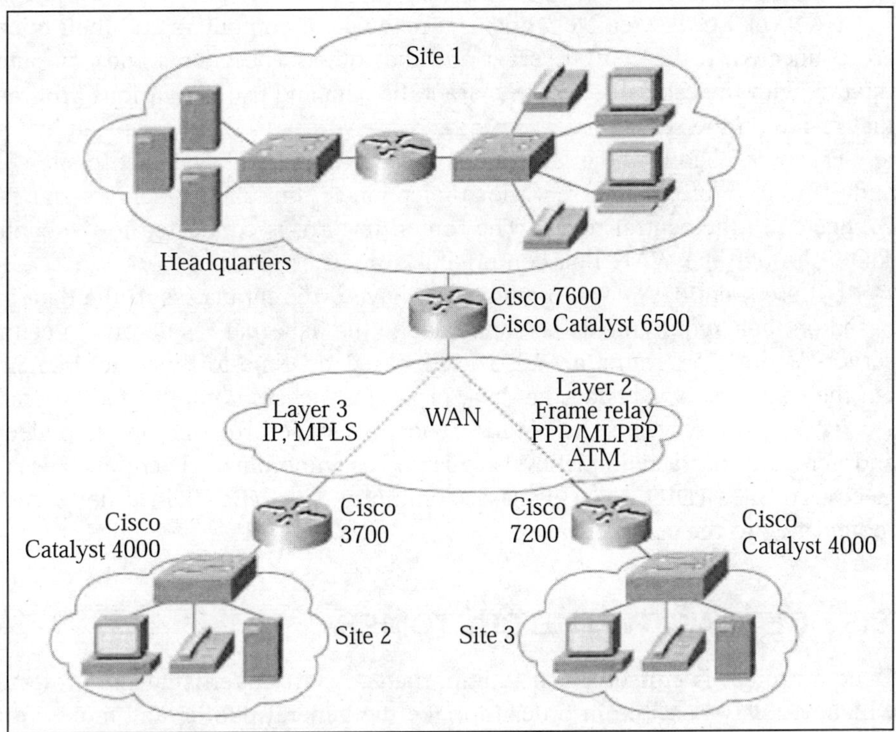

Fig. 9.7 LAN and WAN integration of various offices.

9.4.1 Networking Technology

With the increasing degree of networking within organizations, there is a change in the manner data resides inside the organization. In a fully networked organization the data and programs reside on a central server and the people in the organization have an access to the data from the consoles they have. They can access the data, use programs, make changes and re-store the data back on the central server, based on the kind of access they have. Some people having only view access cannot make any changes to the data that resides. Others have greater access, and can change the data, based on the newer developments. Access is given to the users based on their seniority, position and responsibility within the organization. For example, those responsible for finance will have access to the financial data; similarly, the marketing personnel will have access to the marketing and sales data, and so on.

WAN (or Wide Area Network) is a networking system that connects various places to a central server. It is a system based on routers and servers. There are linkages (optical fibre or copper) between the various routers to connect various sites. The sites are connected to the central server through the various linkages between the routers and server. The WAN uses MPLS technology to connect various sites to the central server.

LAN (or Local Area Network) is a network of computers and their clients are connected to the central server and the router. The clients and computers interact with the central server to extract the data and use the various programs that reside on the server.

Figure 9.7 shows the organization of WAN and LAN systems. In sites 1, 2 and 3 in the figure, there are various telephones, thin clients, servers and PCs connected to the central router. The router, in turn, is connected to the central router through the WAN link comprising fibre or copper link.

Different entities in the organization have different access to the data and based on their requirements use and change the data that reside on the central server. Various programs are also used based on time-to-time requirements. On the central server reside the data, programs, access defaults, entity details, etc. The central server is the biggest repository of information and knowledge and generally has a redundancy because of its importance. There are Disaster Recovery Sites (DR) and Business Continuity Sites (BCP) in order to have redundancy to the central server.

9.5 GETTING TO THE CUSTOMER

Once a project is conceived, it is important to start advertising the project in whichever way possible in order to make the general public, and more so the potential customers, aware of the new product and service that will be available soon.

9.5.1 Marketing

There are various stages of marketing. For instance, when the product or service is about to be initiated, awareness and advertisement should begin and assume greater intensity as the product nears its launch as depicted in Fig. 9.8. Similarly in smaller projects, the relevant clients and users are to be kept informed.

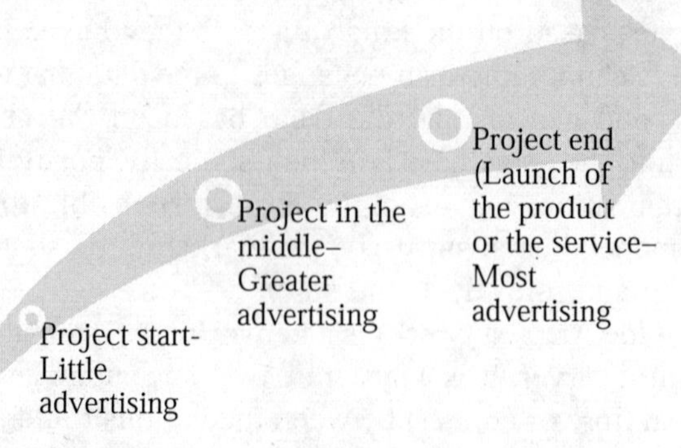

Fig. 9.8 Stages in marketing.

At the same time it should be ensured that the sales of existing products from the same company are not negatively influenced. For instance, the objective of a smaller project can be to improve the look of an already existing car in the market. The project manager should start advertising just before the new-look car will be available to the general public; otherwise the sales of the already available cars with the old look will drop drastically as the people will start waiting for the new-look car. Thus, when and how to conduct a marketing campaign are important strategic decisions for the company's survival and growth.

9.5.2 Advertising

The advertising of today is considerably different from the advertising of the past, when not many avenues were available for marketing. Today with the increasing availability of Internet, most companies are using web advertising to advertise their products. The means for advertising and marketing that are available today include advertisements through the web, pamphlets, mobile phones, television, radio and magazines, depending on the target customers and cost involved (Fig. 9.9).

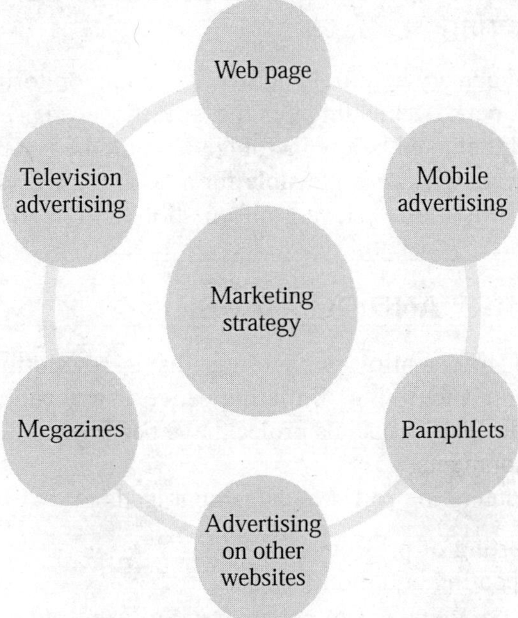

Fig. 9.9 Marketing of products and services.

Most companies prefer to make pre-project delivery promotions. The promotion talks about the product or the service that will be available in the near future. For example, people were already aware of the Nano car even before it was launched. Tatas, the promoters of the car, were advertising it as the least expensive car available on the face of this earth.

Many companies also develop websites and web pages to promote their products and services that will be launched in the near future. Web pages and websites play an important role in advertising and marketing today. With most customers having access to computers and Internet, it becomes increasingly important to have a very good project/product/service website. The website should talk about the various products available and their delivery methods. The website needs to project the following kinds of information:

- History of the company
- The accomplishments of the company
- The products/services available
- The delivery periods
- Promotional schemes
- Presence of the company
- The future products
- The newer projects

9.5.3 Role of Computers and Networking in Online Project Monitoring

Computers could be very helpful in networking and monitoring online a number of on-going projects. Depending on the specific needs, an issue resolution sheet of the kind indicated below in Table 9.2 could be generated and centrally available to indicate who is responsible for a task, from whom sanctions are to be sought and to whom the relevant information is to be given.

9.6 SUMMARY AND CONCLUSIONS

Computers and information technology have revolutionized our means of communication and living. Initiating, advertising and informing various stakeholders of developments in a project have become easy, quick and efficient with these developments.

Use of computers in project management leads to

- Easy sorting of project activities
- Easy updating and monitoring
- Advanced analysis (time–cost trade-offs, resource analysis and cost control)

Computer packages vary in their features and capabilities.

There has been a trend towards both proliferation and evolution in software packages. Networking and the IT revolution can provide useful information sharing and exchange between multi-site projects.

Table 9.2 Issue resolution sheet

Date	*Importance*	*Category*	*Timeline*	*Raised to*	*Copy sent to*	*Issue*	*Issue resolution*	*Issue resolution*	*Issue resolution*
		Project level/Site level					*Client*	*Project consultants*	*Vendor*
20/09/09	High	Project level	6 months	Client	Project leader/ steering committee/ project consultants	Sub-qaulity computer peripherals used	The peripherals must be replaced within the project timelines with new quality equipments	The replacement must be done at the earliest because the new equipments are being deployed as and when those are supplied	The new peripherals that will be supplied henceforth will be the same quality as mentioned in the RFP. The old equipments will be replaced soon

A number of commercially available packages are currently available and a comparison of existing computer software packages has been made.

MS Project is a widely used, user-friendly package for planning and implementing projects from Microsoft.

Ultimately, all computer software is a tool available to the project manager which can assist him, but the responsibility of managing the project is entirely his own.

PROBLEMS

1. How have information technology and the advent of computers revolutionized project management?
2. What are the features that you would look for in buying a computer package for
   (a) a small household business?
   (b) an organization located in one city?
   (c) an organization spread geographically over the whole globe?
3. Comment on the role of data security and confidentiality when computers are used for project tracking and monitoring of a project at multiple sites. How can one ensure that information is not passed to unwanted users?
4. You are about to launch a new product in the market. Design an appropriate website highlighting the objective and special features of your project, the date of launch and any special marketing drives you can think of to promote your product to prospective customers.
5. What is the role of a status reporting site for a multi-site project? Indicate the typical information that you would include to facilitate the execution of the project.
6. Conduct a literature survey on the Internet to identify the various computer packages that are commercially available. Summarize their features, costs and vendors.

CHAPTER

10

Behavioural and Contractual Issues

10.1 GETTING PROJECTS DONE

A project, as we have seen earlier, is a collection of tasks with well-defined responsibilities allotted to different individuals, agencies, organizations or groups. A task thus has to be completed with

- Requisite quality and product specifications
- Using the available resources (with minimum wastage)
- Least time and cost overruns
- A respect for the precedence restrictions among jobs
- Accommodation of unforeseen risks in the environment (these environmental risks may be economic, social, political, technological or of any other variety)

These are often formidably conflicting and demanding requirements, often not possible to achieve simultaneously by a single individual or agency. Hence, projects have to be undertaken by a number of individuals or agencies and the human issues involved in coordinating the work are of paramount importance in the successful implementation of projects. Contractual obligations and mutual understanding and coordination in this kind of scenario become really necessary to bind the project executive, the vendors and the client to achieve the objectives of all the parties concerned.

A contract, properly defined, is an anchor for both the project beneficiary on the one hand and the project executor(s) on the other. This may be likened to a rubber band analogy depicted in Fig. 10.1. The rubber band may be imagined to be anchored by the project's desired objectives and only a limited flexibility is available to all the involved parties to develop a contractual framework in which the work is to be carried out, without breaking or stressing the band too much. Both formal and informal contracts may be of relevance in the execution of projects, though as the projects become bigger, with higher stakes and the involvement of multiple agencies and experts, formal legal contracts are a necessary part of stating responsibilities and commitment to the work scope, quality specifications and schedules. Depending on the nature of the contract and its importance, suitable penalty clauses for non-adherence to the terms of the contract by either party could also be included.

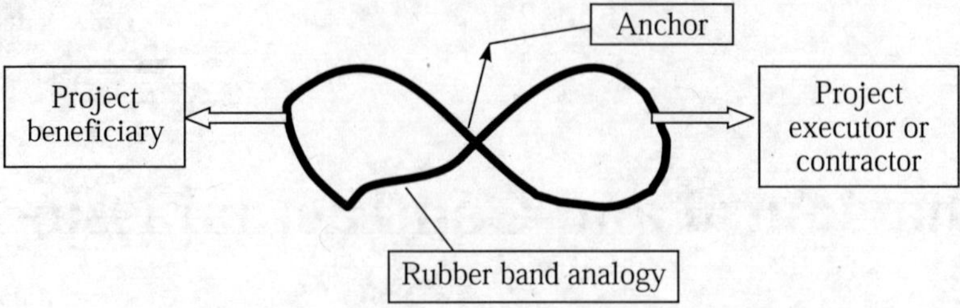

Fig. 10.1 A project contract (Rubber band analogy).

This, in a nutshell, is the importance of project contracts which must be carefully worded in legal, precise and just language to defend the interests of all the concerned parties.

Generally, a system of legislation exists from the lower to the highest courts whose job is to dispense justice. But the point that must not be denied is that justice must not be delayed, for as is often said, justice delayed is justice denied. And in the smooth running of any project, the resort to legal wrangling ought to be absent or at least minimized. This is generally possible with the development of a good team spirit among members and with a proper transparent and honest relationship with the various contractors. Since it is the people who are working on the project, human relationships are extremely important and mutual concern is the key to completing quality projects within the stated goals of time and cost.

There could be many legal problems that arise in the initiation, planning and execution of work for which resort to proper legal contracts and provisions may be made to. For instance, some of the laws pertaining to the management of projects and protection provided by the law could be as follows:

- Landlord vs. tenant in rental disputes
- Evacuation vs. rehabilitation of the underprivileged in projects
- Payment for compensation for an accident at work
- Rules for hiring and layoff of staff
- Tax concessions for donations and special usage
- Depreciation, accounting and audit procedures for new investments

10.2 IMPORTANCE OF CONTRACTS IN PROJECTS

It is rare that a large project like the setting up of a refinery or the building of a road network could be managed and conducted by a single person or an agency. A number of expert agencies have to be involved to carry out those portions of the project where the expertise and economics of time and cost work out best.

For these reasons projects or portions thereof are sub-contracted to different contractors who have the relevant experience and skill to carry out the required functions. Contract management is thus a very important aspect of practical project execution. Contracts for large projects are generally legal bindings on both the client and the contractor detailing the quantum of work, the detailed specifications, the price schedule and the expected phasing of the work to be done. Contract management typically involves

(i) Preparing a detailed statement of what exactly is required to be done.
(ii) Communicating this note inviting quotations (NIQ) to competent contenders with appropriate time to respond and submit their bids.
(iii) Examining and shortlisting quotations (invariably in large government projects the practice of awarding the contract to the lowest bidder (L1) consistent with the required specifications is followed as the norm).
(iv) Negotiations with the prospective bidders (generally the top three, unless it is a proprietary item with a limited number of quotations).
(v) Award of the contract.

The contract should specify how the work is to be performed and monitored. How are disputes to be resolved? There are generally some penalty clauses included in the legal document to ensure conformance to quality and schedule requirements.

It is, however, important that a proper professional relationship be developed between the various contractors and client for the efficient implementation of the project. In this context, the importance of teamwork and proper leadership cannot be overemphasized. Since ultimately it is the people who are carrying out the work, all the issues pertaining to human psychology, motivation, ego and culture play a significant role in the project execution stage.

10.3 TEAMWORK IN PROJECT MANAGEMENT

Projects are managed by *people working together as a team.* At this juncture, it is important to understand the distinction between a team and a group of people. A team is generally united in its purpose. Each individual in the team aligns his/her activities to the accomplishment of the project goal and should recognize his role or duty in the entire team. In a group of individuals, each one may hold his own point of view and there need not be consensus amongst the individuals regarding the specific goal that the group of people is trying to achieve. Friends chatting together on a social function could be likened to a group, whereas the same trying to solve a social or a financial problem jointly could be more likened to a team. Team building for a project manager is the first essential art of educating, training and aligning people in the direction of the project.

Making a good team requires effort and training on the part of those responsible for the project. In physical terms, one might use the analogy of magnetizing an iron bar by rubbing it unidirectionally with a powerful magnet.

As depicted in Fig. 10.2, the orientation of different people (likened to individual magnets) may be random in a group, but as the process of magnetization is accomplished a greater and a more uniform orientation in all the individuals develops. By this alignment of team members a commitment to the common project goal is sought to be achieved so that the individuals understand their roles and perform together in a harmonious orchestra while the project is conducted. It is the primary task of the project manager or leader to be able to carry his team with him and explain to each member what is expected from him/her in the entire project exercise.

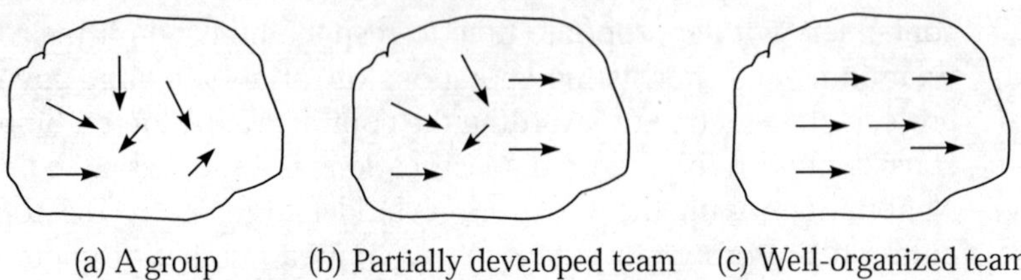

(a) A group (b) Partially developed team (c) Well-organized team

Fig. 10.2 Development of a team.

Network techniques should *not* be viewed as merely mathematical tools for planning and controlling the schedule for special projects. The major advantage of the network and its visual representation is that it gives an overall idea of the whole work to the project team and becomes a very effective medium to communicate, refine and reach a consensus on the scope of the entire work. Moreover, each stakeholder gets a clear idea of his/her involvement or expectation from the whole project.

This is the reason that network techniques should be an integral part of the *total process of team building*, where different contenders understand the project objective(s) and their individual roles in the whole game.

10.4 TEAM VS. GROUP

Whenever a new project is contemplated, the people with the right experience and capabilities are generally identified and included in the initial stages. The project team is usually a *new, temporary group* without previous experience of working together. This group of people has to grapple with the initial problems, understand the project scope and endeavour to become an effective team. This is a cooperative effort in which the project leader has to play a significant role in understanding the strengths, weaknesses and sensibilities of his team members. The initial time spent in developing a good working relationship and a proper atmosphere for work goes a long way in the success of the final project.

Complex projects require complex teams with a *set of work rules and norms*. These work rules may be formally imposed by the culture prevailing in the organization, but are constantly under change through informal interactions as the project proceeds. It needs to be understood that the informal working relationships that develop as the members work together are very important and often govern the commitment and success of the project team.

High degree of learning and interdependency requires *well functioning and cohesive teams.* This can develop in practice with mutual trust and recognition of the strengths and capabilities of various members. An atmosphere where members can freely communicate and discuss their problems with one another without fear or ego clashes is the ideal prerequisite for this kind of behaviour.

10.5 ATTRIBUTES OF A GOOD PROJECT TEAM

A good project team requires many qualities to foster an atmosphere of effective working. Chiefly among these qualities are

- **Commitment to a common goal:** The goal must be clearly understood by all the members of the team and each member should play his role in the achievement of the common goal. Often in developing a proper team the individual goals or desires of the members have to be subordinated to the common goal of the team.
- **Integrity:** Honesty and integrity in the members of a project team is a necessary quality for transparent and effective operations. People should be clear about commitment and devotion to the project goals and should try to meet the overall project objectives by their honest and whole-hearted commitment to their respective roles in the entire project.
- **Openness:** An atmosphere of openness where members can freely communicate with each other for information, advice and assistance in the performance of their tasks is a major help in the performance of a good project team. In an open system, each member should know clearly what his responsibilities are and should also be able to realize the responsibilities of his colleagues. A team works best in the atmosphere of mutual give and take with understanding that all the partners are involved in the common goal of executing the same project.
- **Competence:** The importance of competence of the members in the project cannot be overemphasized. People with different specializations have to cooperate to produce the end result. Ego conflicts among specialists with considerations like who is more important to the project often cause project delays, harm the quality and dent the reputation of the organization conducting the project. Thus, though individual competence in functional areas is necessary, a recognition of the contribution and competence of all the members is necessary in the members. A training and understanding of people skills is also a very essential part of the project manager's job.

- **Trust:** Mutual trust could perhaps be considered a central trait for the formation and success of any team. Team members should develop trust in each other and be able to bond with each other by relying on the strengths of their colleagues. There should be a realistic assessment of the weaknesses and limitations of the members, and attempts should always be made to improve the overall performance through encouragement, example and proper training.
- **Loyalty:** Loyalty to the project group with the capability to maintain the company secrets and key statistics is a very important consideration in project performance. In an uncertain economic climate with high attrition rates of employees among organizations, this factor is becoming increasingly important. Loyalty is considered an essential part of business ethics and is an employee asset which any progressive organization would cherish.
- **Consistency:** Consistency in maintaining business standards of quality, lead time and customer service governs the overall reputation and branding of the team or the organization. It is only through consistently reliable performance that a company or a project organization would be able to sustain and grow. The client of today with his discrimination and the wide ranging choices would prefer customers with whom his relationships have been consistently desirable.

An effective team thus requires all these qualities. A diagrammatic representation of these various attributes is given in Fig. 10.3. Trust is here exhibited as a central quality as it would foster and encourage the development of the other qualities indicated above.

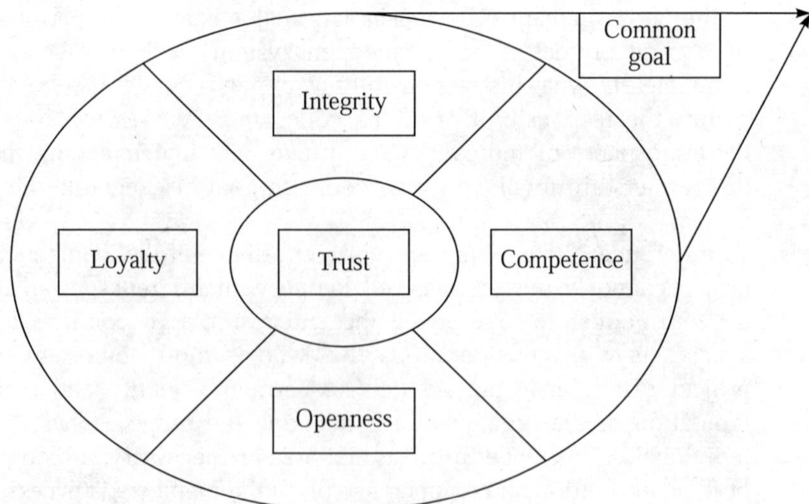

Fig. 10.3 Attributes of an effective team.

10.6 FORMATION OF EFFECTIVE TEAMS

Team formation is a process in project management which proceeds generally through the various stages of forming, storming, developing norms of behaviour and performing.

When a project is conceived and planned for implementation, an initial project team is identified with a project leader.

In the preliminary meetings and introductions of various members, the project leader explains the broad project goals and a "Rough Network" outlining the overall task to be performed is proposed.

Some issues that can typically be debated at this stage include questions like

- Who else should be in the team?
- Without concern for budget restrictions, what would each member contribute?

The group would construct an idealized network (one they would implement if they could do what they wanted).

This would be done with the participation of team members, giving them an opportunity to know each other's views.

Involvement of people right from the goal setting stage nurtures commitment and continuity.

The project members would generally iterate towards a realistic plan through negotiations with each other and other partners or specialists.

Here the practical constraints and limitations would be brought up by the members from their own areas of expertise and experience.

This is a participative process.

Continue the process of negotiation until a feasible solution is found (operationally viable and within the budget).

This network becomes the initial project plan with which project execution begins.

When people from different departments are assembled for a project they form a temporary social system and as it is new there is no system of customs that indicate proper behaviour while working on that project.

Each person brings his/her own set of customs, beliefs and perceptions to the project.

Hence what tends to operate and govern the behaviour of the members is the "Group Mind" wherein the viewpoints of all the project participants are blended together.

The discussion and the relationships are generally strengthened by a common set of objectives and motives.

All projects involve both explicit and implicit contracts. To initiate a plan or a project an explicit project plan has to be drawn up. However, as people continue to work together, they develop their own implicit methods of working and quite often working relations mature to such an extent that formalism and written requests from each other may be replaced by oral or personal requests.

A heterogeneous group has no commonality of motives. And since most projects begin with new project members it is the role of the project leader to bring people together, explain the project objectives and delineate the role of individual participants in the whole process.

The initial project plan is the explicit contract for the team. Working towards building that network helps to develop the implicit contracts which are necessary for a smooth working team.

Studies indicate that heterogeneous groups tend to be more productive than homogeneous groups. This is primarily because of the complementary nature of the skillset involved in people from different backgrounds and the possibility of developing innovative and new solutions by examining various aspects of the problem.

10.7 STAGES OF TEAM FORMATION

A *team* is a heterogeneous group with the objective of completing a project or a task. Since people are involved with their backgrounds, beliefs and egos, the formation and the success of a project team goes through various stages and may be treated as an organic process. The team faces different problems and objectives at different stages of the project and these may be summarized in the stages of forming, storming, norming and performing as outlined below.

10.7.1 Forming

Depending on the chosen project, a team leader and the core members of the team are identified. During the 1st or the 2nd meeting of the project team, these people understand the project scope and also develop opinions about each other, trying to assess each individual's strengths, weaknesses and possible contributions to the project.

It must be stressed that there is a gradual transition from this set of individuals, to first a group which is generally wary and cautious of each other's intentions and capabilities. The purpose of the project is debated and a suitable definition or a title is assigned to the project which serves to bring the participants into a common group. The progression of this group to an effective team occurs as more interactions take place, people start placing greater trust in each other and understanding their own roles vis-à-vis the roles of their colleagues in the whole project. In this initial phase, the project leader performs the role of introducing the project scope, bringing the project members together and explaining the individual roles that different people, groups or organizations will play in the whole project. Generally, the overall budget, time constraints and goals are explained but no specific allocations are made at this stage. A project has a projected and limited life span. And the project team members have complementary rather than competing skills. It is to be understood that a project is a *temporary* alliance created for a specific purpose or *objective*, which is generally dissolved once the aim has been achieved.

10.7.2 Storming

Invariably after the formation of the initial project team, a conflict stage arises in which the team members negotiate for assets and iterate towards the initial project plan. This is the stage when people start opening up and clarifying their doubts, asserting their egos and establishing their perceived roles in the whole project. Many worthwhile suggestions and comments may come up during this phase and a preliminary consensus on purposes and means is generated. Discussion and conflict could arise on

- Leadership and other roles
- Norms of work and behaviour
- Personal agenda/interpersonal hostilities

This may, however, be viewed as a necessary phase where wrappers are removed, the project tasks assume greater visibility and clarity and there is emergence of clear responsibilities of the total work and the individuals who will manage them.

10.7.3 Norming

After the stage of conflicts, negotiations and task allocation, the project group establishes the norms and practices for performing its tasks. In this stage, the manner of completion of the initial project plan and commitment to activities at the level of assets is negotiated. Some of the typical questions that are resolved are

- When and how should the group work?
- How to take decisions?
- What type of behaviour?
- Appropriate degree of openness, trust and confidence

These factors which are governed partly by the prevailing organizational culture and partly by what the external members bring from their experiences are responsible for the group ethics and norms that the project grows and develops with. Any organization would have its own methods and procedures of working, its internal bureaucracy and also the informal relationships that would tend to provide resilience and flexibility to operations. This governing culture would vary from organization to organization and would invariably be the key to success and competitiveness of the organization. It is here that the transition from a formal group to a team has taken place and the effectiveness of the team is determined by its smooth and understanding coordination in the performance of the project.

10.7.4 Performing

This is the stage where the plan is executed. Included in this stage are the procurement of the right resources, their mobilization, getting the right people in place and coordinating with the appropriate agencies for timely completion of predecessor activities. Environmental factors, contingencies and unforeseen features could play a significant role in project implementation. This is where the skills of improvisation, innovation and constant alertness and resourcefulness of the team members play an important part. Because of the level of trust and the explicit contacts built up, changes can be implemented more smoothly. It may now be assumed that the group of individuals who had initially assembled to perform the project have matured into a well-functioning team and imbibed the values and culture which the association was aimed at developing. The success of the team is dependent on recognition of the overall values and commitment to the goals, a spirit of give and take and a sense of pride in the achievement of all the members rather than of an individual. Although the project leader is often credited or blamed for the performance of the whole team, it must be appreciated that the role of the project leader is to motivate, set the right examples and facilitate the process of his team mates. The styles and demands of leadership vary during the different stages of growth of the project team and it is a challenge for the project manager to change his roles and respond to the changing needs of his team members.

10.8 ADVANTAGES OF PARTICIPATION

The principal benefit of planning comes from engaging in it—the "process" is important. A major consequence of participation is seen as a reduction of problems associated with implementing plans.

Total involvement using both the left and the right hemispheres of the human brain is one of the major gains of people engaging together and looking at the project both holistically and with reference to the details they are likely to engage in. It is well known that the human brain has two halves—the left and the right each capable of performing a certain subset of human tasks efficiently. For instance the left side is the rational or logical part which handles language, mathematics, analytical and logical type of thinking used in constructing network diagrams. The right side, on the other hand, is the one for intuitive thinking wherein synthesis, or putting the parts together by realizing the whole, simultaneous relations and dependencies are handled. Participation is thus viewed as an activity wherein members develop the opportunity to handle both sides of the brain and come to innovative, complete and unconventional results and solutions more quickly and effectively.

By concentrating on the details of constructing a network and then standing back to study the entire network, team members exercise both sides of their brain and construct a more complete image of the entire project.

Once the initial project plan is realized each member of the team should reiterate his/her part in the plan in the presence of all other team members.

In this way each person can realize how each others' activity relates to his/her own activity, which is a left brain process, while simultaneously realizing how each activity relates to the whole, thus completing the right brain synthesis.

10.9 THE ROLE OF LEADERSHIP

Project management is more the management of the *team* of people than the management of the tasks. The *team* goes through various stages in its *development and maturity*, as we have seen above. In consonance with the requirements of the team at these various stages, the project leadership too needs to grow and mature. The kind of leadership is related to the tasks and the levels of their maturity. At a preliminary level the tasks have to be structured for each individual, so that each person knows what is expected of him/her. This structuring is based on the total work content and the work breakdown structure. It is thus one of the first tasks of the project leader to communicate and assign the proper work to different participants in the project. This initial phase of project leadership may be termed as *structuring*.

The four leadership styles are as follows:

S1 Structuring

- Organize and direct the work of others
- Make each person accountable
- Demonstrate and clarify any difficulties that project staff might experience

S2 Coaching

Once the task responsibilities are given, the project manager's responsibility shifts to ensuring that the tasks are being properly performed. For accomplishing this, the project leader's role changes into one involving the following activities:

- *Tutoring:* This involves making interventions in situations where difficulties arise and to facilitate the project by giving guidance, support and appropriate provision for resources like manpower, money and machines.
- *Joint effort:* In order to strengthen the team spirit, the idea that the project is the joint responsibility of the team wherein members are expected to cooperate with one another is extremely important. The project leader can encourage this attitude by his own interest and participation. Leadership by participation and concern rather than by position of authority is likely to be more effective in building effective teams.
- *Role model:* In keeping with the above spirit, a project leader should be a role model whose examples and instructions the project members willingly follow.

S3 Encouraging

When the project members mature and perform their tasks with understanding, their motivation can be kept up by suitable encouragement from the project leader. This encouragement may take the form of

- Greater responsibility with doer
- Recognizing and praising good work

S4 Delegating

Finally, when the project manager develops confidence in his team members he should treat them with dignity and respect and delegate part of his duties to them by the following means

- Assign task responsibility and let others carry it out
- Motivate by giving control and showing respect

10.10 SUMMARY AND CONCLUSIONS

Project contracts are the legal means to bind the various stakeholders such as contractors, vendors and clients with their respective roles and responsibilities in the project. Both formal and informal projects have their role to play, but for projects with wide scope, cost and duration, formal contracts become necessary.

The process of awarding contracts is based on a bidding process from amongst the eligible and competent bids, followed by negotiations before the contract is awarded.

Process used for designing a network may be more important than the network itself in project management.

This process synthesizes the project and helps build a *project culture* while team members become accustomed to *working together.*

It also helps to build a more *effective team* as members begin to *trust one another.*

This process helps to release large amounts of creativity as team members *idealize* and use *both* the left and right brain activities.

As the *project team matures* through the stages of *forming, storming, norming* and *performing,* the project manager too has to adopt *appropriate leadership styles.*

The four leadership styles of *structuring, coaching, encouraging* and *delegating* are relevant as the task relevant maturity level increases.

PROBLEMS

1. Distinguish between formal and informal contracts. Outline their importance in getting projects done, giving suitable examples.

2. In evacuating land for a particular construction project, which parties would enter into a contract and what would be the kind of conditions that you would like to include in the contract?
3. In outsourcing a portion of the work of your project to a third party vendor, what kind of contract would you enter into? Write a sample contract.
4. How is a team different from a group of people?
5. Comment on the behavioural characteristics needed to make a successful team.
6. What are the typical kinds of conflicts that may arise in a project at different stages? How would a project manager resolve them?
7. What are the stages and problems in the development of a team?
8. What are the qualities needed in a good project manager?
9. What is the role of a project leader? Comment on how the leadership roles change with maturity of the tasks in a project.
10. Leaders are born, not made. Do you agree? Which aspects of leadership can and cannot be cultivated?

CHAPTER

11

Project Organization, Implementation and Closure

11.1 INTRODUCTION

The key issues discussed in this chapter include the organizational and human factors which are essential for the success of a project. Once the technical planning and specialized inputs in the overall project plan have been completed, the execution has to be supported by a proper organizational structure which would facilitate the performance of the member teams, the right leadership and motivation by the project leader and ensuring the solution of both the strategic and tactical governance of the project. An understanding and resolution of conflicts that may arise due to improper role definition, ego clashes or other unforeseen circumstances lend uncertainties and challenges for the project team which have to be resolved through people management skills in most of the cases. This chapter is organized in the following major topics:

- Organizational structures for projects
- Selection of the project manager
- Leadership and motivation
- Conflict management
- Communication
- Variety and nature of practical problems

11.2 THE FUNCTIONAL ORGANIZATION

In order to implement a project a special kind of organization is needed. The functional organization, a typical hierarchical structure, is used for a conventional organization manufacturing goods or services. As shown in Fig. 11.1, the classical (functional) organization is headed by a chief executive and the various functional division heads of engineering, operations, finance and marketing report to him. Each division may have one or more departments under its control. And these individual departments could be divided into sections where specialized work is being performed. The major advantage of such an arrangement is that people are organized into their routine functions with each one doing his job. This, however, encourages bureaucracy and lethargy in the system. Some of the major advantages and disadvantages of such an organizational structure are summarized below.

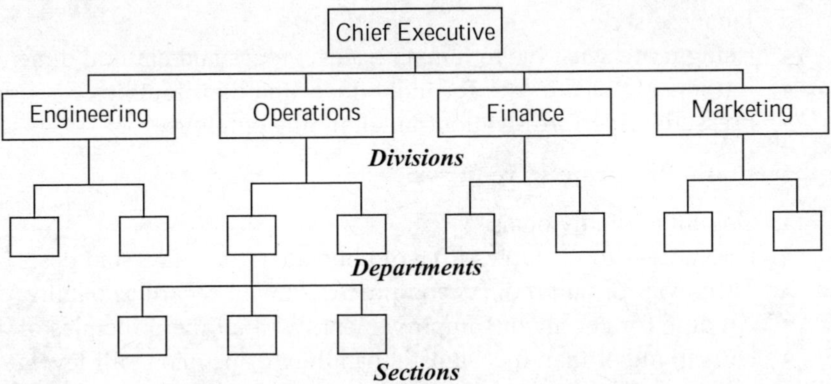

Fig. 11.1 Functional organization.

Advantages

- Flexibility in use of manpower
- Many projects can share functional expertise
- Continuity of technical expertise
- Functional divisions provide normal path for career growth

Disadvantages

- Low priority to projects
- Not problem oriented, may overemphasize a particular function
- No direct touch with client
- No single person may be responsible for the project

As people rise from the bottom, they acquire greater skills and experience and are promoted to the top till they reach their levels of incompetence (the Peter Principle).

A service organization, on the other hand, requires greater customer interactions and hence is more porous to facilitate interaction with customers at all levels.

A totally porous or transparent organization would be one in which the boundary totally disappears and what is inside is exactly what is visible outside. This may be termed as the *transparent organization* or the *least viscous organization.*

It is clear that in the information age of today, boundaries are becoming more and more porous. The major challenges in managing such organizations are

- Retention of talent in view of global opportunities
- Ensuring the security of propriety data when an employee is not committed for long to serve the organization
- Increased competition among big players
- Devising incentives for employees to be faithful, as in the conventional Japanese style
- Being more sensitive to human needs, values and cultural dimensions
- Introducing health care for individuals and their families
- Pressure to perform without breaking the employee

Implementation of projects requires

- Committed individuals
- Free access to resources to avoid bureaucratic delays and costs
- Strict control on products and processes with regard to quality
- An urge for continuous improvement, with all the principles of TQM
- Human rather than mechanistic handling of people at all levels

There are no short cuts to achieve quality in this competitive world, but the effort is well worthwhile to make the world a better place to live in through carefully chosen projects, well planned and implemented with a sense of purpose.

11.3 PURE PROJECT ORGANIZATION

Since each project is unique and requires its own attention and resources, a project structure with the project manager at the helm of affairs assisted by a group of the required functional managers would be an ideal or pure project organization (Fig. 11.2). This kind of organization would be a temporary one depending on the scope and duration of the project. Some of the major advantages and limitations of this project organization are given below.

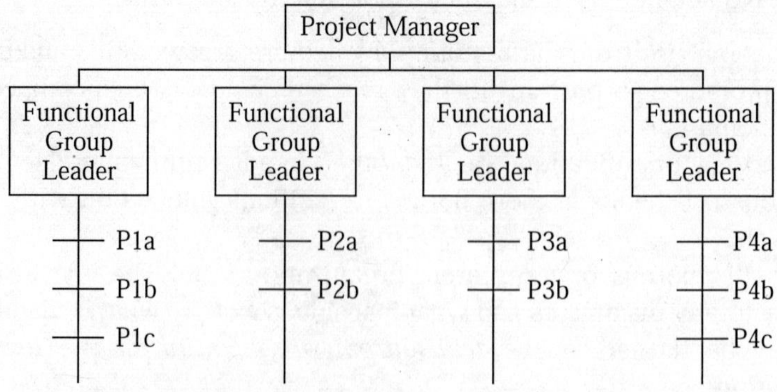

Fig. 11.2 Pure project organization.

Advantages

- Complete line authority over project
- Strong communication
- Personnel demonstrate loyalty to project
- Rapid reaction time
- Flexibility

Disadvantages

- Cost prohibitive for multiple projects
- Tendency to retain personnel on project after they are needed
- Technology suffers without strong functional groups

Although this kind of organization structure could be adopted for projects with reasonable lengths of time, it would be cumbersome to create and disband new structures on arrival of new projects and completion of old ones. This lack of stability is one of the deterrents for this kind of project structure. And this is one of the major reasons for the emergence of the *matrix organization*, which is specially suited to provide stability and continuity to project personnel while enabling them to handle multiple projects.

11.4 MATRIX ORGANIZATION

The matrix organization is the one that is generally suited for organizations engaged in multiple projects. In this organization headed by a general manager, the various functional heads are ordered vertically as in a functional organization. Apart from this, each project manager has a team drawn from the various functions as shown in Fig. 11.3. The arrangement looks like a matrix and hence the name. Some of the major advantages and disadvantages of the matrix organization structure are highlighted below.

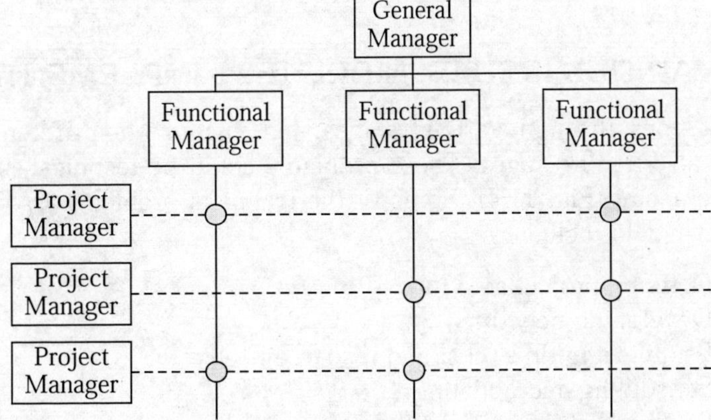

Fig. 11.3 Matrix organization.

Advantages

- Project manager has the authority to handle the project
- Rapid responses are possible to changing circumstances.
- Sharing persons reduces cost
- Conflict resolution is earlier

Disadvantages

- Multidimensional work and information flow
- Dual reporting
- Continuously changing priorities
- Difficulties in monitoring and control
- Each person has a “home” after project completion

Although each person retains his functional specialization, he can be drawn into a project by the project manager if his expertise is required and thus he is relieved of his functional obligations during the period. He then reports to the project manager during the execution of the project and when the project is over, he returns to his safe haven in the functional hierarchy of the project. Thus, career growth and continuity are guaranteed for the employee and the disadvantage of disbanding the project team in a pure project structure is obviated. To a large extent, the matrix organization is an attempt to capture the stability of the functional organization along with the exigencies of new and emerging projects. This is perhaps the reason why such organizational structures are adopted by organizations handling multiple projects. However, the major disadvantage of this scheme is that of dual reporting, because an employee is required to report to the project manager and implicitly to his boss in the functional organization. This could lead to interpersonal conflicts. This is where the role of teamwork and people management is all the more important. After all it is the people who have to work together to realize the company goals and the working environment should be healthy and conducive to cooperative working.

11.5 VARIOUS ISSUES IN PROJECT IMPLEMENTATION

A project goes through various stages and encounters different kinds of problems at different stages. These problems could be technical, behavioural or environmental (Fig. 11.4). Some of the technical problems associated with the project would include

- Defining project activities
- Developing network
- Establishing time, cost and resource needs
- Scheduling and updating
- Preparing and understanding engineering drawings
- Placing order for technical equipment

- Installing and checking equipment
- Reviewing performance

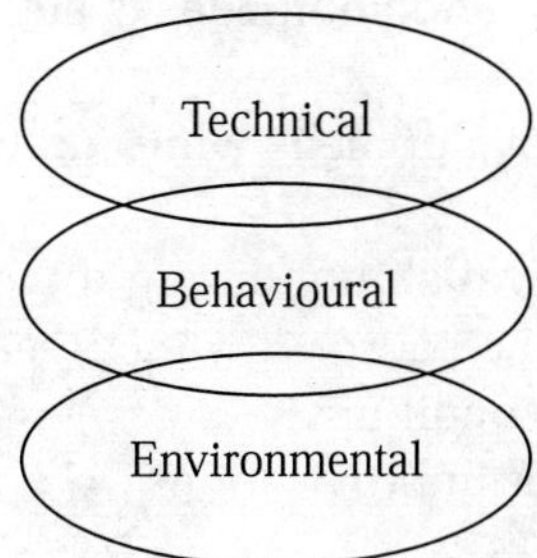

Fig. 11.4 Nature of problems in projects.

The solution to these technical problems would require the expertise of specialists who have had training and experience on similar kinds of projects. Apart from the specific technical problems, each project would face behavioural problems of a more generic type including the following major aspects:

- Team building based on project needs
- Leadership and motivation
- Communication
- Conflict management
- Project organization
- Reward and recognition systems
- Tact, marketing and public relations

In addition to the technical and behavioural problems, there could be problems unique to the environmental factors prevailing at the time the project is being contemplated or executed. Some of the environmental problems could be

- Awareness of the market trends
  - Major competitors
  - Vendors for major items
  - Fluctuations in prices, supplies and lead times
- Government regulations and changes
  - New legislation
- New technology
  - Computer software
  - Equipment

The nature of problems that may arise in the various stages of a project could be diverse. Some examples of the problems that the project manager and his staff are confronted with are listed below.

- Organizational/behavioural issues over authority delegation
- Financial matters relating to budgets, overspending and incorrect estimation

- Legal matters
- Engineering standards and their interpretation
- Construction/installation bottlenecks due to non-availability of men or equipment
- Site evacuation/development while drawing site boundaries or construction
- Labour unrest/unavailability during the progress of the work
- Non-availability of resources owing to seasonal stocks and competition
- Adverse weather conditions
- Ad hoc/on the spot improvisations

These tend to result in

- Uncertainties of time, cost, and resource estimates of a job
- Inclusion/dropping of a job (alternatives)
- Delays in schedules
- Overruns in costs

For overcoming these problems the project manager should have the following capabilities:

- Honesty and integrity
- Understanding of personnel problems
- Understanding of project technology
- Business management competence
  - Management principles
  - Communication ability
- Alertness and quickness
- Versatility
- Energy and toughness
- Decision-making ability

11.6 CONFLICT MANAGEMENT IN PROJECTS

As indicated earlier, the project involves a number of people working together and there is bound to be some conflict among the various stakeholders which the project manager has to manage. The sources of conflict may vary over the project life cycle, and may be due to a variety of reasons, at different stages. The conflict from various sources over the project life cycle is depicted in Fig. 11.5

A project manager should ask himself

- Do I make it easy for employees to talk to me?
- Am I sympathetic to their problems?
- Do I attempt to improve human relations?
- Do I make an extra effort to remember names and faces?

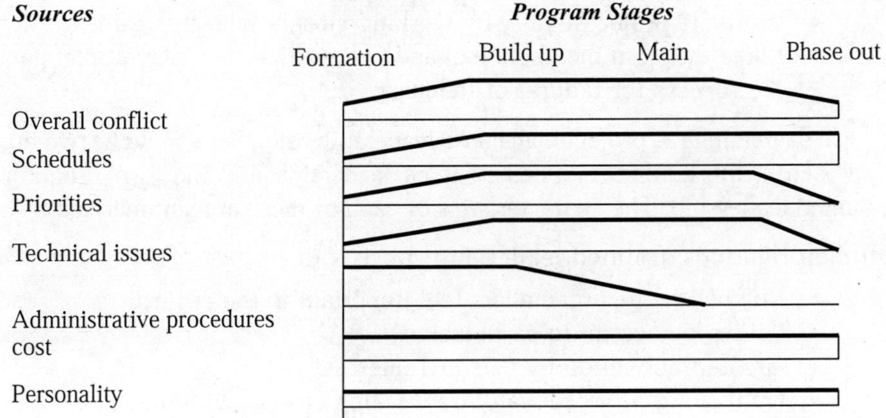

Fig. 11.5 Conflicts over the project life cycle.

And on the basis of this evaluation, the project manager should

- Convert win–lose proposition to a win–win proposition.
- Be a good listener.
- Encourage openness and emotional expression.
- Be able to convince, communicate and negotiate with others.
- Streamline administrative procedures.
- Seek and be open about technical opinions of specialists.
- Perform staffing and resource allocations on demand and merit.
- Handle costs and budgets meticulously.
- Adhere to schedules as far as possible.
- Try to avoid interpersonal and personality clashes.

11.7 COMMUNICATION AND LEADERSHIP STYLES

Communication is the key to effective implementation of a project. Members must be kept informed about their roles, responsibilities and developments that take place from day to day. This gives them a sense of participation and ownership and motivates them to contribute their best. For this purpose, the project manager should take care of the following points:

- Allow each member to contribute in his own way (support, challenge and counter your point of view).
- Make the decision in a meeting.
- Test for commitment to the decision.
- Assign roles and responsibilities.
- Take periodic feedback from concerned individuals.
- Make the team members feel important in the project.
- Give due credit to participants.
- Greater motivation by personal interest.

- Cultivate project loyalty by working closely with the team.
- Make the team members feel and believe that they play a vital part in the success (or failure) of the team.

In exercising the project manager's leadership role, there could be two broad approaches: the human relations oriented leadership and the formal authority oriented leadership. The characteristics of each of these are summarized below.

Human relations oriented leadership consists in

- Making the team members feel important in the project.
- Giving due credit to participants.
- Greater motivation by personal interest.
- Cultivating project loyalty by working closely with the team.
- Making the team members feel and believe that they play a vital part in the success (or failure) of the team.

Formal authority oriented leadership operates by

- Pointing out how great the loss will be if cooperation is not forthcoming.
- Threatening to precipitate high level intervention and do it if necessary.
- Convincing the members that what is good for the company is good for them.
- Maintaining control over expenditures.
- Delegating authority to get the work done.

11.8 PROJECT CLOSURE AND LESSONS FOR THE FUTURE

A project, as we have already seen, is a temporary activity undertaken to accomplish an objective. After the project objective is accomplished, the project must be wound up. In effect, the project staff has to hand over the project to the user group, which may be the operations group for a newly erected factory or the customers in case of a service project. This process of handing over, settling all the financial and accounting records, training the user on how to operate the desired services constitutes the aspects of project closure. Shifting, transferring of manpower and resources to their respective places and placing on record the proper procedures of operations in the form of training manuals or conducting training sessions for users are important aspects of the project winding up stage.

The project winding up stage must not be ignored for it is akin to the pudding in a meal. Moreover, this is the stage at which the customer or actual user comes in close contact with the project and compares his/her expectations with the real output. This is thus a great opportunity for both the client and the project staff to review their performance and establish long-term contacts for future projects.

Some of the major activities before the completion of a project include

- Accounting and report writing

  - Taking stock of performance, time and cost
  - Preparing final report (contractual or otherwise)
- Handing over project to user
  - Training of users and gradual withdrawal
- Disbanding of project team
  - Dragging of the project
  - Uncertainties over fate of individuals

The learnings from the project experience are valuable and provide a wealth of experience for handling similar projects in the future. The following are some areas where the project team becomes richer:

- Appreciating the difficulties faced at various stages of the project.
- Obtaining more realistic estimates of time, cost and resource requirements for various activities and work packages.
- Human relations and people management skills.

These learnings should be

- documented and available to future users
- publicized through seminars and presentations

The project experience typically encourages working as a team and provides technical exposure through interactions with consultants, suppliers/vendors, subcontractors and clients. A variety of issues and skills are needed and developed during the execution of a project. Some of these are

- Dealing with people
- Communicating objectives, work allocation, etc.
- Interpersonal conflicts
- Motivation and leadership
- Other behavioural issues
- Creativity and situational decision making
- Dealing with a dynamic environment through the various stages of the project
- Project selection and goal setting
- Planning for schedules, cost and resources
- Implementation including monitoring and control
- Completion and winding up

A project is a temporary entity that comes into existence to achieve some personal, organizational, technological or other environmental goal. Once the goal has been accomplished, the project ceases to exist. This is why the matrix structure of project organization is best suited for organizations engaged in doing multiple projects. As soon as a project is over, the individuals get absorbed in the mainstream of their functional specialization and prepare to take the next project when it comes into being. In this way, new projects are born and old ones are completed in due course whilst the talent of the personnel is utilized without being frittered away.

11.9 SUMMARY AND CONCLUSIONS

The broad steps in any project may be summarized as follows:

(a) Identification of the need or desire
(b) Pre-planning and tentative team selection with a leader
(c) Work breakdown structure through negotiations with the project team
(d) Allocation of responsibilities, development of network and its display
(e) Project scheduling with a timetable for action assuming suitable durations of jobs
(f) Consideration of resources—men, machines, materials and money, through time–cost trade-offs, resource aggregation, resource levelling, limited resource allocation or resource substitution
(g) Critical chain concepts and their applications
(h) Implementation including project monitoring and control
(i) Closure, accounting and report writing
(j) Handing over the project to the user and associated human and technical problems
(k) Training sessions for clients
(l) Documentation of learning or a presentation to the group for future projects

Since a project is handled by a team of people, the organizational and behavioral aspects are very essential for its success.

The organization structure adopted for doing projects has considerable impact on project performance.

- The traditional functional structure is suited for repetitive activities and is bureaucratic in structure, lacking the flexibility for projects.
- The pure project structure is specially designed for the project at hand but has problems of set-up and winding up in a limited life span.
- The matrix structure is the one commonly employed by project organizations because it permits the flexibility required for handling multiple projects as well as the functional growth of the personnel involved. However, the major drawback of this structure is its dual reporting.

The selection of the right project manager plays a crucial role in

- Building an effective project team
- Providing leadership and motivating the team members
- Addressing the multifarious problems faced in practical project settings
- Managing interpersonal conflicts in the life cycle of a project
- Coordinating the project with proper communication and planning

A project is a time-bound plan to achieve an objective. Once the objectives of the project are met, the project has to be wound up. During project closure, issues of winding up of resources of manpower and other resources, financial and cost accounting, training of personnel and documenting the lessons for the future are some of the major concerns. Moreover, since this stage presents the final deliverables to the customer, it must be well managed with proper concern for future relationship building between the client and the project staff.

Major issues of concern to managers and researchers

- Representation and modelling for visualization and analysis
- Scheduling activities subject to resource constraints
- Financial issues related either to project compression or to cash flows
- Uncertainty in activity durations as well as in resource availabilities and/or cash flows, and how to cope with it
- Risk management in projects through priority setting and defining margins for cost and time
- Human and organizational aspects

PROBLEMS

1. What is a functional organization and why is it not suitable for projects?
2. What is the difference in the role and training required for a project manager as compared to the head of a functional organization?
3. How does a pure project organization differ from a functional organization?
4. What is the matrix organization structure? What are its strengths and limitations for handling multiple projects?
5. Comment on the various technical, commercial and environmental issues in the management of projects.
6. How and why do interpersonal conflicts arise in projects? Comment on the nature of these conflicts over the life cycle of the project. How can the project manager mitigate these conflicts for the smooth implementation of a project?
7. What are the problems during project closure? Why do projects tend to drag along and what can be done by the project manager at this stage?
8. Considering the life cycle of a project, would you consider project management to be an art or a science? Comment on where the human and behavioural aspects dominate compared to the technical and knowledge components.

Bibliography

I. BOOKS AND DISSERTATIONS

Ahuja, H.N., *Project Management*, Wiley, New York, 1984.

Anderson, E.S., K.V. Grude and T. Haung, *Goal Directed Project Management* (2nd ed.), Kogan Page India Private Ltd, 1999.

Bhatnagar, S.K., *Network Analysis Techniques*, Wiley-Eastern, New Delhi, 1986.

Chandra, P., *Projects: Planning, Analysis, Selection, Implementation & Review* (4th ed.), Tata-McGraw Hill, New Delhi, 1995.

Dean, B.V. (ed), *Project Management: Methods and Studies*, North Holland, Amsterdam, 1985.

Elmaghraby, S.E., *Activity Networks: Project Planning and Control by Network Models*, Wiley, New York, 1977.

Ford, L.R. and D.R. Fulkerson, *Flows in Networks*, Princeton University Press, Princeton, N.J., 1966.

Goldratt, El. M. and J. Cox, *The Goal* (2nd ed.), Gower Publishing, Hampshire, U.K., 1993.

Goldratt, El. M., *The Goal II: It's Not Luck*, Productivity & Quality Publishing Private Limited, T. Nagar, Madras, 2005.

Goldratt, El. M., *The Critical Chain*, the North River Publishing Corporation, Great Barrington, 1997.

Havranek, T.J., *Modern Project Management Techniques for the Environmental Remediation Industry*, St. Lucie Press, Boca Raton, Florida, 1999.

Hwang, C.L. and K. Yoon, *Multi Attribute Decision Making: Methods and Applications—A State of Art Survey, Lecture Notes in Economics and Mathematical Systems No. 186*, Springer Verlag, Berlin Heidelberg, 1981.

Iri, M., *Network Flows, Transportation and Scheduling*, Academic Press, Tokyo, 1977.

Kanda, A., *Project Planning with Renewable and Non-Renewable Resources*, unpublished Ph.D dissertation, Mechanical Engg Department, IIT, Delhi, 1985.

Kerzner, H., *Project Management: A Systems Approach to Planning, Scheduling and Control*, Van Nostrand Reinhold, New York, 1989.

Leach, L., *Critical Chain Project Management* (2nd ed.), Artech House Publishers, Boston, 2004.

Mittal, M.L., *Multi-Project Scheduling with Resource Transfers*, unpublished Ph.D dissertation, Mechanical Engg Dept., IIT, Delhi, 2005.

Moder, J.J., C.R. Phillips and E.W. Davis, *Project Management with CPM, PERT and Precedence Diagramming* (3rd ed.), Tata-McGraw Hill, New Delhi, 1983.

Nagarajan, K., *Project Management*, New Age International (P) Limited, New Delhi, 2001.

Nicholas, J.M., *Managing Business and Engineering Projects: Concepts and Implementation*, Prentice-Hall Inc., New Jersey, 1990.

Philips, Don T. and A. Garcia Diaz, *Fundamentals of Network Analysis*, Prentice-Hall Inc., New York, 1981.

Randolph, W.A. and B.Z. Posner, *Effective Project Planning and Management: Getting the Job Done*, Prentice-Hall of India, 1993.

Rickett, J.A., *Reaching the Goal*, IBM, 2008.

Saaty, T.L., *The Analytic Hierarchy Process*, RWS Publications, Pittsburgh, P.A., 5213, USA, 1990.

Srinath, L.S., *PERT and CPM: Principles and Applications* (3rd ed.), East West Press, 1989.

Shtub, A., J.F. Bard and S.G. Loberson, *Project Management: Engineering, Technology and Implementation*, Prentice-Hall Inc., New Jersey, 1994.

Whitehouse, *G.E., Systems Analysis and Design Using Network Techniques*, Prentice-Hall Inc., New York, 1977.

Wiest, J.D. and F.K. Levy, *A Management Guide to PERT/CPM with GERT/PDM/DCPM and Other Networks* (2nd ed.), Prentice-Hall of India, 1977.

Wysocki, K.R., R. Beck Jr and D.B. Crane, *Effective Project Management*, (2nd ed), Wiley, New York, 2001.

II. SELECTED RESEARCH PAPERS

Abeyasinghe, M.C.L., Greenwood, G.J., and Johansen, D.E. (2001) "An efficient method for scheduling construction projects with resource constraints", *International Journal of Project management*, vol. 19, pp 9-45.

Anavi-Isakow, S., and Golaney, B. (2003) "Managing multi-project environments through constant work-in-process", *International Journal of Project Management*, vol. 21, pp 9–18.

Ahn, T., and Erenguc, S.S. (1998) "The resource constrained project scheduling problem with multiple crashable modes: A heuristic procedure", *European Journal of Operational Research*, vol. 107, pp 250–259.

Alvarez-Valdés, R., and Tamarit, J.M. (1989) "Heuristic algorithms for resource constrained project scheduling: A review and an empirical analysis", Advance in Project Scheduling, Edited by R. Slowinski and J. Weglarz, Elsevier, Amsterdam, pp 113–134.

Ash, R., and Smith-Daniels, D.E. (1999) "The effects of learning, forgetting, and relearning on decision rule performance in multiproject scheduling", *Decision Sciences*, vol. 30, no. 1, pp 47–82.

Blazewicz, J. (1981) "Solving the resource constrained deadline scheduling problem via reduction to the network flow problem", *European Journal of Operational Research*, vol. 6, no. 1, pp 75–79.

Cooper, D. (1976) "Heuristics for scheduling resource constrained projects: An experimental investigation", *Management Science*, vol. 22, no. 11, pp 1186–1194.

Davis, E.W. (1966) "Resource allocation in project network models–A survey", *Journal of Industrial Engineering*, vol. 17, no. 4, pp 177–188.

Davis, E.W. (1968) "An exact algorithm for the multiple constrained resource constraints project scheduling problem", Unpublished Ph.D. thesis, Yale University.

Davis, E.W. (1973) "Project scheduling under resource constraints—Historical review and categorization of procedures", *IIE Transaction*, vol. 7, no. 2, pp 297–312.

Davis, E.W., and Heidorn, G.E. (1971) "An algorithm for optimal project scheduling under multiple resource constraints", *Management Science*, vol. 17, pp 803–816.

Davis, E.W., and Patterson, J.H. (1975) "A comparison of heuristic and optimum solutions in resource constrained project scheduling", *Management Science*, vol. 21, no. 8, pp 944–955.

Demeulemeester, E., De Reyck, B., and Herroelen, W.S. (2000) "The discrete time/resource trade-off problem in project networks: A branch and bound approach", *IIE Transactions*, vol. 32, pp 1059–1069.

Depuy, G.W., and Whitehouse, G.E. (2001) "A simple and effective heuristic for resource constrained project scheduling problem", *International Journal of Production Research*, vol. 39, no. 14, pp 3275–3287.

Doersch, R.H., and Patterson, J.H. (1977) "Scheduling a project to maximize its net present value: A zero-one programming approach", *Management Science*, vol. 23, no. 8, pp 882–889.

Elmaghraby, S.E. (1995) "Activity nets: A guided tour through some recent developments", *European Journal of Operational Research*, vol. 82, pp 383–408.

Elmaghraby, S.E., and Herroelen, W.S. (1990) "The scheduling of activities to maximize the net present value of projects", *European Journal of Operational Research*, vol. 49, pp 35–49.

Elmaghraby, S.E.E., Herroelen, W.S., and Leus, R. (2003) Note on the paper 'Resource-constrained project management using enhanced theory of constraint' by Wei et al. *International Journal of Project Management*, 21 pp 301–305, Pergamon.

Elsayed, E.A. (1982) "Algorithms for project scheduling with resource constraints", *International Journal of Production Research*, vol. 20, no. 1, pp 95–103.

Hartmann, S., and Kolisch, R. (2000) "Experimental evaluation of state-of-the-art heuristics for the resource-constrained project scheduling problem", *European Journal of Operational Research*, vol. 127, pp 394–407.

Herroelen, W.S., and Leus, R. (2004) "Robust and reactive project scheduling: A review and classification of procedures", *International Journal of Production Research*, vol. 42, no. 8, pp 1599–1620.

Herroelen, W.S., and Leus, R. (2005) "Project scheduling under uncertainty: Survey and research potentials", *European Journal of Operational Research*, vol. 165, no. 2, pp 289–306.

Kanda, A., and Rao, U.R.K. (1984) "A network flow procedure for project crashing with penalty nodes," *European Journal of Operational Research*, vol. 16, no. 2, pp 174–182.

Kanda, A., and Singh, N. (1988) "Project crashing with variations in reward and penalty functions: Some mathematical programming formulations," *Engineering Optimization*, vol. 13, no. 4, pp 307–316.

Kolisch, R., and Padman, R. (2001) "An integrated survey of deterministic project scheduling", *Omega*, vol. 29, pp 249–272.

Pritsker, A.A.B., Watters, L.J., and Wolfe, P.M. (1969) "Multiproject scheduling with limited resources: A zero-one programming approach", *Management Science*, vol. 16, pp 93–107.

Smith-Daniels, D.E., and Aquilano, N.J. (1987) "Using a late-start resource-constraint project schedule to improve project net present value", *Decision Sciences*, vol. 18, pp 617–630.

Smith-Daniels, D.E., and Smith-Daniels, V.L. (1987) "Maximizing the net present value of a project subject to materials and capital constraints", *Journal of Operations Management*, vol. 7, no. 1, pp 33–45.

Talbot, F.B. (1982) "Resource constrained project scheduling with time-resource tradeoffs: The non-preemptive case", *Management Science*, vol. 28, pp 1197–1210.

Yang, K.K., and Sum, C.C. (1993) "A comparison of resource allocation and activity scheduling rules in a dynamic multi-project environment", *Journal of Operations Management*, vol. 11, pp 207–218.

III. WEBSITES & CDS

http://nptel.iitm.ac.in (The following two courses were developed as a part of the National Project on Technology Enhanced Learning, NPTEL, in 2007 and are available on the NPTEL official website.)

(a) VIDEO COURSE ON PROJECT AND PRODUCTION MANAGEMENT UNITS: 42
Author: Prof. Arun Kanda

Contains the following 42 lecture video series on Project and Production Management delivered by Prof. Arun Kanda, Mechanical Engineering Department, Indian Institute of Technology Delhi, Hauz Khas, New Delhi 110016.

1. Project and Production Management – An Overview
2. Project Management – An Overview
3. Project Identification and Screening
4. Project Appraisal Part – I
5. Project Appraisal Part – II
6. Project Selection
7. Project Representation
8. Consistency & Redundancy in Project Networks
9. Basic Scheduling with A-O-A Networks
10. Basic Scheduling with A-O-N Networks
11. Project Scheduling with Probabilistic Activity Times
12. Linear Time–Cost Trade-offs in Projects: A Heuristic Approach
13. Project Crashing with Multiple Objectives
14. Resource Profiles and Levelling
15. Limited Resource Allocation
16. Project Monitoring and Control Using PERT/Cost
17. Team Building and Leadership in Projects
18. Organizational and Behavioural Issues
19. Computers in Project Management
20. Project Completion, Review and Future
21. Life Cycle of Production System
22. Role of Models in Production Management
23. Financial Evaluation of Capital Investments
24. Decision Trees and Risk Evaluation
25. Introducing New Products and Services
26. Economic Evaluation of New Products and Services
27. Product Mix
28. Product and Process Design
29. Issues in Location of Facilities
30. Mathematical Models for Facility Location
31. Layout Planning
32. Computerized Layout Planning
33. Product Layouts and Assembly Line Balancing
34. Forecasting
35. The Analysis of Time Series
36. Aggregate Production Planning: Basic Concepts
37. Aggregate Production Planning: Modelling Approaches
38. Basic Inventory Principles
39. Inventory Modelling
40. Material Requirements Planning
41. Scheduling of Job Shops
42. Course Summary and Review

[Developed as a part of the National Project on Technology Enhanced Learning (NPTEL) funded by the Ministry of HRD, Govt of India, 2007]

(b) WEB COURSE ON PROJECT AND PRODUCTION MANAGEMENT 9 MODULES
Authors: Arun Kanda and S.G. Deshmukh

Contains a 9-module web-based course on Project and Production Management with text, illustrations, solved examples, quizzes and unsolved problems developed by Prof. Arun Kanda and Prof. S.G. Deshmukh at the Educational Technology Services Centre at Indian Institute of Technology, Delhi.

1. Project Conception and Appraisal
2. Project Planning
3. Project Crashing and Resource Allocation
4. Project Implementation
5. Strategic Decisions in Production Management
6. Product and Process Selection
7. Facility Layout and Location
8. Forecasting and Aggregate Production Planning
9. Inventory, MRP and Job Shop Scheduling

[Developed as a part of the National Project on Technology Enhanced Learning (NPTEL) funded by the Ministry of HRD, Govt of India, 2008]

Video CDs developed by Prof. Arun Kanda

1. PROJECT MANAGEMENT UNITS: 25
Author: Prof. Arun Kanda

Set of 25 lectures on Project Management, Produced by Educational Technology Services Centre, Indian Institute of Technology, Delhi, 2003 (Available through FITT, IIT, Delhi)

1. Project Management – An Overview
2. Project Identification and Screening
3. Project Appraisal Part – I
4. Project Appraisal Part – II
5. Project Selection
6. Project Representation
7. Consistency & Redundancy in Project Networks
8. Basic Scheduling with A-O-A Networks
9. Basic Scheduling with A-O-N Networks
10. Project Scheduling with Probabilistic Activity Times
11. Alternatives to PERT: Chance Constrained Programming
12. Alternatives to PERT: Project Simulation
13. Issues in Project Simulation
14. Linear Time–Cost Trade-offs in Projects: A Heuristic Approach
15. Linear Time–Cost Trade-offs in Projects: A Network Flow Procedure
16. Non-Linear Time–Cost Trade-offs in Projects
17. Project Crashing with Multiple Objectives

18. Resource Considerations in Projects: Part I
19. Resource Considerations in Projects: Part II
20. Project Monitoring and Control Using PERT/Cost
21. Team Building and Leadership in Projects
22. Organizational and Behavioural Issues in Project Management
23. Ten Rules for Effective Project Management
24. Computers in Project Management
25. Project Completion, Review and Future

2. PRODUCTION MANAGEMENT **UNITS: 23**
Author: Prof. Arun Kanda

Set of 23 lectures on Production Management, Produced by Educational Technology Services Centre, Indian Institute of Technology, Delhi, 2004 (Available through FITT, IIT, Delhi)

1. Project and Production Management–An Overview
2. Life Cycle of Production System
3. Role of Models in Production Management
4. Financial Evaluation of Capital Investments
5. Decision Trees and Risk Evaluation
6. Introducing New Products and Services
7. Economic Evaluation of New Products and Services
8. Product Mix
9. Product and Process Design
10. Issues in Location of Facilities
11. Mathematical Models for Facility Location
12. Layout Planning
13. Computerized Layout Planning
14. Product Layouts
15. Forecasting
16. The Analysis of Time Series
17. Aggregate Production Planning: Basic Concepts
18. Aggregate Production Planning: Modelling Approaches
19. Basic Inventory Principles
20. Inventory Modelling
21. Material Requirements Planning
22. Scheduling of Job Shops
23. Course Summary and Review

Articles on Goldratt's Theory of Constraints and the Critical Chain Methodology

http://www.focusedperformance.com/articles/ccpm.html
http://pqa.net/ProdServices/ccpm/W05002005.html#Introduction
http://finance.groups.yahoo.com/group/CriticalChain/
http://www.cutter.com/research/freestuff/itj0303.pdf

Index